The Paradox of Mass Politics

The Paradox of Mass Politics

Knowledge and Opinion in the American Electorate

W. Russell Neuman

Harvard University Press
Cambridge, Massachusetts, and London, England   1986

Library of Congress Cataloging-in-Publication Data

Neuman, W. Russell.
   The paradox of mass politics.

   Bibliography: p.
   Includes index.
   1. Voting—United States.   2. Elections—United
States.   3. Public opinion—United States.   4. Elite
(Social sciences)—United States.   5. United States—
Politics and government—1945–   .   I. Title.
JK1967.N48   1986   324.973   86-288
ISBN 0-674-65455-2 (alk. paper)
ISBN 0-674-65460-9 (pbk. : alk. paper)

To W.F.N. and M.W.N.

Acknowledgments

THE IDEAS addressed in this book have been following me around as I have studied and taught at the University of California at Berkeley, Yale University, and the Massachusetts Institute of Technology. My colleagues and students, most of whom are haunted by spirits of another sort, have listened to my mutterings and musings with special patience. They have made suggestions and offered alternately, as appropriate, encouraging and discouraging words. Over the years the list of people I should thank has thus grown long.

Ithiel de Sola Pool, William Gamson, Donald Kinder, Gary Marx, Donald Blackmer, Robert Lane, Arthur Stinchcombe, Charles Glock, and Merrill Shanks read the manuscript in its various stages and offered thoughtful comments and suggestions.

The Inter-University Consortium for Political and Social Research provided most of the data. Additional data and help were provided by Herbert McClosky, Jack Citrin, Paul Sniderman, John Pierce, Charles Bann, Deborah Jay, Robert Stumpf, and Stephen Hart. Patricia Ewick, Richard Fryling, James Parker, and Steven Schneider helped with the data analysis. Special thanks are due to Richard Feldman, who was the last of the brave souls to do battle with the collected data sets and who inherited all of the loose ends.

The research was supported at various stages by the Ford Foundation, the National Science Foundation, and the John and Mary R. Markle Foundation. The manuscript was typed with a careful eye and good spirits by Judy Oshida and Joann Wleklinski. I would also like to express appreciation to Aida Donald, Elizabeth Suttell, and Virginia LaPlante at Harvard University Press for their help and encouragement.

Finally, I would like to thank my family, Susan, Sara, and David, who graciously accepted the computer and word processor as members of the family, and who nurtured the author through each of the ups and downs and in-betweens.

Contents

The Paradox of Mass Politics

Introduction

It is a central premise of democratic practice that the citizenry must be both vigilant and vocal about issues which affect them if the system is to work as intended. How much attention do typical citizens pay to the political world around them? Certainly almost every adult follows issues of war and peace, major economic crises, and presidential elections. But what about some of the more complex and remote issues of economic and international policy?

This is a critical question in the study of mass politics and, as it turns out, one that is far from being resolved. Take, for example, the case of two associates of mine who found themselves on a panel at a recent conference of the American Political Science Association. After the usual polite preliminaries, a pointed disagreement emerged between them. Both men are established scholars and shrewd analysts of the American political scene, and each was amazed at the wrong-headedness of the other. How could a thoughtful student of American politics study these issues so long and yet get it so wrong? I was particularly intrigued by each scholar's version of the encounter as presented to me later, because the issues raised go to the heart of what politics is and how it ought to be studied. The two versions express a very different sense of public opinion and how the political influence process works. These differences define a paradox.

The first scholar argued: "The central fact of American politics is the behavior of the political elite. Washington is everything. The vagary of election returns, of course, determines which of two competing members of the elite will occupy a seat in Congress for a few years. But who gets nominated and, more important, what gets decided as policy in the day-to-day workings of the political process are determined in smoke-filled rooms and on golf courses. Public opinion is the inarticulate and blurry backdrop for the realities of political life."

The second scholar responded: "Electoral politics is not the backdrop; it is the essence, the keystone of the political process. The big issues, such as military, economic, and welfare policy, are influenced by the electorate's opinions. There is a complex dialectic between Washington and the rest of the country. Elections need not be held on a daily basis to make officials in Washington pay attention. Woe to the young elected officials who think they can play politics in Washington without actively courting the opinions, preferences, and whims of the folks back home. It is easy for the power junkies close to the citadel in Washington to forget that the rest of the country is out there. In the final analysis, if a policy is not based on public opinion, it won't survive."

The first position was put forward by Michael Robinson, who teaches politics at Georgetown University. He finds it rather difficult to imagine breakfast without *The Washington Post,* let alone living outside Washington. He is uneasy about number-crunching survey research. He focuses instead on how specific political issues are perceived by members of the political and journalistic elite and how political interests and influence bear on the decisions made in Washington. Public opinion seems a vague and distant vapor of half-thought-out, half-hearted opinion compared to the broadly articulated views of the political elite of Washington. Theirs are the opinions that matter.

The second position was put forward by Walter Dean Burnham, who teaches American politics at MIT. His professional career has focused on long-term trends in the American electorate, with special attention to the structure of party politics and historical patterns of realignment. He is a walking goldmine of detailed statistical information on American public opinion and voting.

The two perspectives are equally valid, and neither can replace the other. Yet they lead to seemingly incompatible approaches to the study of politics (Kuhn, 1962). The first leads to case studies of political activists, professional journalists, and politicians, designed to find out their view of the fundamental issues of the day and their strategies for political success. The second leads to the study of election returns and public opinion data, in search of trends and the public mandate as an engine of the democratic process.

The two perspectives differ because they focus attention on different ends of a spectacularly complex communications process between publics and elites. It takes a great deal of initiative, energy, perseverance, and financial and institutional support to be "heard" in Washington. Each of these constraints tests the intensity of opinion of a citizen or citizen group. When a staff interviewer persuades a housewife in Iowa, however, to open the screen door and invite the interviewer into the living room, the situation is unique. It has no precedent before the development of survey research. As the interviewer earnestly leans forward and asks the housewife her opinion of national defense policy, she pauses, looks around the room, shrugs her shoulders, but does offer an opinion.

Until public opinion polling and scientific sampling techniques were invented in the 1920s and 1930s, the voice of the people was the voice of those who chose to speak out—those who voted, wrote letters to editors, went to public meetings, wrote to legislators, or hired professional lobbyists to represent their interests in the corridors of power. Of course, most everyone had a vague sense of public opinion at large from occasional contacts with friends and associates. But since individuals tend to associate with people like themselves, such informal measures were (and continue to be) misleading. The pioneers of survey research were thus shocked, when they systematically assessed the political knowledge of the electorate, to find such low levels of interest and information.

The paradox of mass politics is the gap between the expectation of an informed citizenry put forward by democratic theory and the discomforting reality revealed by systematic survey interviewing. The paradox raises serious questions. How different are the views of those few who actively attempt to influence political decisions on a day-to-day basis from the views of the many who simply monitor the news media half-attentively and occasionally make it to the polls to vote? Do the masses and elites process political information in distinctly different ways? To the extent that there are differences, how do they affect the workings of the democratic process?

These questions are not new. Walter Lippman (*Public Opinion*, 1922) puzzled over how the public could be expected to understand the complexities of international diplomacy and military strategy during the First World War well enough to offer meaningful guidance to their elected officials. Similarly, Joseph Schumpeter (*Capitalism, Socialism, and Democracy*, 1942) concluded that on most political and economic issues the level of reasoning of the average citizen is primitive, even infantile. The well-educated are no exception. He cited the example of a lawyer who has been professionally trained to evaluate evidence carefully and critically as it is introduced in the courtroom. This same lawyer, when later in the day it comes time to read a political story in the newspaper, reacts instinctively and primitively to the facts and arguments at hand. Simon (*Administrative Behavior*, 1945) and Downs (*An Economic Theory of Democracy*, 1957) further developed the theory of how people make decisions when they have less than full information and limited time and energy to seek it out.

This book takes a fresh look at these issues, paying particular attention to electoral politics. The starting point is the paradox itself. Major election surveys from the period 1948 to 1980 provide the evidence on the character of the average citizen's political interest and knowledge, cognitive style, political opinions, and awareness of central public issues. Although it is difficult to calibrate the minimum necessary threshold of public knowledge, by most benchmarks the level of public awareness is disturbingly low. Yet all studies of decision-making in Washington indicate that an articulate voice of attentive public opinion is being heard. Where is this voice coming from?

Four theories have attempted to resolve this paradox. The first theory, which emerged from the early voting studies, emphasized that public opinion is *stratified*. Although the average citizen may not be terribly well-informed on an issue, there are opinion leaders within the community who are articulate, active, and indeed well-informed. Through a complex, multilevel communications process, the issues are discussed and evaluated, and ultimately public views are voiced, usually by means of the opinion-leader stratum.

The second theory, also based on the early voting studies, emphasized the *pluralism* of public opinion. Each citizen need not be an expert on each issue. There exist issue publics, or groups of concerned citizens who have a special awareness about and expertise in matters which affect them directly. Veterans track veterans' affairs; businessmen track business regulations. The resolution to the paradox is pluralism.

The third theory, which emerged in the 1970s, concluded that the portrait of the unsophisticated citizen is an artifact of the 1950s, which were an unusually quiescent period in American politics. As a result of the polarized politics of the 1960s, characterized by student and urban unrest and the ideological candidacies of Barry Goldwater and, later, George McGovern, a *changed American voter* emerged. In response to the more intense political environment, the average citizen proved to be more politically concerned, more aware of the issues, and more attuned to ideological disputes.

The fourth and final theory, also from the 1970s, dealt with the technical issues involved in the measurement of ideology, issue voting, and opinion consistency over time. This *methodological critique* asserted simply that the portrait of an unsophisticated citizenry is false, the unfortunate result of errors in measurement.

Although each response is plausible and offers a potentially attractive resolution to the paradox of mass politics, each turns out to be fundamentally flawed. The notion of a two-step flow of information back and forth between opinion leaders and the mass public is incomplete and misleading. The pluralism of opinions and interests that exists among citizens does not in fact correspond to a pluralism of political expertise. Nor has the American voter changed, for patterns of knowledge, interest, and awareness established in the 1950s have proven over time to be remarkably consistent. And the basic findings about low citizen interest and sophistication have persisted, despite methodological adjustments and refinements.

The key to the paradox, it turns out, lies in a reformulation of the first theory, the theory of opinion stratification. Most studies of political stratification have inferred this phenomenon from measures of education, participation, or the expression of opinions. In doing so, they risk a tautology. The central issue is the correlation between political knowledge and either opinion or behavior. To analyze that correlation, one must have an independent measure of political knowledge and sophistication, so as not to entangle the argument hopelessly. Such a measure of political sophistication would assess the individual's interest in political life, knowledge of political institutions, groups, and issues, and conceptual sophistication. This index of political sophistication is here recalculated for each of a series of nine voting studies covering the period 1948–1980.

The theory of political stratification, as well as common sense, would suggest that the more sophisticated members of the citizenry have more numerous, stable, and structured opinions and a more clear-cut ideological position. Surprisingly, the findings derived from the voting studies do not support these hypotheses. The relationship between sophistication and these variables tends to be small or nonexistent. This is a puzzling finding, which represents, in a sense, another paradox within the main paradox. As for the relationship of sophistication to voting and other forms of political participation, the expected strong linkage again turns out to be incomplete and nonlinear. It is not that political sophistication is unrelated to political opinion and behavior. Rather, the linkage is subtle and complex. The theory of political stratification requires a major reformulation.

A central issue concerns the origins of sophistication, or how it is that some citizens become relatively well-informed and involved while others are oblivious to the entire political process. Analysis of the demographic roots of sophistication reveals a spiral process of the acquisition of political knowledge. This is a gradual process in which interest breeds knowledge which, in turn, breeds further interest and knowledge over time. Related issues concern political learning from the mass media and the linkage between sophistication and political alienation and authoritarianism.

Despite the accumulated results of over thirty years of election surveys, there is a nagging sense that the paradox remains unresolved. The system apparently works quite well despite a generally low level of public interest in and knowledge about the political world. A full resolution to the paradox requires a demonstration that the system does indeed work well, which would lead the book into quite a different direction. But the formulation that, under the circumstances, the system works as well as it does focuses attention on how the system works.

There are three elements to an evolving theory of the impact of sophistication on opinion and behavior. The first focuses on the distribution of political sophistication in the mass electorate. It identifies three distinct styles of political involvement, a theory of three publics. The original notion of stratification developed in the voting studies posited a substantial stratum of opinion leaders, generally the better-educated members of the electorate, and implied a gently sloping distribution from the least to the most sophisticated. Actually, there is a large and undifferentiated middle mass, including the great majority of those who have advanced to a college education or beyond. This large central group, perhaps 75 percent of the population, accounts for a number of the surprisingly weak correlations between knowledge and opinion or behavior. At the top of the sophistication distribution is a distinct but very small group of political activists. Their level of knowledge and cognitive style is much like that of professional politicians, journalists, and political analysts. But their numbers are so small, perhaps a few percent of the population, that they hardly influence the results of a representative national survey. They are articulate and active, however, and their views and concerns make up much of what is heard as "public opinion," just as they did before survey sampling was invented. At the bottom of the sophistication continuum is a third distinct group of apoliticals who seldom pay attention to or participate in public affairs. They constitute about a fifth of the population. The key to both the paradox of mass politics and the theory of three publics is a recognition that the bulk of the population is neither political nor apolitical; it lies in between. Most people can be mobilized to political action, they half-attentively monitor the flow of political news, but they run for the most part on a psychological automatic pilot.

The second and third elements of the theory of political sophistication concern the distinctions between issues and nonissues and between attitudes and nonattitudes. Public opinion has been characterized as a sleeping giant. Most of the time it is passive and unresponsive. But when aroused, it has effects on the polity that are significant and immediate. Government officials and representatives deal with literally hundreds of distinct issues in any given week. And they have some sophisticated knowledge of each issue. They may well have taken a position on many, perhaps most of them. They are also aware that tiny but alert and vocal groups of individuals are concerned about each of these issues. But in the public at large there is awareness or concern about only a few of these issues, perhaps a half-dozen or so that receive prominent attention in the media. The key to the democratic process is the fluidity of the public agenda, the possibility that at any minute what was once the concern of a tiny group of activists may suddenly crystallize the attention of the mass electorate and become a matter about which they do indeed have real opinions and real knowledge. The evolving theory, then, emphasizes public opinion as process, the setting of the public agenda, the process by which nonissues become issues, and, at the individual level, the process by which nonopinions become opinions. Therein lies the key to the paradox.

Each of these conclusions and interpretations is subject to challenge. The line between the active elite and the mass public is not clear-cut. New efforts at the assessment of mass political knowledge may reveal that the pluralism of knowledge and interest extends much farther into the mass electorate than the evidence has so far revealed. These concerns, no doubt, will continue to attract the attention of political scientists.

When Michael Robinson and Walter Dean Burnham met at the podium, each was surprised at the wrong-headedness of the other. Robinson, from his study of Washington politics, was convinced that the balance of power lies in the tiny elite of political influentials. Burnham, from his study of the history of electoral coalitions, was convinced that the balance of power lies where it should, in the electorate at large. Not surprisingly, the answer lies in between.

1 | The Paradox

> That is the paradox. Individual voters today seem unable to satisfy the requirements for a democratic system of government outlined by political theorists . . . It seems remarkable that democracies have survived through the centuries.
>
> Bernard Berelson

DEMOCRATIC THEORY has never been terribly explicit about the precise requirements of knowledge and cognitive skill that must be exhibited by each citizen for the system to work as intended. But by most any standard imaginable, the low level of political knowledge and the pervasive inattentiveness of the mass citizenry is a cause for profound concern. It is remarkable that the American democratic system works as well as it does, given the character of the electorate.[1] Public ignorance and apathy seem to be the enduring legacy of twenty-five hundred years of political evolution. This is the paradox of mass politics.

Although the political knowledge of the mass population is a central issue of political theory, it has been studied only indirectly. There are numerous studies of attitudes and voting. Inferences are made about voter rationality from the patterns of agreement on issues between voters and their preferred candidates. Sometimes education or media exposure is used as a proxy measure of political sophistication. But there are few attempts to measure knowledge or understanding. The situation is a little like the discussion of sex in Victorian times. Everybody is interested in the subject. There are many allusions to it. But they are all inexplicit and oblique.

Voting researchers have been reluctant to tackle "the more pessimistic

1. It may seem that there is no paradox at all because the political system works poorly and is in need of fundamental reform. Certainly elements of the political system might bear improvement. But this particular political system, in persisting for over 200 years, has exhibited both stability and a capacity for change in weathering both civil and international conflicts of major proportions and numerous political and social crises. Throughout this history both the mass public and the political elite have developed a sense of the dominant direction of public opinion and a shared belief that it ought to influence public policy and that it does. All things considered, notably other national histories, the American democratic tradition has fared pretty well.

aspects of their data" (Burdick, 1959). Gradually, as the result of inference from fragments of data, the low parameters of political sophistication and interest have come to be accepted as a fundamental given of American electoral behavior: "Surely the most familiar fact to arise from sample surveys in all countries is that popular levels of information about public affairs are, from the point of view of the informed observer, astonishingly low" (Converse, 1975, p. 79). The massive National Election Study series (NES), administered first by the Center for Political Studies at the University of Michigan and now a nation-wide board of researchers, serves as a central database for this research community. The series includes over 2500 items about the personal characteristics, attitudes, and behavior of a representative sample of American citizens. Yet only ten of these items deal directly with political knowledge. Furthermore, the linkage between knowledge and opinion has not been carefully analyzed. Ironically, the issue of mass political sophistication has moved from a puzzling discovery to a familiar cliché without ever being the subject of sustained empirical research.

Assessing the sophistication of the mass citizenry raises five basic questions. The first question focuses on the salience of politics for the typical voter. What does the accumulated data on citizen interest and attentiveness reveal? The answer is not a mystery, as indicated by the heading "Citizen Apathy." The second question addresses the level of factual political knowledge most citizens acquire. This is the core of what is meant here by the term *political sophistication*. A random collection of political facts is by itself, however, unlikely to serve an individual very well. Facts need to be structured and put in context. Accordingly, the structuring of political thought represents the third question to be addressed. The last two questions involve patterns of political opinion-holding, regarding both the nature of the opinions themselves and their role in the electoral calculus of the typical voter.

Citizen Apathy

Apathy dominates American mass politics. This has probably been true since the time of Alexis de Tocqueville, although in his time, as in ours, one is likely to get a contrary impression as a result of the tiny minority of politically active and outspoken individuals who receive all of the attention. Survey research, however, through random sampling captures the less vocal and more representative citizen and reveals that the public is profoundly uninterested in the political world.

In the 1930s scientific sampling began to reveal the character of the previously silent citizen. The term *silent majority* might be appropriate were it not generally used as a conservative polemic. The early voting research produced puzzling findings: "An assumption underlying the theory of democracy is that the citizenry has a strong motivation for participation in political life. But it is a curious quality of voting behavior that for large numbers of people motivation is weak if not almost absent . . . Most voters, organized or unorganized, are not in a position to foresee the distant and indirect consequences for themselves, let alone for society. The ballot is cast, and for most people that is the end of it. If their side is defeated, 'it doesn't really matter.' " (Berelson et al., 1954, p. 306).

Berelson's study documented that two-thirds of the citizenry have only moderate or no interest in politics. The same parameter of interest was found by University of Michigan researchers in the following two elections (Campbell et al., 1960). Such figures are not the result simply of a large number of nonvoters, for 61 percent of active voters describe themselves as only "moderately" or "not at all" interested in politics (p. 31).

The low salience of politics in American life was also noted in research on civil liberties during the McCarthy era. In answer to an open-ended question about problems facing the country at the height of the publicity about McCarthy's accusations, only 2 percent of respondents volunteered any reference to domestic or international Communism. Although a larger number were certainly aware of the issues McCarthy was raising, only one in 50 thought them important enough to mention (Stouffer, 1955). Another study of American opinion revealed that only 5 percent of respondents' fears about the future contain any political content whatsoever, as do only 2 percent of their hopes for the future. Their primary concerns, hopes, and fears focus on concrete elements of their personal lives rather than on the abstractions of politics (Cantril, 1965). Only during times of war, depression, or bizarre episodes such as Watergate does even a sizable majority of the mass public seem to pay much attention to political life.

The level of attention to politics is so low in the mass public that events must be "starkly visible" to have an impact on opinions. There appears to be a distinct threshold of public awareness. As a result, impressions of the political parties derived from the Depression and the Second World War continued to influence opinions through the 1950s, because no new events had sufficient dramatic appeal to break through the apathy barrier of most citizens and stimulate new thinking (Campbell et al., 1960, p. 60). This basic fact of mass politics has taken on the character of a given, an assumed premise of mass political trends. But the fact of political apathy remains as important now as it was when first demonstrated.

Citizen apathy is reflected by the low rates of voter turnout. Since the beginning of the twentieth century, turnout has averaged only 59 percent of eligible voters in presidential election years and only 42 percent in nonpresidential election years (Burnham, 1965). The low point was 1974 when only 38 percent of the voters made it to the polls. In primary elections, which are critical determinants of who will ultimately be elected, turnout stands at levels of only one-half that of regular elections (Ranney, 1972).

If turnout rates provide meager evidence of voter interest, data on other political activities from the NES provide even less. Twelve percent of the adult population report signing a petition, 5 percent report contributing to a political candidate, 4 percent have sent a letter to a government official, and only 2 percent have demonstrated for a political cause.[2] All in all, the number of politically active citizens is very small, or roughly one in twenty Americans. Even within the narrow stratum of the politically active the primary motive for participation is not a political one. A primary satisfaction of political activists derives from the friendships and collegial activities of political life rather than any abstract political motives (Verba and Nie, 1972).

The early voting studies emphasized a number of factors, particularly the modest educational background of the average voter and the ambiguous connection between political action and personal consequences. One study emphasizing the factor of cognitive limitations concluded that many people find politics "downright confusing" and simply lack the conceptual tools to make sense out of the chaos of day-to-day politics. When those with an impoverished political understanding do participate in politics, they tend to rely on the concrete cue of political party affiliation inherited from their parents. To the extent that psychological

2. The fact that roughly one in 8 Americans reports having signed a petition represents an exaggerated measure of motivated political activity. This is a reflection of the psychology of petition signing. Many people, when approached in a shopping center or on the streets to sign a petition, are more apt to sign than to ask questions or to explain why they have little interest in the issue. Even within the narrow stratum of the politically active, the primary motive for participation is not a political one.

party affiliation substitutes for thinking issues through and evaluating candidates on their own merits, it challenges the basic premises of the electoral system (Campbell et al., 1960).

For many people, politics appears to be a rather threatening enterprise:

While some people may enhance their egos through victory in political argument, there are others who, facing the prospect of revealing factual ignorance or committing gross logical errors, seek to avoid the feeling of defeat, abashment, humiliation, or other discomfiture by staying far away from such discussions . . . One woman observing that her husband and in-laws discussed politics, was asked whether she joined in the discussions. "No, since I don't understand too much about politics, I just keep my mouth closed . . . People should know what they are talking about and this takes an education which goes beyond the high school level. I don't think I am capable enough to take an active part (in politics). I just feel that I lack the ability . . . I don't know what would be required of me. My husband and I talk it over, of course, but I don't talk it over in public because I don't know enough. I wish I knew more. Sometimes I'd like to say something." (Rosenberg, 1954, pp. 353–354)

Many other people write politics off as incomprehensible. The NES studies include the agree-disagree item: "Sometimes politics and government seem so complicated that a person like me can't really understand what is going on." The question was designed to tap political estrangement and identify those pathologically alienated and marginal citizens who had withdrawn from political life. As it turned out, however, 71 percent of the sample agreed with the item when it was first asked in 1952, and the proportion has since remained remarkably constant. In retrospect, such a collective response seems more reasonable than pathological. In fact, in recent years increasing numbers of voters have become convinced that government officials do not understand a great deal more about the enduring problems facing this nation than they do (Figure 1.1).

Still another factor in public apathy is the belief that it is futile to try to influence political decisions. One group of citizens remarked: "Voting doesn't make much of a difference. What can an individual do about it? He can't really do much . . . My vote will always count, yet one vote one way or another doesn't make much of a difference . . . Well it seems almost useless to do a lot of work for the national group when there are so many other people for it and when you really won't have much to say about what happens anyway. A lot of those people are a lot better than I am and a lot of them have more pull" (Rosenberg, 1954, pp.

Figure 1.1. Citizen Apathy: Is Politics Comprehensible? *Source:* National Election Studies (NES).

355–356). Even when people discuss local politics, they emphasize the futility of trying to affect decisions in a meaningful way. At the national level, the perception that one vote will not make much of a difference is widespread.

This attitude is reinforced by the belief that most of the available candidates offer less than a meaningful choice. On average, one-third of the population freely admit they do not care who wins the presidential election (Figure 1.2). In 1976 that number rose dramatically to 50 percent of the population. Well above two-thirds of the population agree with the statement, "Generally speaking those reelected to Congress in Washington lose touch with the people pretty quickly" (Miller et al., 1975).

Cynicism and withdrawal from politics, although more pronounced in recent years, is not a new and unique phenomena. For a large number

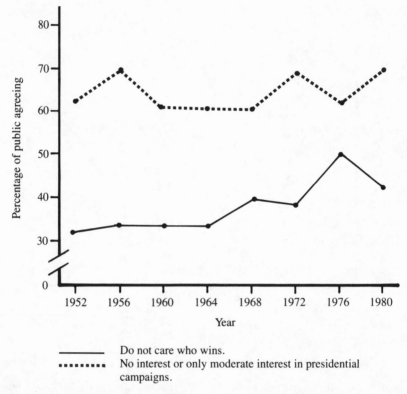

Figure 1.2. Citizen Apathy: Ambivalence about Electoral Outcomes. *Source:*
NES.

of Americans, voting has largely been defined as a ritualistic and symbolic activity rather than a means to an identifiable political end. Low
interest in politics is not the exception or even a recent phenomenon
but rather the norm of American political life.

Low Levels of Public Knowledge

The inevitable outgrowth of widespread political apathy is a fundamental
public ignorance of the central facts of political life. Such levels of public
knowledge and awareness do not jibe with the long-standing democratic
ideal: "The democratic citizen is expected to be well informed about
political affairs. He is supposed to know what the issues are, what their

history is, what the relevant facts are, what alternatives are proposed, what the party stands for, what the likely consequences are. By such standards the voter falls short. Even when he has the motivation, he finds it difficult to make decisions on the basis of full information when the subject is relatively simple and approximate; how can he do so when it is complex and remote?" (Berelson et al., 1954, p. 308).

The study of political knowledge, unlike most other dimensions of political sophistication, is unique. Such abstract phenomena as a citizen's level of ideological awareness or the importance of political issues in voting decisions are difficult to identify precisely and measure meaningfully. But there are domains of basic factual knowledge which, unlike opinions, allow for veridical measurement. When unknowing citizens give vague responses to factual questions, they reveal just as much about themselves as when they give correct answers.

Unfortunately, because the tradition of survey research emphasizes the development and maintenance of rapport with respondents, researchers are reluctant to ask factually oriented knowledge questions for fear of embarrassing interviewees. As a result, direct measurement of political knowledge is rare. Yet the available data show overwhelmingly that even the basic facts of political history, the fundamental structure of political institutions, and current political figures and events escape the cognizance of the great majority of the electorate. Moreover, the media coverage of politics and interpersonal conversations peak at election time. Thus, since most of the studies were conducted at the height of an election campaign, these results may represent a relatively conservative estimate of public ignorance.

The basic fact of political relevance to the voter is the names of political candidates. Simple recognition of the candidates' names represents the minimum necessary awareness for a functional political life. It is difficult to imagine an individual with a sophisticated sense of a candidate's policy positions, background, and political style who is unable to identify the candidate's name. After all, a great deal of political advertising, from bumper stickers and billboards to television spots, does little more than put the candidate's name in front of the public. Over the past two decades, however, on average 56 percent of the population have been unable to identify any congressional candidate in their district at the height of the congressional campaign. Thus a majority of citizens are unable even to guess at or approximate the names of any congressional candidate, including the incumbent, who in many cases has been serving the district for many years (Figure 1.3). On the average, only 22 percent are able to name both of the major party candidates in contested races in their district.

Perhaps the Senate presents a fairer test, since congressional districting is complex. A senatorial race puts the full power of the local and regional media at the disposal of the candidates. But again, 56 percent of the populace cannot name either senatorial candidate at the height of the campaign.

It is true that a respondent might forget momentarily or confuse names. Perhaps with some prompting many would ultimately recognize names, faces, and even positions of current candidates. But a candidate's name remains the basic medium of political currency. The fact that a consistent majority cannot recall the names of congressional candidates might well be taken as a benchmark of the mass public's interest in politics.

The findings on public knowledge of basic political facts and concepts are similar (Figure 1.4). Even the most vivid concepts of political life, such as the cold war, are recognized by only a little over half the electorate. Other fundamental concepts of domestic policy, including such basic symbols of policy polarization as the welfare state, are recognized

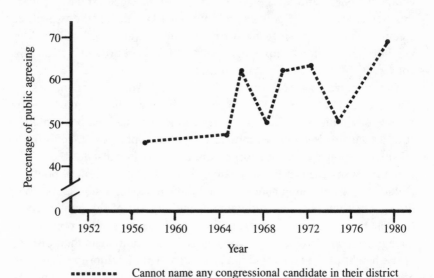

-------- Cannot name any congressional candidate in their district during the election campaign.

Figure 1.3. Public Knowledge of Congressional Candidates. *Source:* NES.

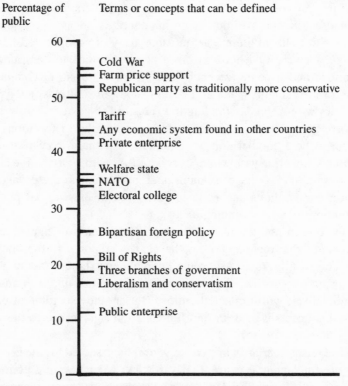

Percentage of public

Terms or concepts that can be defined

Figure 1.4. Public Knowledge of Political Terms and Concepts. *Source:* Erskine, 1963; Compton Advertising, 1975.

by only one in three citizens; the Bill of Rights is recognized by only one in five. As a rule, the most prominent political terms are understood by about half the population, typical political terms are recognized by about one in three, and the more abstract, complex, or specialized terms are familiar to about one in five.

Unstructured Political Thinking

The low level of public concern and knowledge about political affairs apparently leads to a free-floating jumble of unanchored opinions and perceptions in the political thinking. The public's lack of understanding of fundamental political concepts helps to explain the persistence of apathy and the low level of knowledge in the face of a continuous and full flow of political information from newspapers, magazines, and the broadcast media. Without anchoring concepts, ideas, and symbols, the events of political life are a confusing array of unconnected facts. One needs a conceptual hook in one's head on which to hang new information, and a cognitive cubbyhole in which to store, compare, and contrast arguments made at different times on similar issues. Watching politics without understanding the rules of the game is like watching a sporting event without any knowledge of its rules or traditions: it may seem to be a competition of some sort, but there is no way to know who is competing with whom over what. As with sports, large segments of the population have no emotional investment in these ongoing political competitions and manage quite well in life without paying any attention to who is winning or losing.

Interest in politics or the recall of specific facts or figures may well fluctuate from one election to the next in response to the intensity or closeness of the race. And some people may exhibit a fashionable cynicism and argue that they do not follow politics or that none of the candidates is worth much attention. But an understanding of basic political concepts is of prior and fundamental significance to the viability of a mass democracy.

The terms *liberalism* and *conservatism* have served for the last century as the fundamental conceptual yardsticks for measuring political life. Most parties, political leaders, policy positions, court decisions, and political arguments can be located along these traditional dimensions. The liberal-conservative continuum in politics corresponds to monetary units in economic analysis. Theory and empirical analysis in economics are strengthened by the precision and clarity of the central variable, money, whether measured in units of dollars or rubles. Theories of supply and demand, taxation, and economic equality all use the same metric for understanding economic processes. In a parallel sense, the liberal-conservative continuum spans the specific issues of politics and serves as its primary, if less precise, unit of analysis. Thus, as the comprehension of economics is seemingly impossible without a concept and metric of price, political life is incomprehensible without some sense of its central continuum.

Yet only one in five citizens are able to define liberalism and conservatism in enough breadth to subsume multiple issues in the full sense of an anchoring concept, and only half of these, or about 10 percent of the sample, offer acceptable definitions (Figure 1.5). This top 10 percent exhibit some sophistication in their response by identifying such things

Percentage of population	No. of voting age citizens (millions)	Definition
10	17	Broad and philosophical, a passing grade.
7	12	Incomplete, not quite a passing grade.
36	59	Limited meaning, tied to single issue, usually in terms of spend-save dimension.
10	17	Uncertain, guesswork.
37	61	No political content.

Figure 1.5. Unstructured Political Thinking: Public Understanding of Liberalism and Conservatism. *Source:* Converse, 1964.

as a posture toward change, government involvement in social problems or private enterprise, and issues of socialism or capitalism. The remainder of those who attempt a definition tend to tie it to a simple and concrete example of a particular issue or to the narrow spend-save dimension. But the more typical group, the other 80 percent, offer much narrower definitions or exhibit considerable confusion (Converse, 1964). Responses from the Bay Area Survey depth interviews (Appendix C) are illustrative:

[What do the terms liberal and conservative mean to you?] "Not too much really. For some reason conservative gets identified with the South—identified with drabby looking clothes vs. more something I would wear, drabby clothes, too, but it is just a different type."

"Oh, conservative. Liberal and conservative. Liberal and conservative. I haven't given it much thought. I wouldn't know. I don't know what those words mean! Liberal . . . liberal . . . liberal . . . liberal. And conservative. Well, if a person is liberal with their money they squander their money? Does it fall into that same category? If you're conservative you don't squander so much, you save a little, huh?

Although the terms *liberal* and *conservative* are appropriately used by journalists and political activists on a daily basis, only one in 40 typical citizens appear to use such terms explicitly and spontaneously in the evaluation of candidates and parties. Most voters apparently evaluate candidates in terms of narrow group self-interest, such as whether a particular candidate favors business or labor, or in terms of the nature of the times, such as whether the economy has improved or worsened or a candidate is likely to bring an extended period of peace (Converse, 1964). Hour-long depth interviews with a representative sample of citizens revealed a generally higher use of abstract concepts, with perhaps one in 20 rather than one in 40 citizens using them spontaneously and explicitly (Appendix B). Other studies have concluded that the 1960s and 1970s brought a much richer political environment and more explicitly ideological appeals by candidates (Nie et al., 1976; Miller et al., 1976). Thus when people are given an extensive opportunity or are stimulated by the political environment, they are somewhat more likely to make use of political abstractions (Table 1.1). Still the behavior of the public changes only in degree, not in character. Thus, even with the most lenient definition of those conceptual yardsticks and the maximal opportunity for their use, only one in four members of the mass population make explicit or implicit use of the notion of liberalism or conservatism to organize their thinking and opinions.

Some research has cited the correlation between identifying oneself as a liberal or conservative and supporting specific liberal or conservative policy positions as evidence of an increased ideological sophistication in the electorate (Miller et al., 1976). But on average, 33 percent of the public are unable to place themselves on a liberal-conservative continuum, and 46 percent conveniently place themselves at the midpoint, so that such correlations derive entirely from the opinion of only one in five respondents, or about what would be expected from the other studies.

Further evidence on political thinking in the mass electorate has emerged from the study of attitudes toward such basic democratic principles as civil liberties and the protection of minority rights—the "rules of the game." The characteristic response to abstract issues of democratic the-

Table 1.1. Use of Abstract Political Concepts (%)

Level of conceptualization	1956 Converse	1968 Pierce	1968 Klingemann	1968 Nie et al.	1972 Neuman
Explicit abstract concepts (ideologue)	2.5	5	6	17	13
Implicit abstract concepts (near-ideologue)	9.0	20	17	23	15
Group-interest concepts	42.0	24	33	22	34
Nature-of-times concepts	24.0	29	25	a	30
No issue content	22.5	22	20	7	8

Source: NES 1956, 1968; Converse, 1964; Pierce, 1970; Klingemann, 1973; Nie et al., 1976; Neuman, 1981.

a. The coding scheme used by Nie et al. is not comparable here, as their categorization of references to policy issues and political parties reflects a generally higher level of sophistication and issue attentiveness and would require a new category between near-ideologue and group interest.

ory, for example, is superficial, based primarily on an acquiescence to recognized civic maxims (Prothro and Grigg, 1960). This response is more akin to saluting the flag than to a reasoned respect for due process of law. There is 95 to 98 percent agreement on abstract notions such as that public officials should be chosen by a majority vote, citizens should be able to have an equal influence on government, and minorities should be free to criticize majority decisions. Yet four out of five people would limit voting to taxpayers, over 50 percent agree that a legally elected mayor who is a Communist should not be allowed to take office, and one in four, as of the 1950s, would not allow a black to run for office.

Furthermore, half the electorate feel that, "If Congressional committees stuck strictly to the rules and gave every witness his rights, they would never succeed in exposing the many dangerous subversives they have turned up." One in three agrees that, "The true American way of life is disappearing so fast that we may have to use force to save it," and "It is all right to get around the law if you don't actually break it." One in four agrees that, "The majority has the right to abolish minorities if it wants to," and "There are times when it almost seems better for the people to take the law into their own hands rather than wait for the machinery of government to act" (McClosky, 1964). Although there is general agreement on the clichés of democratic practice, the meaning of these abstractions is not entirely clear to large portions of the electorate.

The mass public apparently responds to political stimuli in fundamentally different ways from those of political elites. The generally held belief among elites that the public understands political abstractions is an optical illusion, generated by the fact that the elite stratum is consumed in political conversation with itself and only rarely has occasion to discuss politics with the apolitical mass citizenry. Even then, elite observers are likely to project their own ideological frames of reference on the utterances of the public. The election of Eisenhower in 1952 was interpreted by many as a shift to conservatism, away from Truman's liberalism. But such an interpretation reflects a fundamental misunderstanding of mass politics, because the public was evaluating the candidates on other and distinctly different criteria. The same mistake was made when the public's rejection of Carter for Reagan in 1980 was interpreted as a profound collective conversion to conservative ideology (Pomper et al., 1981). It is understandable for politicians and political elites to assume that the same kinds of ideological abstractions which motivate them are shared by their supporters, but in fact "the true motivations and comprehensions of the supporters may have little or nothing to do with the distinct beliefs of the endorsed elite" (Converse, 1964, p. 249).

Pseudo Opinions

The fact is that most people have extremely few political opinions. For an array of ten prominent general political issues that confront the country in any given year, for example, the average citizen is likely to have a strong and consistent preference on perhaps one or two of them and virtually no opinion whatsoever on the rest. Yet when an eager survey research interviewer, after driving a considerable distance, sits down in a respondent's living room, clipboard in hand, and starts to ask for opinions on ten political issues, most respondents feel obliged to have an opinion, in effect to help the interviewer out. Even when they are admonished that not all citizens have opinions on all issues and are asked if they have thought about an issue enough to develop an opinion, 80 to 90 percent of the population selects an alternative in response to most questions. In effect, opinions are invented on the spot. Many of these new opinions may even be staunchly defended if challenged by the interviewer. But they are pseudo opinions. They are ephemeral and so weakly tied to the political thinking of the respondent that within a few days or weeks the respondent is as likely to give the opposite answer to the same question.

Studies of these phenomena, also known as nonattitudes, have demonstrated that in response to certain items, only one in five people has a stable, nonrandom opinion, although three-quarters of them insist on offering an opinion (Converse, 1964, 1970). In 1956, 1958, and again in 1960, respondents were asked whether or not the federal government should "leave things like electrical power and housing for private businessmen to handle." They were first asked whether they had an opinion on the matter and, if so, what their opinion was. The reference to direct government involvement in businesses such as power and housing was designed to tap basic beliefs about the role of govenment in private enterprise, an issue central to the liberalism-conservatism continuum. Thus these opinions should be unlikely to change over time in response to day-to-day events in the political environment. The item had a particularly high proportion of "don't know" responses (24 percent) and a particularly low correlation over time (a tau beta coefficient of .28). It became a test-case item.

The over-time correlations between 1956 and 1958 and between 1958 and 1960 were identical. So was the correlation between 1956 and 1960, a four-year interval. If meaningful attitude change was under way, one would expect the correlation spanning the entire four years to be lower than either two-year interval.

One interpretation of this intriguing datum is that the correlation was the product of one small group of respondents who had meaningful and consistent opinions on this issue throughout the four years and the random churn of a larger group of respondents with nonattitudes. To test this interpretation, one could examine those respondents who had reversed their opinions between 1956 and 1958. For that group one would expect the correlation between 1958 and 1960 to be near zero. It turns out to be .004. Accordingly, one would expect the remaining respondents who had given consistent answers between 1956 and 1958 to reflect a mix of those with true and consistent attitudes and those with nonattitudes who had simply given the same answer by chance. The 1958–1960 over-time correlation for this group reveals the overall percentage of true attitudes for the item, 18 percent of the total sample.

The results for the other seven opinion items that were repeated in 1956, 1958, and 1960 were surprisingly similar. The correlation for the random group between the second and the third waves of the panel for these other items rarely exceeded .09. Thus, not only is the power and housing item a critical test with a somewhat abstract referent, but virtually all of the central political issues measured over time vary only in slight degree from that benchmark. Similar findings have been found in more recent studies (Converse and Markus, 1979).

One especially intriguing test of nonattitudes is to ask respondents about nonissues. Anecdotal evidence confirms the enthusiasm of respondents to offer opinions on nonexistent legislative proposals. In one study, 70 percent of the respondents offered an opinion favoring or disapproving a nonexistent Metallic Metals Act (Gill, 1947). More recent and more rigorously conducted studies indicate that the number offering opinions on nonissues is not quite so high.

When respondents were asked their opinion on the repeal of a fictitious Public Affairs Act, 33 percent conjured up a response (Bishop et al., 1980). Respondents were not giving entirely meaningless answers but were drawing on the context of the interview, which included other political items, to interpret the item as a way to express generalized distrust of government authority. Favoring repeal of the nonexistent act, for example, was correlated with an independent measure of interpersonal distrust. When respondents were asked about a real but highly obscure matter before Congress, the 1978 Agricultural Trade Act, 31 percent offered an opinion (Schuman and Presser, 1981). They were also queried on their attitude toward the Monetary Control Bill of 1979, another real but equally obscure matter, and 26 percent offered an opinion. These matters were sufficiently obscure to escape the attention of even a devoted *New York Times* reader and were virtually unknown to all members of the general sample. Parallel tests were conducted in which respondents were asked explicitly if they had an opinion on these bills. The proportion of respondents offering opinions went down. Nonetheless, 10 percent in the case of the Agricultural Trade Act and 7 percent in the case of the Monetary Control Bill insisted on offering an opinion.

The off-hand remarks to inteviewers by some respondents reveal the dynamics of the interview process. The respondents seem to be grasping around in a confusing array of complex political positions for an anchoring point from which to interpret these abstract questions: "Favor— though I really don't know what it is"; "You caught me on that. I don't know, but from the sound of it, I favor it." In response to the question on the Monetary Control Bill, for example, they elaborated their position: "That's a bill that has to do with controlling inflation" (favor); "The bill has to do with controlling pay raises" (oppose).

The items about the Monetary Control Bill were asked six months later to explore the stabilities of these pseudo opinions over time. Of those respondents expressing an opinion the first time, only 47 percent still had an opinion six months later. Of the group expressing an opinion at both points in time, the responses were not entirely random, for two-thirds gave consistent responses.[3]

Issueless Politics

Although many citizens are uninterested and have clear-cut opinions on only a few issues, it is critical to the democratic process for the politically active population to evaluate the candidates in terms of those issues on which they do have opinions as they weigh their vote decision. This phenomenon of issue voting is complex and does not permit an unambiguous empirical test. But the research so far raises the strong possibility that electoral decisionmaking for many typical voters represents essentially issueless politics.

One source of evidence is the series of questions about why people vote for or against either presidential candidate or either party which have been asked each election year since 1952 in the National Election Studies. Their open-ended format allows the respondents to articulate any criterion at all, not just those anticipated by the researchers, as a consideration in a voting decision. Most respondents in the 1980 Carter-Reagan campaign, for example, could mention at least one characteristic of the parties or candidates they were considering. Most of the responses, however, referred to clichés about the parties, such as "The Democratic party is for an average guy like me," or to personal characteristics of the candidates.

Evaluations of the candidates' policy positions clearly do not dominate the public's thinking (Table 1.2). About 68 percent of the population can articulate a general issue position of at least one candidate which might influence their vote decision. But only 31 percent can identify an

3. The correlation of the item with itself, measured a half year later, is .29 (tau beta), not too far from the average test-retest correlation of less obscure and more fundamental political attitude items.

Table 1.2. Issueless Politics: Issues and the Vote Decision (%)

Issue references	Total sample	Voters	College-educated
Any general issue associated with either candidate	68	73	81
At least one general issue associated with each candidate	31	36	43
Any specific issue position taken by either candidate	27	30	35
At least one specific issue position taken by each candidate	4	6	7

Source: NES 1980.

issue position for both candidates. These percentages are not dramatically higher for the college educated or the politically active substrata of the population.

Actually most of the responses that are viewed as issue mentions are rather vague references to general policy areas, such as the need for world peace. A typical comment points out the need to do something about taxes or about the Middle East, rather than specifying positions that could guide policymaking. Such comments are nondirective references to general problem areas. A more demanding test of the public's awareness of issues, in which voters identify an actionable policy position on a unique issue—such as applying wage and price controls to stop inflation, increasing defense spending, decriminalizing marijuana use, or mandating sentencing for repeat offenders—reveals that, on average, only 4 percent of the population can associate at least one such issue with each candidate.

Issue voting represents a critical test for democratic practice: "Commentaries on democracy often assume two basic facts about electoral decision: first, that the public is generally in possession of sufficient information regarding the various policy alternatives of the moment to make a rational choice among them . . . and, second, that the election in fact presents the electorate with recognizable partisan alternatives through which it can express its policy preferences." But the empirical analyses leave little room for optimism about the outcome: "There is a great deal of uncertainty and confusion in the public mind as to what specific policies the election of one party over the other would imply. Very few of our respondents have shown a sensitive understanding of the positions of the parties on current policy issues. Even among those people who are relatively familiar with the issues presented in our surveys—and our test of familiarity has been an easy one—there is little agreement as to where the two parties stand" (Campbell et al., 1960, pp. 542–543).

The election of 1956 became the central test case. The charisma of Dwight Eisenhower—his sincerity, integrity, likeableness, and reputation as a military leader—overwhelmed questions of policy and political philosophy in public discussion and the electoral calculus. In short, the electoral decision seemed to be based as much on affect as on issues. Further research revealed that the Eisenhower phenomenon was not exceptional (Kagay and Caldeira, 1975; Margolis, 1977). The relative importance of issue positions has been consistent and moderate over three decades. On the average, voters' comments on why they would vote for one candidate or party over the other mention issues 32 percent of the time. In only one year, 1972, does the mention of issues exceed the mention of personal qualities of the candidates.

There is little hope that the situation will improve as a result of improvements in the campaign process and media coverage, because the critical factor appears to be the cognitive style of the electorate: "In the electorate as a whole the level of attention to politics is so low that what the public is exposed to must be highly visible—even stark—if it is to have an impact on opinion . . . For example, despite a concentration on foreign issues by Mr. Stevenson [in 1952 and 1956] which must have been at least as great as that of any candidate in this country, the public was largely unaware of his position" (Campbell et al., 1960, pp. 60–61).

The actual language used by voters to describe their political thinking further reinforces this perception:

The wife of a worker in a Pittsburgh mattress factory: (personally care which party wins?) "Doesn't make any difference to me. I am not interested in stuff like that. I don't listen to nothing; I don't even read about politics in the paper." A Minnesota fisherman: (care?) "Not a bit." (Anything you like about the Democratic party?) "No, there ain't; don't believe in politics." Wife of a Georgia laborer: (care?) "I guess you'd call me not caring since I've never voted, wouldn't you?" . . . Retired California minister: (care?) "I have never registered or voted because I believe that prayers will do more than votes in keeping this country on the right path." (Key, 1961, p. 189)

More recent interview protocols reveal the same theme, albeit a new perspective on religion and party politics: "(Anything you don't like about the Republican party?) 'Republicans don't believe in Christ— many do the work of Satan, they lie and steal from the poor.' (Anything you dislike about President Ford?) 'It's not right to give speeches on the White House lawn.' (Anything you like about Carter?) 'I like his mother, I like his smile.' (Anything you like about Carter?) 'I don't like any politician, I dislike politics, I am a sports fanatic.' "

The quintessential answer of the apolitical voter is that of a California real estate developer who in 1972 voted not for Richard Nixon but against George McGovern. Was it something McGovern had said or a position he had adopted on a particularly salient issue? Actually, McGovern's staff had run a campaign documentary which preempted a rerun of the "Star Trek" television series. This displacement of "Star Trek" so infuriated the voter, he reported, that his vote for Nixon was unalterably determined at that moment.

If issues are not an important determinant of an electoral outcome, what is? One compelling hypothesis is that political tastes resemble cultural tastes:

For many voters political preferences may be considered analogous to cultural tastes—in music, literature, recreational activities, dress, ethics, speech, social behavior. Consider the parallels between political preferences and general cultural tastes. Both have their origin in ethnic, sectional, class, and family traditions. Both exhibit stability and resistance to change for individuals but flexibility and adjustment over generations for the society as a whole. Both seem to be matters of sentiment and disposition rather than "reasoned references." While both are responsive to changed conditions and unusual stimuli, they are relatively invulnerable to direct argumentation and vulnerable to indirect social influences. Both are characterized more by faith than by conviction and by wishful expectation rather than careful prediction of consequences. The preference for one party rather than another must be highly similar to their preference for one kind of literature or music rather than another and the choice of the same political party every four years may be parallel to the choice of the same old standards of conduct in new social situations. (Berelson et al., 1954, p. 311)

This is an appropriate analogy for the media age. Popular politics is much like popular music. The elite is indeed sensitive to cycles of popular fads and fancies. Political superstars fade from popular attention as quickly as they rise. And throughout it all there is a troubling aura of superficiality.

These five related factors—citizen apathy, low levels of political knowledge, unstructured political thought, pseudo opinions, and issue-less politics—frame the paradox. There is legitimate controversy on each of these points, but taken together, they present a stark portrait of the typical voter.

2 | Alternative Theories of Mass Politics

> The longer one frets with the puzzle of how democratic regimes manage to function, the more plausible it appears that a substantial part of the explanation is to be found in the leadership echelon . . . These political influentials both affect mass opinion and are conditioned in their behavior by it . . . Competitive segments of the leadership echelons normally have their roots in interests or opinion blocks within society. A degree of social diversity thus may be, if not a prerequisite, at least helpful in the construction of leadership appropriate for a democratic regime.
>
> V. O. Key

THERE HAVE been a number of responses to this stark portrait of the typical voter, each seeking to minimize the problem either by questioning the evidence itself or by shifting attention to other ameliorating circumstances. There are merit and wisdom in these arguments worth careful attention. They help in an important way to clarify the issues, but as yet, because of internal flaws and contradictions, they move us only a few steps toward resolving the paradox.

The Theory of Stratified Pluralism

The paradoxical character of the findings on public political sophistication were the source of some frustration for the pioneering researchers in the field of political behavior. They had become increasingly confident of the survey findings documenting the low level of public interest, knowledge and attentiveness and were torn between the desire to establish the validity of the findings for a still skeptical audience, on the one hand, and on the other, the desire to resolve the paradox between the requirements of democratic theory and the reality of citizen inattentiveness. These researchers, like the citizens they studied, shared a common commitment to the values of liberal democracy and felt that, despite the results of the research, somehow the system as a whole did work. But it was not yet clear how the public in aggregate could demonstrate a reasonably balanced and knowledgeable appraisal of the strengths and weaknesses of political candidates and policy options while the individual citizen fell so far short of the democratic ideal.

Their attempt at resolution draws on the concepts of stratification and pluralism (Figure 2.1). The basic notion is to redefine the role of the ideal citizen from that of an omnicompetent individual, interested and

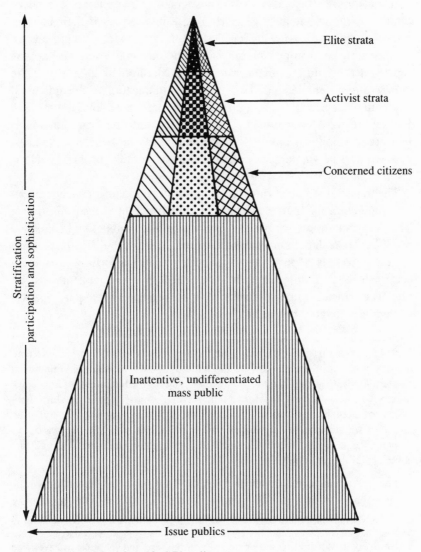

Figure 2.1. Model of Stratified Pluralism.

informed about all issues, to a more realistic model of overlapping and cross-cutting interest publics. On any particular issue there is a smallish subgroup of informed and concerned citizens who actively discuss the issue among themselves, attempt to influence others, and bring their opinions to the attention of the authorities. On other issues the participants are for the most part different. Because of differences in occupation, religious affiliation, geography, race, and personal history, the individuals' personal political agendas vary. Thus, for any given issue, a random sample of the public at large gives a false impression of their inattentiveness and ignorance. This is called the theory of stratified pluralism.[1]

According to stratified pluralism, public inattentiveness and apathy represent the failure of democratic man at the individual level: "If the democratic system depended solely on the qualification of the individual voter, then it seems remarkable that democracies have survived through the centuries. After examining the detailed data on how individuals misperceive political reality or respond to irrelevant social influences, one wonders how a democracy ever solves its political problems" (Berelson et al., 1954, p. 311).

The mistake, in this view, is to misunderstand the concept of an "average citizen." Individuals vary in their concerns and social origins. The determination of public policy is a complex, public, and collective process. To collapse those dynamics into the psyche of an idealized typical citizen is a misleading and unfortunate distortion. In fact, a certain level of indifference on the part of the mass citizenry can be seen as a critically important cushion to absorb the intense participation of highly motivated partisans:

How could a mass democracy work if all people were deeply involved in politics? Lack of interest by some people is not without its benefits, too . . . Extreme interest goes with extreme partisanship and might culminate in rigid fanaticism that could destroy democratic processes if generalized throughout the community . . . Low-interest provides maneuvering room for political shifts necessary for a complex society in a period of rapid change. Compromise might be based on sophisticated awareness of costs and returns—perhaps impossible to demand of a mass socety—but it is more often induced by indifference. (Berelson et al., 1954, pp. 314–315)

This perspective resonates with traditional concerns about mass society, such as what would happen if a demagogue were able to polarize

1. The term *stratified pluralism* is a neologism. It should have a vaguely familiar ring because the two components are frequently used. But the arguments drawn together here as a theory of mass politics have been refined over the years and only recently have come to take an integrated form as textbooks and literature reviews have attempted to make sense of this complex and contradictory collection of findings.

political conflict and previously apolitical citizens, unaware of the "rules of the game," were suddenly mobilized. The direct unmediated contact between national elites and mobilized mass publics without an intervening level of local leaders and experienced political activists is one of the most critical challenges to stable democracy (Kornhauser, 1959).

The model of stratified pluralism is based on four elements: stratified participation in the political system, the central role of opinion leadership, the pluralism of concerns and political expertise, and the mediating role of political parties in aggregating the concerns of the mass citizenry. The first element, stratified participation in the political system, turned out to be one of the most reassuring findings of the early research on mass political behavior. Thus, although there may be a sizable component of "know-nothings," they are not interested in politics and are reluctant to participate (Hyman and Sheatsley, 1947). This hard-core bottom strata of unreachable, nonvoting apoliticals, corresponding to Marx's lumpenproletariat, consists of perhaps 20 percent of the population. At the other end of the participatory continuum is an elite core of activists and influentials, estimated to be about 12 percent of the population, who attend closely to the media and are likely to have an informed and coherent set of political views. Of this strata, 94 percent vote in an average presidential year election (Campbell et al., 1960, p. 264).

The most politically active are better educated, better informed, and more involved in multiple activities, including the discussion of politics with less-informed friends and colleagues. At the extreme, the sophisticated elite have an average of three years of college, while the lowest stratum average only eight years of formal schooling. The elite are also ten times as politically active (Converse, 1964, p. 225). These findings, which are replicated in other political cultures, emerge as a central fact of political life (Almond and Verba, 1963).

The strong norm of equality of political opportunity gives the notion of political stratification a taint of antidemocratic elitism (Key, 1961). But the phenomenon of political stratification is critical to the day-to-day workings of the political system. Different "layers" of opinion are arranged along a continuum of influence and visibility to officials in government, in a kind of "cocoon":

The cocoon of opinion that envelops government may be regarded as a cloudy sort of structure consisting of layers of opinion near to government and others remote from government . . . At any particular time with respect to a given issue, immediate opinion consists of that of the alert, attentive, interested, and informed public. These are the people who talk to officials, write letters to their congressmen, comment in print or on public occasions, nudge other people to action, or who manifest a low-boiling point in other ways. More remote from government is the opinion of persons with lower levels of participation in public affairs, with less attention, less information, and a less immediate concern . . . The outer layers of less-involved opinion, though, may be slow to be aroused, and expressions may be delayed until the next election, or even the next election after that. The direction this opinion will take when it is stirred to action may be unpredictable. What its memory of past actions will be and whether its perceptions will be converted into electoral approbation or animosity are equally imponderable. (Key, 1961, pp. 428–429)

The elite leadership stratum is the missing piece in the paradox of mass democratic systems: "The longer one frets with the puzzle of how democratic regimes manage to function, the more plausible it appears that a substantial part of the explanation is to be found in the motives that actuate the leadership echelon, the values that it holds, in the rules of the political game to which it adheres, in the expectations which it entertains about its own status in society, and perhaps in some of the objective circumstances both material and institutional, in which it functions" (Key, 1961, p. 537). The development of scientific sampling and survey research turned what was once a "mysterious vapor that emanated from the undifferentiated citizenry" into a subject of disturbing clarity and precision.

The phenomenon of opinion leadership became another important element in the stratified pluralism model. The activist stratum influences not only political leaders but fellow citizens as well through informal discussion. Those who play the role of opinion leaders are more interested in politics, follow political news in the media more attentively, are generally better informed, are better acquainted with the stands of the candidates on issues, have better-developed political opinions, and in turn feel they have a more significant effect on government than their less active associates (Katz and Lazarsfeld, 1955). Opinion leaders are not a narrow ruling elite of some sort but can in fact be found within all walks of life, with different opinion leaders exerting influence on different topics (Key, 1961; Campbell et al., 1960).

In some cases, the opinion leadership role is mechanical, as when union members or spouses accept unthinkingly the official position recommended to them—a phenomenon generally referred to as proxy voting. In other cases, the central dynamic is extended political discussion with issue-specific leaders who crystallize opinion and help less attentive friends and coworkers interpret the complexity of a particular political debate. The political genius of citizens may well reside "less in how well they can judge public politics than in how well they can judge the people who advise them" (Berelson et al., 1954, p. 109). The role of opinion leadership is manifest in the areas of fashion and entertainment as well as political life (Katz and Lazarsfeld, 1955).

The concept of stratified pluralism also includes the notion of multiple issue publics, stressing the variety of concerns within the mass electorate and the notion that individual voters need not be knowledgeable about every issue of political relevance. In this perspective, voters "specialize" in those issues with which they have had experience and have developed an understanding in depth. Thus one would expect veterans to have a special interest in military issues, accountants to follow tax laws closely, American Jews to track policy toward the Middle East with care, and city residents to be especially alert to issues of urban policy. Each such group represents a potential issue public.

The concept of pluralism, with roots in de Tocqueville's (1856) observation about the uniquely activist and group-oriented consciousness of the American body politic as well as in the philosophy of the *Federalist Papers,* emphasizes the existence of multiple centers of power which function to counterbalance each other and prevent the central institutions of government from becoming overly dominant. Alliances are flexible and allow for a majority to be reconstituted from different groups for each issue. As a result, citizens gain respect for the system, accepting losses, playing by the rules, and thereby developing an appreciation of the need to protect minority views. Such cross-cutting political cleavages are seen to moderate political passions, reinforcing a practical orientation toward compromise and bargaining (Lipset, 1960).

The investigation of pluralist politics originally focused on case studies of the activist strata, especially the interaction of elites and lobbying groups (Truman, 1951; Dahl, 1961). A later study based on survey research reinforced these findings with evidence that for the most part issue concerns are dispersed across the population: "The simple conclusion seems to be that different controversies excite different people to the point of real opinion formation. One man takes an interest in policies bearing on the Negro and is relatively indifferent to or ignorant about controversies in other areas. His neighbor may have a few crystallized opinions on the race issue but he may find the subject of foreign aid very important. Such sharp divisions of interests are part of what the term 'issue public' is intended to convey" (Converse, 1964, p. 246). Thus, a small elite of opinion leaders do not play a unique role of interpreting and articulating the thinking of the mass electorate. Each issue public has its own activist strata members, who jockey for positions of leadership, inform and mobilize potential followers, and hammer out political compromises.

The stratified pluralism perspective also focuses on the mediating role of the party system in facilitating the political process. The party system is identified as a critical two-way linkage mechanism, a means of communicating information to the public and, in turn, coordinating, channeling, and moderating demands of issue publics. The role of party is "as a supplier of cues by which the individual may evaluate the elements of politics. The fact that most elements of national politics are far removed from the world of the common citizen forces the individual to depend on sources of information from which he may learn indirectly what he cannot know as a matter of direct experience. Moreover, the complexities of politics and government increase the importance of having relatively simple cues to evaluate what cannot be matters of personal knowledge" (Campbell et al., 1960, p. 128).

Another function of party is to mold consensus. By incorporating within a single political group different religious, regional, and class groups, parties make the system as a whole more stable (Lipset and Rokkan, 1967; Key, 1961). A related notion is that of party leaders as role models. One irony of public opinion is the fact that a great majority would like simultaneously to increase spending on welfare issues and to cut taxes even at the expense of important things that ought to be done. The role of elites is to manage the interrelated policies in a coherent manner and win public consent by drawing attention to their interrelatedness. Thus any measure of voter information on current issues may underestimate the accumulated thinking and past judgments that are reflected in the "standing decision" of party affiliation (Key, 1961).

One of the most concerning aspects of an uninformed electorate is its malleability, or even gullibility. The theory of mass society, for example, warns of the susceptibility of an unattached, uninformed mass citizenry to the vague promises and abstract symbolism of a potential demogogue (Kornhauser, 1959). But the American party system provides a bulwark against such threats. Individuals judge candidates not only by their promises but also by the past achievements of their party (Campbell et al., 1960; Key, 1966; Fiorina, 1981). Many of the central constructs used by political scientists to characterize the role of party structure reflect the stabilizing influence theme. They include the concept of the normal vote, the distinction between long-term and short-term forces influencing the voter, and the notion of a cognitive mass of accumulated political judgments which draw an explicit analogy to the concepts of physical mass and inertia (Converse, 1962; Campbell et al., 1966).

Each of these elements—stratified participation, opinion leadership, pluralism, and the mediating role of political parties—would appear to take the edge off the paradox of mass politics. The problem is not as bad as it first appears. The diagnosis of an uninformed average voter may be cause for concern, but the ultimate question is the working of the political system in aggregate. The patient at hand is the body politic, not the individual voter.

Stratified pluralism represents a relatively persuasive set of arguments and resonates with the more hopeful side of the liberal democratic instincts. Curiously, however, the theory has never been formalized and tested empirically, partly because of another response to the paradox positing a changed American voter.

The theory of stratified pluralism turns out to be a kind of deus ex machina. In the ancient Greek theater, the plot occasionally became overly complex. When it was time for the play to end and the moral to be crystal clear, the playwright would rely on the artifice of having a God-character appear and make everything right, to punish hubris and reward the virtuous. Apparently, as the tradition developed, some sort of dramatic puppet was hung from strings over the back of the stage; thus "deus ex machina," God from the machine. The theory of stratified pluralism has the same quality of a hurried and awkward attempt at resolution. It was added on, superimposed on, the basic structure of the data. A close examination of the theory, as originally formulated, and the accumulated research findings reveals a number of fundamental inconsistencies. The critical failure concerns the presumed link between knowledge and opinion. It turns out that the expression, stability, and structuring of opinion vary only slightly between the less and the more sophisticated segments of the mass population. Furthermore, the phenomenon of opinion leadership and a flow of information from the better to the less informed does not fit the hypothesis. Most political discussion takes place between people on equal levels of political interest. People who are highly interested and informed about politics talk a great deal with people like themselves about such issues. Those at the lower end of the stratification curve do not talk much about politics, and when they do, they are likely to consult someone of a similar background (Rogers, 1973). As a result, the notion of informal information flow and opinion leadership will need to be reformulated.

Another missing element of the stratification model is a theory of motivation, of how individuals are mobilized to become more interested and knowledgeable about the political system. Information needs to be gathered not only on what role opinion leaders and party activists play but on how individuals are recruited to those functions and, in turn, why so few people end up playing such roles.

The pluralism element of the stratified pluralism model also turns out to be problematic. Part of the problem is methodological. Pluralism is not a phenomenon that is easily assessed by traditional survey research methods. Surveys are optimized to provide data on the attitudes of large numbers of people toward commonly understood issues. They elicit responses from as many people as possible and discourage or omit from analysis don't-know or no-opinion responses. Survey research results are reported most often in terms of population means or correlations, with the focus on central tendencies. Pluralism as a concept, however, focuses more on differential patterns for unique issue-public subgroups. The survey tradition thus stands as an institutionalized impediment to the study of pluralism.

The notion of issue publics, for example, has only a fragmentary empirical basis. One of its theoretical underpinnings is the notion of self-interest, or utility-maximizing political behavior by unique economic, ethnic, or geographic subgroups. An issue public is more attentive to a particular issue because it has more to gain or lose. Although this would seem to be self-evident, the evidence for self-interest calculations is weak and contradictory. The unemployed are not particularly active or vocal on unemployment issues, the relationship between economic deprivation and attitudes is "surprisingly weak," and social class has virtually no relationship to economic policy preferences (Schlozman and Verba, 1979). There is no relationship between attitudes toward the conflict in Vietnam and the direct involvement of close relatives or friends in the conflict (Lau et al., 1978). And various self-interest measures have little effect in determining either policy preferences or voting behavior (Sears et al., 1980). Pluralism extends not just to types of citizens but also to types of issues on the common political agenda.

The model of stratified pluralism, then, is incomplete, contradicted in several respects by the available data, and not easily evaluated with survey research data. But it provides fertile ground for a reformulated analysis. The model is not wrong, but it is incomplete.

The Theory of the Changing American Voter

The theory of the changing American voter attempts to resolve the paradox of mass politics by ignoring the aggregate workings of the political system and returning to the question of the sophistication and competence of the individual voter. The central argument of this theory is that the earlier conclusions about voting were not incorrect but rather historically limited. They were based on data collected during the presidential elections of 1952 and 1956, in which Dwight Eisenhower converted his charismatic appeal as a military leader and his noncontroversial centrist positions into a political landslide. The 1950s were thus politically quiescent. The divisive, politically dramatic issues and events of the 1960s, however, transformed the electorate.[2]

The American public in the mid-seventies differs in fundamental ways from the public of the fifties. In the 1950s the public was only mildly involved in politics, was relatively content with the political process, and had long-term commitments to one or the other of the major parties. Today it is more politically aroused, more detached from political parties than at any time in the past forty years, and deeply dissatisfied with the political process . . . The American people have changed in more fundamental ways, in their basic assumptions about the American polity and in the way in which they relate to that polity. They have changed

2. It is helpful briefly to describe the time line of these developments in the literature. The classic voting literature which became subject to critique spanned the period 1954–1964, from *Voting* (1954) through *The American Voter* (1960) to Converse's seminal work on belief systems (1964). Throughout the 1950s and 1960s the basic and convergent ideas of these studies became crystallized in textbooks. The next stage began in the late 1960s with articles by Field and Anderson (1969) and John Pierce (1970) which reanalyze the Michigan data of the 1950s and draw explicit comparisons between those original findings and the differing patterns that became apparent in the elections of 1964 and 1968. Field and Anderson at Stanford and Pierce at Minnesota, working independently, converged on similar arguments. They did not find themselves in fundamental disagreement with Converse's original analysis of overall low levels of sophistication and ideological perception, but they argued that the citizenry is responsive to the ideological cues of candidates and that in 1964 there were distinct increases in the ideological response of the public reacting to the Goldwater candidacy. The primary literature revolving around the notion of the new American voter was published in the mid-1970s. The central figure was Nie, who with Anderson (1974) and Verba and Petrocik (1976, rev. 1979) published major arguments and empirical findings of the new American voter perspective. The work of Pomper (1972, 1975) and Miller et al. (1976) also represents this school of thought.

not only in *what* they think of political matters, but in *how* they think about political matters. (Nie et al., 1976, pp. 1–3)

The primary evidence for this reevaluation of the American voter came from two dramatic research findings. First, there was an apparent two and one-half fold increase in the size of the ideologically sophisticated stratum of voters, from 12½ percent in 1956 to 33 percent in 1972 (Nie et al., 1979). Second, there was evidence of a threefold increase in the structuring and organization of attitudes from 1960 to 1964 (Figure 2.2).

The changing American voter model postulates that this dramatic shift in voting behavior and attitude structure was caused by five basic elements: new candidates, new issues, new voters, the changing role of the parties, and the growth of the mass media. On the emergence of new

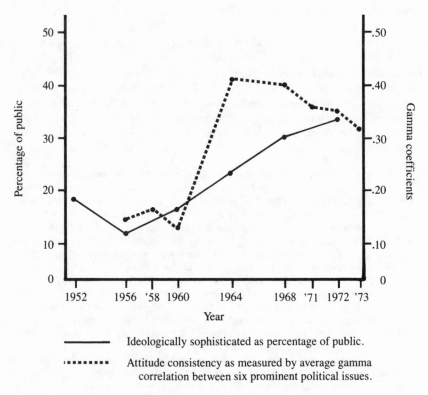

——————— Ideologically sophisticated as percentage of public.

▪▪▪▪▪▪▪▪▪ Attitude consistency as measured by average gamma correlation between six prominent political issues.

Figure 2.2. Evidence for Changing American Voter. *Source:* Nie et al., 1976, 1981.

candidates, the model pivots on the argument that the Eisenhower era was uniquely nonideological. Eisenhower was a national hero, a man above politics who tried deliberately to diffuse potentially controversial issues (Nie et al., 1976). This was the "issue-less '50s," as the national Democratic leadership of Lyndon Johnson and Sam Rayburn diffused the attempts of the Democratic Policy Council to define new domestic policy goals for the Democratic party and openly to confront Eisenhower on matters of national policy. The only real contest in 1956 was the battle between Democratic party loyalties and the attraction of a popular folk hero (Miller et al., 1976).

The Kennedy-Nixon election of 1960 was a transition point. Sharp differences on domestic and international issues emerged from the campaign speeches and the debates, which stimulated the interest level of the public. But the issues were not yet divisive and polarized. Real movement toward polarization resulted from the Kennedy legislative program, which in 1963–1964 was crystallized by Johnson into the war on poverty and a new push for civil rights.

A critical factor was Barry Goldwater, whose ideological references and distinctly conservative platform in 1964 served as a catalyst to a new issue awareness in the mass public (Pomper, 1972). The change in a mass political behavior persisted into the early 1970s, reinforced by the George Wallace candidacy of 1968 and the George McGovern candidacy of 1972. The spectacular change in the quality of mass attitudes toward questions of public policy, sometimes identified as the "new politics," was essentially the articulation of new issues by political leaders (Miller and Levitin, 1976).

Another central element of the new American voter model is the emergence of new issues, independent of the traditional economic and class alignments of the Roosevelt era, including race, crime, war, and urban and student protests (Scammon and Wattenberg, 1970). Polarizations on these social issues led to a new cleavage structure of liberals versus the silent majority (Miller and Levitin, 1976).

The turmoil of 1960s politics was not followed by a regression toward apathy and a blander, apolitical politics. The conflicts in the urban ghettos and on the university campuses left a significant and enduring imprint: "The new portrait of the voter is drawn in permanent oils, not erasable crayons. The total system has changed, not only individual voters. Recent turmoils can be seen not as passing events but as evidence of a major change, the political modernization of the United States" (Pomper, 1972, p. 13). Racial problems were the most divisive social issue to emerge since the Second World War (Nie et al., 1976). Vietnam and the draft generated a unique political environment in which a new cohort of voters came to political consciousness. These issues divided the citizenry on the ultimate questions of who should live and who should die (Pomper, 1972).

Not simply new issues but the redefinition of old ones contributed heavily to the changing voter. There was an apparent increase in correlations between abstract principles of civil liberties and specific items about protection of free speech for unpopular minority groups from the 1950s to the 1960s as the issues became redefined and integrated into basic ideological issues (Nie and Andersen, 1974). It also appeared that a greater number of issues were part of the public agenda (Nie et al., 1976). Not only were issues more salient but their linkage to the basic positions of the two major parties was increasingly clear to the great majority of voters (Pomper, 1972).

One other element in the changing American voter model was the contribution of new young voters to the electoral process. Having come to political consciousness in the late 1960s with the unique circumstances of the social turmoil and particularly the war in Vietnam influencing their world view, the younger voters were much less likely than their elders to be strongly identified with one of the political parties (Abramson, 1976; Converse, 1976). Their unique lifestyle and alienation from the central institutions of American politics made them especially alert and policy-sensitive voters. They were also, as a group, increasingly well-educated. Thus the successive waves of new cohorts entering the electorate are seen as another reinforcing element in the general pattern of rising sophistication.

Another related element of the changing American voter model is the shifting role of political parties. Identification with a political party was a much less significant element in the electoral calculus of the voters of the 1960s and 1970s than of the 1950s. The number of references to party ties in evaluating candidates fell to half that found in the 1950s, while the number of references to candidate issue positions grew from 49 percent in 1952 to a peak of 77 percent in 1964 (Nie et al., 1976). At the same time, the correlation between party identification and the vote fell precipitously (Figure 2.3).

Television and the mass media are the final element in the changing American voter theory. The introduction of television created a new level of political sophistication and added a new dimension to campaign attentiveness. Part of the impact of television is its ability to bring po-

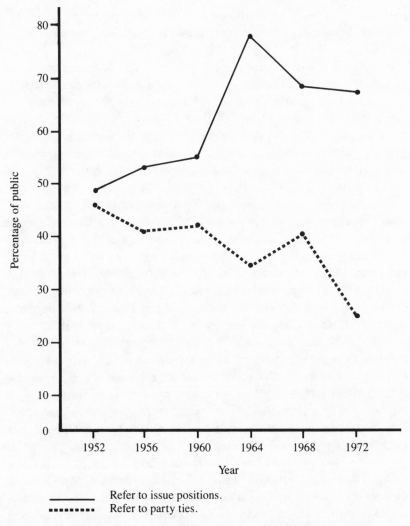

Refer to issue positions.
Refer to party ties.

Figure 2.3. Changing Role of Political Parties. *Source:* Nie et al., 1976.

litical stimuli to a broader segment of the population, diminishing class and educational differences in attentiveness (Nie et al., 1976). The media are a costless and reliable source of political information (Pomper, 1975). Television integrates politics into the entertainment mode, making it less dry and more meaningful, effective, and dramatic than in previous eras (Mendelsohn and Crespi, 1970). In addition, the media may present issues in a way that clarifies the connections across the issues. Thus, not just new media but new manners of presenting political news contribute to these overall patterns (Nie et al., 1976).

The model of the changed American voter unfortunately turns out to be for the most part a brouhaha over a series of methodological artifacts. Some important lessons have been learned about the interaction between the individual citizen and the political environment. As candidates arise and articulate policy differences, the public will respond. The measured proportion of the mass public that thinks in ideological terms also varies up and down within a limited range in response to the political environment.

But the theory greatly exaggerates the amount of change and postulates fundamental shifts in the political psychology of the mass public when the fact of the matter is that the American voter has not changed dramatically and the paradox of mass politics is still very much alive. It turns out that this literature hinges on the unfortunate coincidence in a change in survey item format in 1964 which led to an apparently dramatic upturn in the structuring of political attitudes (Figure 2.2). Strangely, the data are at consistently low levels for the elections of 1952, 1956, or 1960, and then, coincidental with the changing question format and the "ideological" campaign of Barry Goldwater, the interopinion correlations rise dramatically and remain at roughly similar levels throughout the 1960s and 1970s. This "Goldwater effect" is a central irony of the changing voter hypothesis. It is "rather incredible" to assign so much political impact in the fundamental political beliefs of the public to a single candidacy (Pierce and Sullivan, 1980, p. 22). Indeed, that this theory is on its face a rather unlikely one should have concerned the changed voter theorists more. The other causal explanations put forward do not correspond with this dramatic disruptive shift in 1964. The proportions of younger voters and of well-educated voters were very gradual trends which would have led to a much more modulated and continuous change if they were primary causal factors. Furthermore, the language of all these theorists suggested that increased political interest was part of this process of change, yet all had easy access to measures of political interest which clearly indicated no significant change throughout the period.[3]

3. A flurry of articles in 1978–1979 finally put the matter to rest, showing that the apparent shift is primarily a methodological artifact. Sullivan et al. (1978) argued that the best way of testing the methodological artifact issue was to collect new data randomly assigning respondents to pre-1964 and post-1964 formats to see, holding everything else

It is understandably exhilarating to attempt to demonstrate significant changes in the political system. If change is found, it can be projected to even more dramatic changes in the future and can encourage speculation on various consequences. Theory building about change also has a seductive ad hoc quality. Because the change generates a new hypothesis, one tends to test the hypothesis on the very data that created it in the first place. Such practices counsel caution.

The Methodological Critique

The methodological critique attempts to dismiss the paradox of mass politics as a false alarm. Proponents of this view argue that reinterpreting the original data from the 1950s or developing new more sophisticated measures, produces evidence that the mass public is much more sophisticated and issue-oriented than originally apparent. The methodological literature draws on complex methodological arguments and is particularly quarrelsome and self-contradictory. But there are important lessons to be learned both from what the critique says about the nature of the paradox and from its failure to resolve that paradox.

The critique correctly points out that extreme caution is necessary in drawing inferences about the sophistication and knowledge of the mass public from data on how closely opinions and behavior correlate. The data do not provide unambiguous evidence that the public is unthinking or unknowing. The special irony, however, is that most proponents of this critique in short order turn to another datum to interpret it as evidence that the public is indeed thoughtful, knowing, and alert. The critique is confounded by three fallacies.

The first is the single-measure fallacy. One should hesitate to make sweeping statements about public sophistication on the basis of any single measure. By focusing on the methodological fine points of a particular measurement approach, both those criticized and the critics themselves lose sight of the broader issues. It is a forest-and-trees prob-lem. Review of the critique, however, reveals a most interesting pattern (Table 2.1). Each of the five elements of the paradox of mass politics—

constant, whether the new question format led to estimates of higher interopinion correlations. Indeed it did. The average gamma for the pre-1964 format was 18.6, compared to 29.5 for the post-1964 format. Bishop et al. (1978, 1980) analyzing a new national sample collected in 1973 using the old pre-1964 format, found identical interitem correlations of .22 for both 1960 and 1973. Converse and Markus (1979) found a similar result in studying item stability over time. They concluded that, when item formats were the same, there were strikingly similar patterns of opinion stability in both the 1950s and the 1970s.

Table 2.1. Methodological Controversy over Political Sophistication

Element of paradox	Primary methodology	Clear link between methodology and conclusion of low public sophistication	Methodological controversy
Citizen apathy	Political interest, attentiveness, concern over political outcomes	Yes	No
Low levels of public knowledge	Political knowledge	Yes	No
Unstructured political thinking	Opinion intercorrelations, open-ended items	Moderate	Moderate
Psuedo opinions	Opinion self-correlation over time	Moderate	Moderate
Issueless politics	Opinion-vote correlations, open-ended items	Problematic	Substantial

citizen apathy, low levels of public knowledge, unstructured political thinking, pseudo opinions, and issueless politics—has a primary methodology on which the findings are based. The measures of citizen apathy and public knowledge are straightforward and self-evident. There are few ambiguities in the linkage between the data and the theoretical conclusions. These findings are, in effect, ignored by the critics. For the remaining elements, however, problems of interpretation arise, and it is here that the critics focus their attention, but only on one measure at a time. Suggesting an alternative interpretation or locating another fragment of data, the critics conclude that they have "rescued the mass public from its unduly imposed state of opinionlessness" or "redeemed" the American voter (Bennett, 1975, p. 9; Bishop et al., 1978, p. 252). This is a little like the aphorism of the blind men and the elephant. One person feels the trunk, another the body, still another the tail, and they argue endlessly about the true nature of the elephant. As one observer has put it, in these polarized debates the two sides "never address exactly the same phenomenon" (Stimson, 1975, p. 395).

Certain methodological approaches by their nature lead to an impression of higher levels of public sophistication. Thus, for example, 12-hour depth interviews give respondents an especially ample opportunity to articulate connections between opinions and the reasoning behind them, which may well lead to an impression of at least modest sophistication (Lane, 1962, 1973). Analyzing the responses of individuals to a few open-ended questions about two candidates and their parties gives those individuals a relatively limited opportunity to articulate such connections and a correspondingly more conservative estimate of public sophistication (Converse, 1964, 1975; Neuman, 1981). The truth of the matter lies somewhere between the estimates generated by each method.

In another example, two scholars used a different strategy for calculating the percentage of the population exhibiting evidence of sophisticated issue-voting. Because different bases were used for the percentaging, their estimates varied by 40 percentage points (Pomper, 1972, 1975, 1977; Margolis, 1977). Another researcher developed an ingenious method to calculate evidence of sophisticated issue-voting from studying deviant case groups who have opinions at variance with their party affiliation. But since these groups represented only 48 out of the 1500 respondents, they generated an exaggerated sense of the true level of issue voting in the population (Repass, 1971; Margolis, 1977).

There are no clear benchmarks for assessing political sophistication. The research generates numerous parameters, such as the proportion of knowledge items answered correctly, the percentage of respondents with stable opinions, or some measure of interopinion correlation. Such parameters are then judged to be either devastating or encouraging, depending on the perspective of the analyst. This is an unpromising format for establishing scientific consensus.

The second fallacy of the methodological critique is the measurement error fallacy. The basic data on which the phenomena of nonattitudes and pseudo opinions are based involve the correlation of an item with itself over time. The critics conclude that the low correlations usually found—generally in the range of .20 to .50—should be interpreted as measurement errors rather than respondent errors because they reflect "the inaccuracy with which the underlying attitude is reflected by the survey instrument. If survey questions are vague, then even perfectly stable respondents will appear to be inconsistent. The variation of their responses, therefore, represents errors of observations by the researchers. It is clear that this latter sort of variability is much less serious for democratic theory: it reflects a flaw in the survey research method rather than the responses of the subjects" (Achen, 1975, p. 1221).

Critics offer a variety of methodological techniques for correcting measurement error, moving the estimated stability coefficients up to levels of .80 to 1.00 (Pierce and Rose, 1974; Achen, 1975; Judd and Milburn, 1980). But ironically, there is no independent basis for determining whether response instability is a result of the vagueness of the respondents' thinking or the vagueness of the survey question. In each case the error corrections are based on the simple assertion that the problem lies not with the respondent but elsewhere. Achen, for example, argues that better-educated respondents do not have more stable opinions. One expects the better informed to have more stable opinions, and thus if they do not, it must be the fault of a vague question. But this finding falls far short of providing evidence that more clearly worded survey questions would lead to higher levels of opinion stability over time. There is doubtless some mix of measurement error and respondent instability in the data, but the question of how much of each cannot be resolved by assertion. It will require independent measurement and new approaches to data collection.

The third fallacy of the methodological critique, like the second, revolves around the interpretation of correlation coefficients. It is labeled the inference-from-correlation fallacy. The conclusions on the structure of political thinking, pseudo opinions, and issueless politics all rest on correlational data. The critics argue appropriately that if a number of opinion items are not highly correlated in the general population, this is hardly infallible evidence of low sophistication or a lack of understanding of ideological constructs. The relevant ideological principles utilized may vary from individual to individual (Coveyou and Pierson, 1971; Marcus et al., 1974; Popkin et al., 1976; Neuman, 1981).[4] But

4. One study develops the illustration: "This point may be illustrated by a simple hypothetical example involving two people, Abel and Baker. Abel may not support federal aid to education on the rationale that aid involves the federal government in an area which he feels ought to be the explicit domain of the local government. Yet he might logically support federal aid for building roads, reasoning that it improves the economy and does not conflict with the issue of location of political authority. Therefore Abel, and others who think like him, would find the responses to these two specific issues negatively correlated. For Baker both issues might evoke as the important criterion the principle of greater government concern for social welfare of the citizenry, and he would therefore support federal funding in both areas. In this situation the pattern of responses to two specific political attitudes would be positively correlated. Yet, does Baker show a higher degree of structure than Abel?" (Marcus et al., 1974, p. 407).

ironically, the methodological critique, having just questioned the meaningfulness of interpreting interopinion correlations as evidence of sophistication, makes just such an inference when relying on some alternative methodology. The new data are again seen as evidence of higher levels of ideological sophistication.

The critics use sophisticated multidimensional scaling techniques as well as traditional Guttman scaling and factor analysis (Luttbeg, 1968; Coveyou and Pierson, 1971; Marcus et al., 1974; Stimson, 1975). They experiment with new formulations of philosophical and rhetorical opinion questions (Bennett, 1975). They develop new ways of defining the elite versus mass opinion (Luttbeg, 1968; Brown, 1970). They explore whether attitude structuring might be different at nonelection periods (Marcus et al., 1974). But as yet no one has found a way out of the briar patch of attempting to infer sophistication from patterns of opinion correlation.

In the case of unstructured political thinking and pseudo opinions, most of the conclusions are drawn from simple correlations among attitudes. Issue voting, however, enters into the realm of multivariate modeling, complex linkages between attitudes and party affiliation and voting behavior. The potential for methodological confusion is overwhelming. Conclusions about political sophistication drawn from aggregated attitude-vote correlations, or the lack thereof, are extremely problematic. Again, ironically, the methodological approach encourages the self-contradictory task of identifying this problematic in other research and then finding evidence for much higher levels of mass political sophistication from some other methodological derivative of the correlation between attitudes and voting behavior.

Basically, the issue is one of partitioning the variance among a series of independent variables which purport to explain the vote decision. Unfortunately a number of patterns of vote-attitude correlation can be interpreted as evidence of low sophistication or of sophisticated issue-voting, depending on the perspective of the analyst.[5] The linkage between theories of sophistication and data of this sort is simply too loose to be meaningful.

The question is complicated by including the evaluation of candidates'

5. If one wishes to demonstrate that party identification has more effect than issues on the vote, one should control for covariation of party and vote and demonstrate that issue proximity explains a limited amount of the residual variance. If, instead, one would like to demonstrate that issues make a difference, one might run through a dozen issues and repeatedly show that each one has a small but statistically significant correlation with the vote over and above party affiliation.

personal qualities. Such personal qualities as Eisenhower's military background or avuncular qualities are seen as less appropriate criteria for voters to consider than are policy statements. But clear-cut policy statements are rare, and candidates' personal competence and leadership abilities are legitimate criteria. Reliance on the personal qualities of candidates is not in itself evidence of unsophisticated political thought, nor does it preclude issue voting.

Inferences about issue voting are further complicated by problems of causal direction. Respondents' issue proximity with a particular candidate may be more influenced by candidate preference than the other way around (Brody and Page, 1972). Ambiguity about the positions of most candidates, which is a natural outgrowth of traditionally vague campaign rhetoric, means that misperception or confusion about policy positions is not necessarily the fault of the voter.

The methodological critique of issue voting raises another important point. If the measured correspondence between voters' issue preferences and their preferred candidates is weak, it could be because the voters are unaware of the candidates' stands on issues. Or it could be simply that the analysts picked the wrong issues. Researchers generally base their conclusions on a set of six to eight issues which they see as important themes of the campaign. But such issues might be beside the point for a significant proportion of the electorate (Schapiro, 1969; Boyd, 1972).

The Paradox Deepens

Each of the three schools of thought that have emerged in response to the paradox of mass politics—the theory of stratified pluralism, the theory of the changing American voter, and the methodological critique—has failed to resolve the paradox. The failure in each case is significant.

The most promising of the three responses to the paradox is the notion of stratified pluralism. Although some of its original assumptions are not supported by the data, the overall theoretical structure is a fertile starting point for reformulating a theory of mass political sophistication.

Democratic theory provides no clear numerical benchmarks against which to assess the acceptable quality of public sophistication. There is no magical number against which to measure a citizen's political thought. The task at hand is to shift from a descriptive to a causal analysis of the linkage between knowledge and opinion and of the conditions and circumstances that nurture the growth of sophistication and participation.

3 | The Link between Sophistication and Opinion

Belief systems have never surrendered easily to empirical study or quantification.

Philip Converse

WINSTON CHURCHILL commented in 1939 on the unpredictability of Russia's role in world affairs, calling it "a riddle wrapped in a mystery inside an enigma." His phrase seems as appropriate to describe the multiple layers of paradox in mass political behavior. It conveys the frustration of unraveling one problem to find another within.

One of the fundamental principles of mass political participation is the notion of an underlying "intelligence of democracy." The related idea that the most politically active citizens have the most stable and well-developed opinions is a central tenet of the stratified pluralism model. It is also, though less explicitly, intertwined in the changing American voter theory and the methodological critique. But within this broad tradition there are hints of a curious gap between knowledge and opinion. Converse (1975), for example, describes setting out on what he thought would be a routine confirmation of the correlation between education and attitude stability over time. He was surprised to find only trifling differences, and that discovery led to a more intensive inquiry. But his efforts to explain why the differences were so small were ultimately unsuccessful. Other scholars uncovered similar findings. Luttbeg (1968) and Brown (1970) concluded that the theory of stratification must somehow have been incorrect. Achen (1975) took such findings as evidence that the opinion items themselves were poorly worded. No one was willing to reconsider the adequacy of the original assumption of a linkage between knowledge and opinion. Part of the problem was that researchers tended to rely on education as a proxy measure of political sophistication. To answer the question directly, one needs a fully developed and independent measure of political sophistication.

Measurement of Political Sophistication

In the research on mass political behavior, the methodological debates over increasingly minute points of measurement technique are reminiscent of the late stages of the Ptolemaic paradigm. Perhaps it is stretching things a bit to attempt an analogy with such a dramatic paradigm shift in the history of astronomy, but the analogy makes up in heuristic value what it lacks in the preciseness of the historical parallel. As the story goes, in the sixteenth century increasingly precise measurement of the movement of the stars and planets wreaked havoc with the dominant geocentric model of the universe passed down from Ptolemy. The apparently retrograde movements of planets were "explained" by having planets revolve around a point in their orbit as a correction factor. If further variations were observed, planets were posited to revolve around points that revolved around points which passed along their primary orbit; that is, there were corrections of corrections. The researchers were sophisticated and resourceful. The diagrams were marvelously complex. But the point is that further refinements were fruitless because the whole enterprise itself was misconceived. The measurement of political sophistication, too, needs a more parsimonious, and hopefully more accurate, model. One might be willing to sacrifice some precision for a broad-scope design that shows first what is revolving around what.

The measurement of political sophistication must be independent and direct, so that the linkage between sophistication and opinion can be meaningfully analyzed. If possible, it should be an integrated index which draws on the full pool of available measures.

The development of the index of political sophistication for this study was an involved process including tabular, correlational, and factor analyses of over 300 candidate items in nine studies involving over 30 waves of field data collection and an aggregated sample size of 11,494 respondents (Appendices A–C).[1] These data sets represent, in effect, many of the large-scale studies from which the accumulated theory of American electoral behavior has emerged (Table 3.1). The strategy involved having a panel of expert judges, primarily faculty and advanced graduate students in political science and sociology, review the full compendium of available indicators and, on the basis of their collective assessment of the relevant theoretical and empirical literature, designate a pool of

1. The appendices describe the nine core data sets used in this study, the process by which the principal measures were derived, and those elements of the theoretical literature that were particularly important to the measurement development process.

Table 3.1. Nine Core Data Sets

Study description	Elmira	Minneapolis (PAR)	Civic Culture	Bay Area Survey (BAS)	NES	NES	NES	NES	NES
Date	1948	1953	1959	1972	1956–60	1964	1968	1972–76	1980
Location	Elmira	Minneapolis	National	San Francisco	National	National	National	National	National
Number of respondents	1029	316	970	143	1966	1571	1557	1320	2622
Principal investigators	Berelson et al.	McClosky	Almond & Verba	Citrin et al.	Campbell et al.	Center for political studies	Center for political studies	Miller et al.	Miller et al.
Panel study	3 waves, 2-month interval	—	—	—	3 waves, 2-year interval	Pre- & post-election	Pre- & post-election	3 waves, 2-year interval	4 waves, 3-month interval, pre- & post-election
Items[a]									
Sophistication									
Salience	13	27	13	6	22	9	11	14	31
Knowledge	22	39	11	12	16	10	8	10	11
Conceptualization	—	—	—	—[b]	16	8	8	24	8
Total	35	66	24	18	54	27	27	48	50
Ideological disposition	2	41	—	43	6	1	6	6	6
Opinions on policy issues	12	—	—	4	32	11	14	24	28
Other demographic attitudinal and behavioral measures	153	37	142	747	743	419	480	2499	902

a. Items repeated in panel studies are counted each time they appear.
b. Depth interviews.

appropriate measures. The pool was analyzed by a series of correlational and factor analyses, which identified three related dimensions of sophistication: political salience (interest, concern, and attentiveness toward politics), political knowledge (familiarity with major political issues and accurate knowledge of prominent political figures and events), and political conceptualization (cognitive organization by means of abstract concepts and the active use of political knowledge in the evaluation of political issues). These three dimensions roughly correspond to the first three normative concerns about the quality of the mass electorate (Table 3.2).[2]

All available indicators for each of the components in each data set were combined to create indices. In turn, the component indices were combined for an overall index of political sophistication for each data set. The data analysis first explores the overall main effect of the political sophistication index and then assesses the three component indicators in search of possible differential effects. Thus, the three factors can be seen as vectors or correlated subcomponents of the underlying construct of political sophistication. In some cases the salience component proves to be empirically most important; in others, knowledge or conceptualization.

Political salience is the initial component. Interest and attentiveness to political life lead to the gradual accumulation of a reservoir of factual knowledge, which in turn manifests itself in political conceptualization, that is, knowledge in use. The three components, however, are unlike Piaget's (1952) or Kohlberg's (1964) sequential stages of cognitive development. A spiraling process model is probably more appropriate, by which interest leads to greater knowledge which in turn stimulates further interest, and so on. The character of each component requires a somewhat different type of measurement (Table 3.3).

Political salience is probably the most familiar operational definition of sophistication. It is the most often used in this research, perhaps because it is the easiest to measure. Yet people are likely to exaggerate

2. The structure and character of the indicators and, accordingly, many of the conclusions from the data analysis are limited by the types of items available. This is an inherent constraint of the secondary analysis of surveys designed for a variety of other purposes. Furthermore, like many studies of American mass politics, the National Election Study series represents the bulk of what is available. Thus any limitations of its items and research designs will have a significant impact. To try to minimize such constraints, a special effort was made to explore other data sets. The findings turned out to be very similar across all data sets (Appendix A), lending credibility to the argument that the basic patterns reported are consistent and robust.

Table 3.2. Components of Political Sophistication

Level of analysis	Component 1	Component 2	Component 3
Normative issue	Citizen apathy	Low levels of public knowledge	Unstructured political thinking
Theory of sophistication	Political salience	Political knowledge	Political conceptualization
Measurement model[a]	Interest (6), attentiveness (18), involvement (40)	Political figures (25), issue familiarity (10), structure of gov. (26), political groups (11)	Differentiation, integration[b]
Exemplary survey items	"Generally speaking, how interested are you in politics: great deal, somewhat, not at all?" (Interest) "Do you read about the campaign in a newspaper?" (Attentiveness) "Generally speaking, would you say that you personally care a good deal which party wins the presidential election?" (Involvement)	"Do you happen to recall the names of the candidates for Congress who ran in this district this November?" (Political figures) "What do you think are the major issues between the Republicans and Democrats in this year's presidential election?" (Issue familiarity) "When a new President comes into office, one of the first things he must do is appoint people to cabinet positions. Could you tell me what some of these cabinet positions are?" (Structure of gov.) "Do you think more working-class people will vote Republican, more will vote Democratic, or do you think they will be evenly split?" (Political groups)	"Is there anything you like [don't like] about the Democratic party [Republican party, Democratic candidate, Republican candidate]?"

a. The number of unique available items appears in parentheses.
b. Conceptual differentiation is the number of discrete elements of political information utilized by individuals, and conceptual integration is the level of explicit organization of ideas and information within abstract or ideological constructs. Both are measured from open-ended responses to questions which have respondents evaluate the political parties and current presidential candidates.

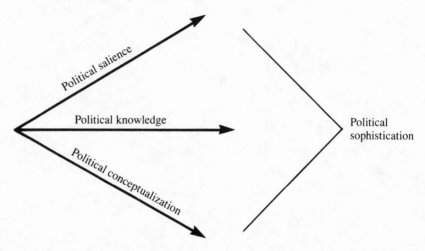

Figure 3.1. Components of Political Sophistication.

Table 3.3. Definition and Measurement of Political Sophistication

Element of sophistication	Definition	Measurement			Coverage in literature
		Type	Difficulty	Format	
Salience	Predisposition to acquire knowledge	Subjective (self-report)	Straight-forward	Closed-ended	Frequent
Knowledge	Knowledge as resource	Objective	Moderate difficulty	Closed-ended	Less frequent
Conceptualization	Knowledge in use	Objective	Difficult	Open-ended	Infrequent

socially desirable characteristics, such as political interest, in describing themselves. Thus, these items may tap a perceived sense of the civic virtue of political interest as well as interest itself. Since large portions of the mass population describe themselves as marginally or not at all interested in politics, the potential measurement problem is not insurmountable. In most cases an exaggerated report of interest in politics probably reflects more ambiguity and self-delusion than the outright attempt to mislead an interviewer.

The measures of political knowledge represent the core indicators of the sophistication domain. A shortcoming of this measurement is that too few questions have been asked. Survey researchers are traditionally cautious about disrupting rapport with respondents and are thus reluctant to ask questions which might prove embarrassing. Another potential shortcoming of the measurement of this component is the textbookish quality of some of the available items. For example, one might have simply forgotten a congressional candidate's name or might not recall immediately that a senator's term is six years. There are political facts of greater significance. But most candidates make it their business to make their name available to all who will pay attention, and thus recognition of the candidates' names would seem to be an appropriate measure. Also, such matters as a six-year Senate term are likely to be internalized as part of the ongoing process of incidental learning in following American politics.

Political conceptualization is the most complex component of sophistication and the most difficult to measure (Appendix B). This measure reflects the propensity of an individual to use facts and abstract constructs in evaluating things political. Thus, for example, less sophisticated political observers might feel that all politicians are pretty much the same. Indeed, numerous catchphrases in common political discourse reflect this perception. But with increased attention to the political sphere, individuals become increasingly aware of what differentiates the candidates and parties. They become familiar with the various wings of the parties, the political actors' past histories, and the structural position of the various actors within the government. Conceptual differentiation and integration are complementary notions. There is a natural spiraling progression of increased sophistication as one moves back and forth between a more highly differentiated perception of the political world and a more active use of abstract concepts to make sense out of this diversity. A broad-based, multimethod, direct measure of political sophistication, rather than one inferred from patterns of opinion structuring, makes it possible to explore the critical linkage between the two.

Opinion Holding

In practical terms, the link between political sophistication and the expression of political opinion is surprisingly weak. This is a counterintuitive finding, but it emerges as a central finding of the present study.

The first-order empirical analysis reveals, as intuition would dictate, a positive correlation between the index of political sophistication and an index of opinion holding for each of the available data sets. Opinion holding is measured as a simple additive index of the number of political opinion items in which the respondent chooses to express an opinion rather than opt for a no-opinion or don't-know response. The average correlation (Pearson) between opinion holding and political sophistication is .51 across the core data sets. Although this appears to be a substantial correlation, it is artifactual and misleading (Figure 3.2). The key finding is that there is very little variation in opinion holding. Almost everybody, almost every time, responds to an opinion question by offering an opinion. This is a central and troubling fact of survey research methodology. Across the nine core data sets, respondents expressed

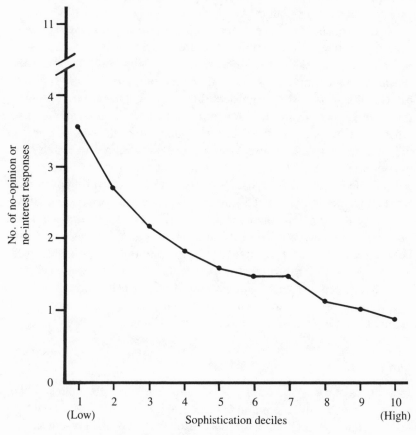

Figure 3.2. Sophistication and Opinion Holding. *Source:* NES 1956–1980.

opinions nine times out of ten. Only a tiny fraction selected the no-opinion option as many as three or more times out of ten. Even when respondents were assured by interviewers that it was not necessary to have an opinion on every issue and were explicitly asked if they had an opinion on a particular issue before their opinion was solicited, respondents offered opinions on an average of eight times out of ten.

There were an average of 11 issue items per study on topics ranging from the economy to civil rights. Respondents on average opted for the no-opinion or no-interest response 1.8 times out of 11, or roughly 16 percent of the time. But the standard deviation was very small. Fully 80 percent of the people answered nine or more of the 11 questions. Thus, though the correlation coefficient computed by the traditional formula indicates a healthy and statistically significant .53 correlation, and the traditional cut-off graph, illustrating only the range of 0–4 no-opinion responses, reveals a nicely modulated curve, the relationship has little practical significance because of the invariance in opinion response. If the full range of 11 items were used in the figure, it would give a better idea of the pattern—a relatively flat line at the bottom of the graph.

To phrase the question in a slightly different way, out of all the opinions expressed, 52 percent came from the top half of the sophistication continuum, and 48 percent came from the bottom half. This would seem to be a textbook example of the need to interpret correlation coefficients with care, especially in cases such as this which are characterized by limited variance.[3] Moreover, the relationship between sophistication and opinion holding is nonlinear. There is almost no difference in the average rate of opinion expression among the top four sophistication groups. The curve becomes steeper for the bottom group, which

3. Ordinarily in cases where variation is artificially constrained, correlation coefficients underestimate the true relationship. If that were true here, the overall correlation coefficient of .51 between opinion holding and sophistication would underestimate rather than exaggerate the link. This, however, is not an artifact of a particular study but rather an inherent characteristic of the survey method. Respondents are reluctant to admit they have no opinion. The number of people who freely admit that they have pre-existing opinions on only a few of the many issues put before them in an interview is so small that the apparent correlation between sophistication and opinion holding is of little practical significance. Perhaps a better way of putting it is to draw on the traditional comparison between slope and correlation coefficients (Tufte, 1974; Stolzenberg and Land, 1983). The difference in slope between the highest and lowest sophistication deciles is about two expressed opinions out of a potential 15. The difference between the top and bottom halves is about one expressed opinion out of a potential 15. Thus, although the correlation coefficient calculates out to an impressive figure, the practical significance in terms of which strata of the populace express opinions in surveys is really quite small.

sets itself apart with a distinctive candor and owns up to not having a crystallized opinion on every subject. Perhaps the distinguishing feature of this apolitical group is that its members simply have not been socialized into the belief that they ought to have such opinions, and accordingly they have no reluctance to say so. This distinctive behavior of the bottom strata of sophistication is a clue to resolving the paradox of mass politics.

Incidentally, all three components of the sophistication index are equally correlated with variation and opinion holding. Salience correlates .23, knowledge correlates .20, and conceptualization correlates .21 with opinion holding averaged over the core studies. Opinion holding, such as it is, seems to be an additive function of all three components of sophistication, because the overall sophistication index correlates .51 with opinion holding. A full regression analysis with education, age, and other demographic factors was also calculated to see if there were any intervening variables of particular interest. Education is positively correlated with opinion holding, and sex is negatively correlated, but neither has a significant independent effect over and above the correlation of sophistication with opinion holding.

An important caveat here concerns the equation of opinion holding with the expression of an opinion in a survey research setting. They are not necessarily the same thing. There are many significant ways whereby the holding and articulation of opinions may vary between the more and less sophisticated strata of the populace, which are obscured by the opinion-giving context of the survey interview. Nonetheless, as public opinion finds its voice in the utterances of individuals at meetings, in letters to the editor, and in the act of voting itself, there is a formality of the setting, an expectation that one will indeed have an opinion that parallels the survey interview setting. Although opinion expression in a survey and opinion holding in the deeper sense are not the same thing, they are closely enough related to be a cause for concern.

This finding influences the stratified pluralism thesis by setting a strong constraint on the notion of issue publics, especially the idea that only those individuals who have thought about and are knowledgeable about an issue will voice an opinion or attempt to influence policy. The proportion who express political opinions depends on the question wording, the interview setting, the questions that went before, and the type of topic. But based on these data, the 80–80 rule is a conservative estimate: 80 percent of the people will voice an opinion 80 percent of the time. In addition, the 20 percent who choose not to offer an opinion reflect only in modest degree those within the populace who are less politically informed.

Opinion Stability

The lack of a meaningful link between political sophistication and opinion holding could be a fluke of some sort, an artifact of the interview process, or the product of a shared sense of civic mindedness in American political culture. The correlation between sophistication and the stability of expressed opinions over time is a more critical test of the knowledge-opinion link. It is well known that there is a great deal of noise in the measurement process (Converse, 1964; Key, 1961; Schuman and Presser, 1981). It becomes increasingly evident to those who have pored over the results of surveys, especially panel surveys, that public opinion consists of some important trends of opinion against a background of constant churn. Perhaps this churn is an inherent and natural "Brownian movement" of opinion and belief. The key to the model of stratified pluralism is then to find the link between sophistication and opinion stability in that potential elite of opinion leadership which provides continuity and consistency and, in times of change, exists as the bellweather stratum.

But in this case there is even less evidence of the link. Indeed, there is significant variation. Although the opinions of some respondents are much more consistent over time than others, the opinions of the more sophisticated of the citizenry are not significantly more stable.

In four studies, which include a variety of item formats, types of issues, and historical circumstances, the result is the same: either no relationship or a surprisingly weak correlation between the sophistication indices and the stability of expressed opinion over time. The Elmira study, which measured opinion stability over a period of several months, includes two items on domestic politics, one concerning approval or disapproval of labor unions and the other concerning the benefits of price controls. Two items also concern foreign affairs, one on respondents favoring the Jews or the Arabs in Palestine and the other on their appraisal of world tensions and the likelihood of war. The average test-retest coefficient of attitude stability on these four issues for the sample as a whole is .44 (tau-beta). The most sophisticated quartile has an average coefficient of only .45, which is substantively and statistically undifferentiable from .44. On two of the items the middle rather than the high sophistication stratum exhibits the highest attitude stability.

The pattern is the same in the National Election Study of 1980. In this case, for a full national sample, four issues were measured in three waves three months apart on a seven-point scale: the trade-off between inflation, unemployment, and welfare; educational spending; foreign policy toward the Soviet Union; and defense spending. The average stability coefficient from the first wave to the last is .44 for the lowest sophistication quartile and only .48 for the highest. It is not clear whether that small difference is to some degree due to the fact that the more sophisticated respondents are literally better able to remember the opinion responses they selected several months before. A better test is the examination of stability over a period of several years, although it is complicated by the increased prospect of true opinion change.

The National Election Studies of the 1950s and 1970s provide the answer. The 1956-1958-1960 panel utilizes Likert items on five domestic policy issues and three foreign policy ones. The average continuity coefficient for the lowest sophistication quartile is .27 (Tau-Beta), compared to .32 for the highest. In the 1972-1974-1976 panel six domestic issues,

Table 3.4. Sophistication and Opinion Stability: Percentage of Opinions Stable over Time (N)

Study	Item format	Sophistication		
		Low	Medium	High
Elmira 1948	Multiple choice	59	63	65
2 waves	4-point scale	(211)	(478)	(250)
2-month interval				
NES 1956–60	Likert-style	39	36	36
3 waves	5-point scale	(281)	(592)	(289)
2-year interval				
NES 1972–76	NES	42	44	44
3 waves	7-point scale[a]	(330)	(660)	(330)
2-year interval				
NES 1980	NES	44	52	55
3 waves	7-point scale	(656)	(1311)	(655)
3-month interval				
Average across all studies		46	49	50

a. For the 7-point scales of NES 1972–1976 and 1980 *stable* was defined as responding with the same or an adjacent scale point each time the question was asked.

measured with the seven-point scale format, reveal a somewhat higher differential between the lowest and highest sophistication quartiles: .42 and .55 respectively. Because of the difficulties associated with the interpretation of coefficients, especially the controversy over comparing different question formats, several other formulations are explored to estimate opinion stability.

Perhaps the most straightforward measure of opinion stability is the percent of respondents offering the same opinion each time they are asked (Table 3.4). The results are comparable across the various studies. In the 1956–1960 panel the lowest sophistication quartile actually has the highest level of opinion stability. But the differences are not significant in any case.

The phenomenon of extreme instability of opinion reinforces this pattern (Table 3.5). The fact that three of the studies measure opinion at three points in time makes it possible to identify those individuals who flip-flop back and forth—agreeing, then disagreeing, then agreeing again—or the converse. Analysis of opinion stability is complicated by the fact that some of the instability might be interpreted as true opinion change. The double reversal of opinion phenomenon, although rela-

Table 3.5. Sophistication and Opinion Double Reversal (%)

| Study | Item format | Subject | Sophistication | | |
			Low	Medium	High
NES 1956–58–60	Likert-style	5 domestic issues	7	8	9
3 waves	5-point scale	3 foreign policy	8	6	5
2-year interval					
N = 1163					
NES 1972–74–76	NES	6 domestic issues	5	5	5
3 waves	7-point scale				
2-year interval					
N = 1320					
NES 1980	NES	2 domestic issues	7	8	10
3 waves	7-point scale	2 foreign policy	31	16	14
3-month interval					
N = 1008					
Average across all items			9	8	8

tively rare, is a critical test, because such movement can hardly be based on philosophically or historically grounded opinion change. This strategy of analysis, though similar to the black-and-white model and the model of three-wave stability, is intuitively and mathematically more straight-forward (Converse, 1970; Wiley and Wiley, 1970). As before, there is no significant or persistent difference in the incidence of truly volatile opinion expression among different strata of political sophistication.

The 1956-1958-1960 panel includes Converse's test-case item on attitudes toward power and housing, which served as the basis for his estimates of random opinion. Use of his formulas shows that the majority of random responders, or some 56 percent, come from the more, not the less sophisticated half of the sample.

One last possibility is that opinion stability is linked to only one component of the sophistication index. The subcomponent of conceptualization, for example, which is based on the individuals' use and understanding of abstract political concepts, might reveal a significant link with opinion stability over time, while the more general components of political salience and knowledge do not. Each of the analyses was rerun separately for each of the three subcomponents, but the verdict remained the same.

The pattern is clear. It is consistent across different policy issues, different time periods in recent American political history, different item formats, different test-retest intervals, different samples, different methods for computing attitude stability, and different measures of political sophistication. Political opinions, as best as they can be measured in a survey setting, are subject to substantial churn and volatility. Furthermore, there is little evidence that the opinions of the most politically sophisticated stratum of the electorate are significantly less volatile than people at the very bottom of the sophistication continuum.

Opinion Structure

The failure of the data to support the hypothesis that the more sophisticated are more opinionated and have more stable opinions diminishes confidence in the related hypothesis that opinions of the more sophisticated are more tightly organized and highly correlated with each other. This is with good reason. Again, the data fail to confirm an intuitively obvious phenomenon. And again, the pattern is clear in each of the data sets, so that it cannot be the unique result of a particular group of measures or a particular historical setting. The analysis compares the average levels of intercorrelation of traditionally defined liberal-conservative policy issues for different sophistication subgroups. When there were two measures of the same issue, only one was included so that the analysis would clearly be based only on interissue rather than test-retest correlations.

Opinion structuring as measured by the average interitem correlations is roughly the same at all levels of sophistication (Table 3.6).[4] The pattern

Table 3.6. Sophistication and Opinion Constraint

	Average interitem correlation (Pearson) Sophistication		
Study	Low	Medium	High
Elmira			
5 domestic issues	.00	.06	.17
NES 1956–60			
5 domestic issues	.14	.17	.25
3 foreign affairs issues	.26	.16	.14
NES 1964			
6 domestic issues	.25	.27	.34
3 foreign affairs issues	.22	.14	.17
NES 1968			
6 domestic issues	.30	.35	.33
4 foreign affairs issues	.14	.11	.14
NES 1972–76			
8 domestic issues	.22	.22	.29
NES 1980			
7 domestic issues	.22	.21	.38
Overall Average	.19	.19	.25

4. Such interitem correlational measures of attitude structuring, though problematic, continue to be frequently used. One particularly interesting psychologically grounded theory of political opinion and survey responses is based on the premise that the more sophisticated respondents give more stable and structured responses (Zaller, 1984). Several factors might explain the differences between his conclusions and those reported here, including the use of more abstract issue referents, a different treatment of no-opinion responses, and a different perspective on what qualifies as a large difference. Most of the research reveals little or no difference between low- and high-sophistication strata on opinion consistency and stability. But the question of which types of issues generate the greatest differences has yet to be pursued.

varies somewhat from study to study and between domestic and international issues. But again, the more sophisticated do not demonstrate dramatically higher levels of opinion constraint.

Because these are summary measures, however, the real differences in the organization of opinions between sophistication subgroups might be hidden in the intercorrelation matrices themselves. Accordingly, each of the matrices was reviewed and factor analyzed separately for the low-, medium-, and high-sophistication subgroups. Overall, the matrices and factor analyses for the different subgroups were quite uniform. Foreign affairs issues, however, tend to be more highly correlated for the less sophisticated. This runs counter to expectations, because such issues involve more abstract and remote questions than domestic questions. Another pattern corresponding more closely to original expectations is that the less sophisticated use the concrete referent of race to organize opinion to a somewhat greater degree. But the patterns are never very distinct. The similarity of patterns of attitude constraint for both low- and high-sophistication subgroups is illustrated by a typical set of interitem matrices used in the analysis (Table 3.7). The use of race, for example, by the less sophisticated as an anchoring point for opinions rather than more abstract principles of government involvement is in evidence here. But the other domestic items are no more highly correlated for the low sophistication group.

These results raise fundamental questions about the stratification of public opinion. This is not an entirely new issue to professional political pollsters. Of all the problems of their profession, the most difficult and enduring is not that of getting respondents to answer questions and express preferences for one candidate or another. Most respondents oblige willingly. And it is not projecting estimates from small samples. The mathematics of statistical inference are well developed and widely understood. The most frustrating problem is trying to estimate which of those who have expressed a preference for one candidate over another care enough about their expressed opinion actually to vote. If those favoring one candidate are less likely to act on the basis of their preference, the survey findings could easily predict the wrong winner. On election day there will be a clear-cut behavioral dividing line between those who voted and those who did not. The paradox lies in the limited ability to predict who will be on which side of that line.

Correspondingly, some individuals have opinions that are relatively more stable and organized than other people's opinions. But the theory of political stratification based on an underlying sophistication continuum does not make it possible to predict which is which. For reasons

Table 3.7. Sophistication and Opinion Constraint: Interitem Correlations (Pearson)

	Domestic issues					
Low sophistication (Lowest quartile)	1	2	3	4	5	6
1. Guaranteed employment	—					
2. Socialized medicine	.36	—				
3. Federal aid to education	.14	.23	—			
4. Nondiscrimination in employment	.38	.24	.36	—		
5. School desegregation	.29	.07	.25	.63	—	
6. Public accommodations desegregation	.16	.09	.31	.47	.55	—
High sophistication (top quartile)	1	2	3	4	5	6
1. Guaranteed employment	—					
2. Socialized medicine	.32	—				
3. Federal aid to education	.40	.32	—			
4. Nondiscrimination in employment	.43	.21	.34	—		
5. School desegregation	.36	.26	.40	.43	—	
6. Public accommodations desegregation	.24	.17	.21	.39	.44	—
	Foreign affairs issues					
Low sophistication (lowest quartile)	1	2	3	4		
1. Foreign aid	—					
2. Talk with Communists	.18	—				
3. Trade with Communists	.20	.33	—			
4. Vietnam	.32	−.09	−.08	—		
High sophistication (top quartile)	1	2	3	4		
1. Foreign aid	—					
2. Talk with Communists	.22	—				
3. Trade with Communists	.20	.35	—			
4. Vietnam	.09	−.01	−.01	—		

Source: NES 1968.

not yet clear, those who are more interested, knowledgeable, and cognitively sophisticated do not have significantly more stable or organized political opinions.

Issue Publics

The other element of the stratified pluralism mode, issue pluralism, must also be addressed. Perhaps attention to specific issue publics holds the key to sorting out who in the mass polity will have predictably more consistent and constrained opinions. If individuals in fact have widely varied concerns and areas of expertise in political life, the central analytic tool—the notion of a measurable, generalized continuum of political sophistication—is not the most appropriate test of the question. The existence of issue publics implies issue-specific sophistication. Accordingly, a straightforward empirical test was made of the link between issue-specific interest or knowledge and issue-specific opinion stability. Patterns of opinion expression would have been a less critical test, because the bulk of the population is more than willing to express opinions on almost any political question raised.

There are several ways to test the issue publics hypothesis. One might consider the traditional emphasis of the pluralist perspective on clearly identifiable cultural and demographic groups. Specialized interest and knowledge are implied by demographic group membership. Thus, one could explore whether black Americans have more focused and stable opinions on policy issues that are of special relevance to the black community. This approach is termed demographic group pluralism. Another form of the pluralist model emphasizes the mechanisms of organized interest groups, such as the American Legion, the Sierra Club, the American Civil Liberties Union, or the National Rifle Association. This approach is called interest group pluralism. Still another approach to identifying interest subgroups is to ask, in an open-ended format, which issues are of specific concern to a citizen. One common question in the National Election Studies, concerning the most important problems facing the country, allows for a test along these lines. An individual need not be born into a unique demographic category or join an organized group but may simply express a special interest in a particular policy question. This model is referred to as issue publics pluralism. It is of particular relevance to issue voing because of the inappropriateness of correlating issue preferences and candidate preferences as an indicator of voter "rationality" without an independent measure of the salience of that issue to the voter (Shapiro, 1969). The issue publics test focuses on just that phenomena, the small subgroups for whom specific issues are of particular salience.

Tests were run of the demographic group, interest group, and issue publics hypotheses. The data came from only a sampling of issues, so that these findings do not necessarily hold for all issues, all groups, and all times. But the result is the same in each case. The data do not support the hypothesis. Those citizens who, by reason of demographic or interest group affiliation or the identification of an issue as having special significance to them, are no more likely than the rest of the population to express opinions or maintain stable opinions over time.

On the demographic variables, those who have had recent direct experience with unemployment have no more frequent or more consistent opinions on unemployment policy. In fact, it works out the other way around, perhaps as a result of the interaction with other demographic variables. Those who have not experienced unemployment are more likely to express opinions and are slightly more likely to have stable opinions. There are similar results on redistributive welfare policy, where lower income groups through self-interest might be expected to be especially vocal and consistent. Again the data fall the other way (Schlozman and Verba, 1979; Kinder and Sears, 1985). Although these conclusions are constrained by the limited data available, the fact of the matter is that there are relatively few prominent political issues for which demographic group affiliations are particularly significant. This is as much a problem of the underlying theory as of the availability of data.

It is true that southerners, Hispanics, young people, and other familiar groups that are commonly used in polling and political journalism do have identifiably different opinions on numerous issues. But in most cases these are incidental or are indirectly derived from their group affiliation. At any point in time, the proportion of central issues on the national political agenda which impact them directly or unambiguously is rare. There may be a crisis in the administration and funding of social security which will impact the self-interests of the young and old differently. There may be a relatively minor bill in Congress on bilingual education or immigration which will directly affect Hispanics. For decades, the American South has been distinguished by its political conservatism, especially concerning racial issues, much of which has its roots in the antebellum era. But with the shifts in racial distribution and the dramatic urbanization and industrialization of the South, this is likely to become more of a cultural tradition than a demographically defined sectionalism.

Often, the closer one looks at a specific issue, the less clear is the demographic self-interest connection. Take the issue of age and social security. This was a matter of considerable concern in the early 1980s; in fact, it was a textbook example of a political hot potato. Surprisingly, the polls revealed that young voters are almost as strongly supportive of maintaining current levels of social security allocations as are older Americans. This turns out to be not only because of their interest in having social security available when they will ultimately need it but also because of their financial and emotional ties to their parents' economic condition. Or take the race issue. On a number of specific proposals, such as busing or racially determined hiring quotas, blacks disagree among themselves whether such policies are appropriate and serve the long-range interests of the black community. Another case in point is the strong difference among women over whether the Equal Rights Amendment represents appropriate or counterproductive policy in terms of their interests.

To get an idea of the potential role of group-linked issue opinions, take any series of prominent political issues and array them across the horizontal axis, then array a typical list of demographic variables down the vertical axis, and observe which of the cells are likely to represent a potentially meaningful connection between the issue and the specific life circumstances of a demographic group. Such an exercise, drawing on the six demographic variables and thirteen political issues from the 1972–1976 National Election Studies, reveals potential logical connections only 13 percent of the time. Another list or another analyst might generate a different parameter, but this one provides a rough rule of thumb for the limits of demographically linked pluralism.

Another perspective on the limits of pluralism can be derived from data on interest group affinities. In the 1976 National Election Study a list of 16 categories was put in front of the respondents and they were asked to pick the one to which they felt most closely associated (Table 3.8). This question forces people to identify an affinity group in the form of, "If you have to pick one, which do you pick?" Half of those giving a response locate themselves on a general economic stratification continuum. The majority identify themselves simply as middle-class people. The next most significant category is age, with 22 percent of the respondents identifying themselves with their age group. None of the other demographic groupings generates very high levels of affinity. Given this pattern, the question remains as to how many people define such interest group affinities in political terms. This is a difficult question which would require a fresh research design, but part of the answer lies in the actual participation in organized interest groups.

The available data are even more limited for testing the hypothesis of interest group pluralism. Again the phenomenon of the rarity of data reflects the difficulty of the original hypothesis. The fact of the matter is that direct participation in political action groups is extremely rare. Take the question on the 1980 National Election Study: "Now what

Table 3.8. Interest Group Affinities of American Population

General domain (%)	Specific group (%)	N	Potential interest group
45	6	134	Poor people
	12	291	Working people
	20	481	Middle-class people
	3	83	Business people
	4	107	Farmers
22	12	280	Young people
	10	247	Older people
7	7	161	Women
6	2	57	Catholics
	3	64	Protestants
	1	24	Jews
8	5	109	Whites
	3	64	Blacks
4	1	29	Liberals
	3	83	Conservatives
1	1	22	Southerners
6	6	143	No group

Source: NES 1976.

about political action groups such as groups sponsored by a union or business, or issue groups like the National Rifle Association or National Organization of Women. Did you give money this election year to a political action group or any other group that supported or opposed a particular candidate in the election?" The question asks only if the respondents gave money, usually in response to direct mail appeals, but not necessarily whether they established a formal membership in the organization. Still, only one in 17, or about 6 percent, answer in the affirmative. Thus, from the total sample of over 1000 respondents, only 12 contribute to organizations active in gun control, seven to union PACs, six to business or professional groups, and six to PACs focusing on either side of the abortion issue. On another question asking if respondents have been involved with a sit-in protest or demonstration concerning some national problem, less than 2 percent report involvement. Such small numbers make a meaningful analysis of opinion stability impossible. In the 1972–1976 and 1980 National Election Studies, a comparison of rates of opinion expression and opinion stability between the small group who did join or support various issue groups and the balance of the sample across all available issues reveals no differences.

Finally, on the issue publics hypothesis, the situation is very different. Here the individuals need not have joined or contributed to a particular organization but simply to have identified an issue as being of special concern to them. Because of the open-ended format of the question, any issue is fair game, not just those with which the researchers are concerned. Here respondents do not hesitate to articulate their concerns. The sample, as a whole, averages seven issues or issue areas as being of special concern to them.

After the first cut of the analysis, it looked as if there might be some life yet in the issue publics hypothesis. Bivariate analyses suggested that those who volunteer a special concern with unemployment or inflation are four times as likely to express opinions and four times as likely to have stable opinions on the standard unemployment-inflation opinion item. Those who noted foreign policy concerns are twice as likely to have an opinion and one and a half times as likely to have a stable opinion on policy toward the Soviet Union.

But this turns out to be a measurement artifact. Such artifacts serve as a warning not to look only at the number of expressed opinions and the number of stable opinions as evidence of distinct pluralism. The reality of these numbers lies in the psychological response set of the survey interview. Some interviewees, when asked to give opinions or list important problems, are more forthcoming than others. Given the opportunity to list nine factors, they are inclined to come up with nine. Given the opportunity to express an opinion on an issue in each wave of the survey, they offer an opinion each time. As a result, the likelihood of mentioning any topic as important and of expressing opinions are mathematically related. Thus, for example, if a respondent mentions foreign policy as an important problem, the respondent is more likely to have an opinion on unemployment. This is hardly evidence of unique issue publics. Controlling for the total number of important problems mentioned washes out the relationship between issue-specific salience and issue-specific opinion expression in all cases.

In view of all this, as well as the weak evidence for self-interest calculations, two postures might be assumed (Schlozman and Verba, 1979; Sears et al., 1970). On the one hand, the pluralism notion might simply not be supported by the data. Interest group participation exists in extremely small proportions, and issue publics are mostly artifacts of common political parlance and the psychodynamics of the survey interview and are not terribly relevant to the basic dynamics of mass political thought. On the other hand, the case might not yet be resolved. The nature of small special-interest groups does not lend itself to meaningful analysis by mass sample surveys. They may have an impact on both the political agenda and political outcomes well beyond their numbers.

The second view is more probable. The notion of large-scale, cross-cutting, issue-public pluralism may reflect the wishful thinking of analysts more than the behavior of the mass citizenry. The role of issue pluralism and interest-group pluralism needs to be rethought. It could be a force in day-to-day politics even without being central to the political cognitions of the great majority of citizens.

Cognitive Styles and Political Ideology

An important and puzzling question about the linkage between sophistication and opinion involves the issue of ideology, or whether and to what extent sophistication leads to conservative or liberal opinions. The term *political ideology* is to students of mass political behavior what the red flag is to the bull. At the mere mention of the term scholars flare their nostrils and furrow their brows, ready to do intellectual battle. There is as much controversy and soul-searching about the origins and influence of political ideology in mass publics among researchers as there is about politics among committed ideologues.

The debate is much more than a two-sided one, and this may be the key to the problem. It is not a single problem but a cluster of loosely related issues. How do voters interpret the issue positions of candidates and parties? How do social class origins lead to potential extremism of the left or the right? How do political elites and mass publics differ in their conceptualization of left and right? Are political conservatives by nature authoritarian and perhaps anti-Semitic, or is there an equivalent authoritarianism of the left? What social and demographic factors lead an individual to become increasingly conservative or liberal? Why do older people become increasingly conservative? Why do the well-educated, especially those who teach college, tend to be liberal? Why does the American South lean so heavily toward political conservatism? The debate over these intertwined issues is not often fruitful, because each side defines the issue somewhat differently and tends to argue past the other (Eysenck, 1954; Bell, 1955, 1962; McClosky, 1958; Lipset, 1960, 1968; Rokeach, 1960; Key, 1961; Lane, 1962; Ladd, 1969; Sartori, 1969; Burnham, 1970; Hamilton, 1972; Putnam, 1973). The exchanges in this area are now a familiar ritual of political intellectual life.

One of the more narrowly defined empirical questions is whether the politically sophisticated tend to be more liberal or more conservative. The word *ideology* is operationally defined as the distribution of individuals on the liberal-conservative continuum. Two measures can be used. The first involves simply asking the individuals to place themselves on a seven-point scale from extremely liberal through middle-of-the-road to extremely conservative. The terms are not defined but are left to be interpreted as words in common usage by each respondent. If the terms are vague or irrelevant to some respondents, they would be expected either to place themselves at the mid-point of the scale or to opt for a no-answer response. The second measure is an index of eleven issue items. Each has a commonly accepted liberal and conservative side. Thus, a highly liberal score on the index represents a strong and consistent propensity to give answers on the liberal side. A middle point represents the propensity to give either an intermediate response or a mixture of liberal and conservative answers. The issues range from domestic policy to foreign relations and include many of the salient points of recent political debate, such as busing, social welfare, and relations with Russia.

There are strongly held hypotheses on both sides. The hypothesis on one side holds that sophistication leads to liberalism. One analysis of 539 survey items on a sample of over 1200 respondents from the Minneapolis–St. Paul area, for example, suggests that, "By every means available to us, conservative beliefs are found most frequently among the uninformed, the poorly educated and so far as we can determine, the less-intelligent" (McClosky, 1958, p. 35). The tables are forceful. More than four times as many college-educated and high-political-knowledge respondents fall into the liberal rather than extreme conservative column. In the tradition of the authoritarian personality, such traits as opinion rigidity, closed-mindedness, and concrete orientation to political issues, as well as anti-Semitism and generalized xenophobia, are associated with political and economic conservatism (Adorno et al., 1950; Lipset, 1960; Brown, 1965; Sears, 1969; Selznick and Steinberg, 1969).

Surveys of public opinion on international and foreign policy issues also demonstrate that the better educated and more politically sophisticated tend to be more liberal and less isolationist. Two and one-half times as many grammar school as college-educated respondents score as isolationist (Key, 1961). Higher education also affects the growth of liberal beliefs among college students. Among students at Bennington College in the 1930s increasing liberalism is assocated with high levels of involvement in college life and with the duration of college attendance, and this relationship is still in evidence 30 years later (Newcomb, 1943; Newcomb et al., 1967). Although the analysis is framed in terms of the especially "liberal atmosphere" at Bennington, the link between higher education in general and liberalism is part of a general "liberalization" process. There is also an apparent correlation between sophistication and liberalism (Neuman, 1981). The anchoring concepts of conservative ideology are perhaps fewer in number and less abstract and thus resonate more easily with a conceptual style of the middle and lower strata of political sophistication.

The other hypothesis holds that sophistication leads to conservatism. The central tenet here is the basic correlation between socioeconomic status and conservatism. Business people and professionals whose careers keep them in close day-to-day touch with policymaking and economics are traditionally conservative. As people get older and become more sophisticated about how political and economic systems work, they become less enthusiastic about idealistic reforms and are more inclined toward the status quo. Perhaps they have seen previous reform movements fail. They have developed an increasing appreciation of the complexity of checks and balances in the current system. Thus, in the American context at least, sophistication is said to breed conservatism. In their attitudes on educational systems, medical care for the poor, civil rights, and government involvement in industry, the better educated are consistently more conservative, and the correlations are higher than would be expected from the intervening effects of education's correlation with occupation and income (Key, 1961). Parallel results are reported in other studies (Free and Cantril, 1968; Erikson et al., 1980).

Both hypotheses, however, oversimplify matters. The truth is that whether sophistication leads to increased liberalism or conservatism depends on the issue. In most cases there is no relationship between liberal or conservative positions and political sophistication. The differences by education, for example, between liberalism and conservatism are for the most part small and statistically insignificant (Free and Cantril, 1968).

Despite these uncertain conclusions, the potential linkage of increased political knowledge and sophistication to particular liberal or conservative viewpoints is of critical importance to the democratic process. In many ways, it lies at the root of concern over mass society, especially the weakness of democracy to simplistic demagogic appeals. How complex problems get simplified into political slogans and parables is extremely important, as in the public understanding of the trade-offs between the twin problems of inflation and unemployment. At some times simplified catchphrases may resonate more with the liberal side of an issue, and at other times more with the conservative.

The issues used in testing the link between sophistication and liberalism or conservatism help to explain why some evidence supports the first hypothesis while other data support the second. The studies showing a link between low sophistication and conservative authoritarianism rely heavily on abstract political statements and simplistic maxims. They are not concrete, currently debated, two-sided policy issues. Not surprisingly, those who agree with such statements as, "If people would talk less and work more, everybody would be better off," and, "People are getting soft and weak from so much coddling and babying," reflect an intuitive and perhaps apolitical conservatism not necessarily akin to the ideological beliefs that attract people to the conservative side of a concrete policy issue (Adorno et al., 1950; McClosky, 1958). The criticism regarding the acquiescence response bias of the authoritarianism studies reflects a recognition of this problem (Christie and Jahoda, 1954). The study of religious prejudice, for example, attempts to isolate out the phenomenon of political simplism itself and relate it to anti-Semitism, political beliefs, and demographic variables (Selznick and Steinberg, 1969).

Furthermore, few studies actually relate political sophistication to political opinions and beliefs. Most studies use education as a proxy indicator for sophistication, which complicates the analysis. Thus, to a great extent the basic hypothesis has yet to be tested. If the less sophisticated and the more sophisticated strata of the polity are coming to have increasingly polarized positions on current political issues, it could have dire implications for the political process.

On the liberalism-conservatism continuum, more Americans tend to identify themselves as conservative than liberal (Table 3.9). The ratio of conservatives to liberals is about five to three. But the ratio is virtually identical for each level of sophistication. Several other distinctions help to put this finding in perspective. Only 62 percent of the respondents opt to place themselves on the continuum in the first place. And a substantial portion of those who place themselves on the continuum feel

Table 3.9. Sophistication and Self-Identification of Liberalism-Conservatism (%)

Sophistication	Extremely liberal	Liberal	Slightly liberal	Middle of road	Slightly conservative	Conservative	Extremely conservative	Proportion of sample placing self on scale	(N)
Low	3	10	10	40	20	15	4	30	(404)
Medium	2	5	15	37	20	18	3	64	(807)
High	3	15	13	19	24	24	3	92	(403)
Overall	3	9	14	31	21	20	3	62	(1614)

Source: NES 1980.

most comfortable at dead center, the middle of the road, which in some ways is a further indication of no opinion. Thus, excluding the middle-of-the-road group, only 43 percent place themselves substantively on the liberalism-conservativism scale. Only 3 percent identify themselves as extremely liberal, and another 3 percent identify themselves as extremely conservative. But the tendency to place oneself on the scale, and to do so outside of the midpoint, increases dramatically with higher levels of sophistication. Only 30 percent of the lowest sophistication quartile place themselves on the continuum, versus 92 percent on the highest sophistication quartile. The proportion at the midpoint falls from 40 percent for the low sophistication group to only 19 percent for the high sophistication group. This makes sense, since part of the operational definition of political sophistication is the ability to interpret abstract political concepts like liberalism and conservatism. But the central conclusion about sophistication and the directionality of ideology remains a straightforward null finding. As the population becomes increasingly sophisticated with time, there is no evidence that it will move in aggregate toward the left or right.

Although many people are vague about such terms as *liberal* and *conservative,* most individuals are inclined to express opinions on most policy issues. On such indices, the most sophisticated respondents are neither more liberal nor more conservative (Table 3.10). The ratio between liberals and conservatives remains constant across all levels of sophistication. This index incorporates a variety of questions on domestic and foreign policy topics. The basic operational measure is the

Table 3.10. Sophistication and Policy Opinion Index of Liberalism-Conservatism (%)[a]

Sophistication	Liberal		Middle	Conservative		(N)
	3 or more	1–2		1–2	3 or more	
Low	9	21	38	21	11	(404)
Medium	12	20	25	22	21	(807)
High	23	11	14	21	31	(403)
Overall	14	18	26	22	21	

Source: NES 1980.
a. The proportion of respondents giving the designated number of more liberal than conservative responses, or the reverse, in an index of 11 policy issue items.

ratio of conservative to liberal responses. This ratio controls for any intervening effects of variation in opinion expression on these items. The respondents have a slight propensity to give conservative responses on these issues, providing roughly one more conservative response than liberal response out of eleven items. But this pattern is unrelated to sophistication.

The relationship of sophistication to individual opinions, however, reveals clear and consistent differences between the lower and higher levels of sophistication in the mass public (Table 3.11). On issues of domestic policy which propose federal government involvement to benefit underprivileged groups by redistributive policies or special government sanctions, the more sophisticated respondents are consistently and significantly more conservative. On four such items the more sophisticated are from 17 to 19 percent more conservative. In contrast, on issues that draw on broader values of the political culture, such as those dealing with social change and civil liberties, including prayer in the public school and the role of women in society, the more sophisticated respondents are from 11 to 27 percent more liberal. On items concerning civil rights and foreign affairs there are no differences.

The contrasting pattern of both more conservative and more liberal views calls to mind a possible two-factor explanation—education versus income. It confirms the liberalizing effects of liberal education. Acceptance of the basic liberal tenets of civil and minority political rights and openness to new social values, such as the changing role of women in society, are reinforced by higher education, while the less sophisticated cling to the older, more traditional norms derived in part from early socialization in parental and community values. Increased income and corresponding involvement in the economic system, however, breed both political knowledge and economic conservatism. The question remains as to whether sophistication is correlated with political-economic conservatism independently of such intervening factors as economic level.

To test this two-factor hypothesis, the tables on sophistication and policy opinions were rerun, controlling for education and income. On economic redistributive issues, the sophisticated citizens among the less well-to-do have liberal opinions much more like their less well-to-do fellow citizens than the sophisticated well-off citizens. On political culture issues, however, income makes no difference, for sophisticated citizens at all levels of income are consistently more liberal. Furthermore, those who have become politically attentive and knowledgeable

Table 3.11. Sophistication and Specific Policy Opinions (%)

An example of social welfare/redistributive items (the more sophisticated are more conservative)

Sophistication	"Government in Washington should see to it that every person has a job and a good standard of living."	Undecided	"Government should just let each person get ahead on his own."	(N)
Low	42	22	36	(205)
Medium	29	22	49	(593)
High	27	19	55	(381)

An example of cultural change/civil liberties items (the more sophisticated are more liberal)

"Recently there has been a lot of talk about women's rights. Some people feel that women should have an equal role with men in running business, industry and government. Others feel that women's place is in the home."

Sophistication	Equal role	Undecided	Woman's place in home	(N)
Low	47	22	31	(265)
Medium	62	18	20	(660)
High	73	12	15	(383)

Source: NES 1980.

by a route other than education, the low education-high sophistication group, respond much more like traditional low-sophistication groups on issues such as women's rights and abortion, while the high education– high sophistication group is especially inclined toward the liberal-progressive side of these issues.

The conflicting and confusing findings begin to fall into place. Any balanced index of a full range of policy issues, including both economic and style issues, is likely to show no correlation with sophistication, as the cultural and economic issues will cancel each other out. An emphasis on cultural and civil liberties issues or acquiescence-oriented, simplistic, conservative maxims is likely to find a correlation between sophistication and liberalism (Adorno et al., 1958; McClosky, 1958). Emphasis on economic policy issues will find the reverse (Key, 1961). Also, self-identification on the liberal-conservative continuum, which is an abstract, overarching distinction combining both cultural and economic issues, shows no difference, as the various factors cancel each other out. Perhaps the most important finding of all, the correlation between generalized political sophistication and economic conservatism, is primarily a result of the intervening correlation between sophistication and higher economic status. Elimination of that intervening effect leaves no correlation between sophistication and conservatism.[5]

Pending further research on specialized knowledge, the policy debate should continue to find a full array of both sophisticated and unsophisticated supporters on both sides of each issue. Many citizens will continue to take the middle point on these issues rather than express no opinion. Generally, those who take sides on these issues are more likely than those in the middle to be politically sophisticated and articulate. As the policy battle is joined, the process should generate equally articulate spokespersons on both sides.

---

5. One important issue remains unknown: the possible link between issue-specific knowledge and opinion on a particular issue. Perhaps expertise on foreign policy or taxation may lead to more liberal or more conservative opinions on such issues. The data analysis here has been limited to the measure of generalized political knowledge and conceptual sophistication. The issue-specific knowledge question would require a more specialized research design.

4 | Political Participation

About one-third of the American adult population can be characterized as politically apathetic or passive; in most cases, they are unaware, literally, of the political part of the world around them. Another sixty percent play largely spectator roles in the political process; they watch, they cheer, they vote but they do not do battle. In the purest sense of the word, probably only one or two percent could be called gladiators.

Lester Milbrath

WHAT GOES on inside voting booths around the nation as the curtains swing shut varies in the extreme. Some voters barely remember the candidates and are literally reminded of their names by reading them at the top of the ballot. Others have been actively involved in the campaign, working perhaps eight or twelve hours a day for months as a volunteer or perhaps as a professional journalist. When these politically involved citizens see the candidates' names before them, each name elicits a wealth of associations, images, and ideas from various speeches and statements.

These two types of voters are a study in contrast. In one case, a vote decision emerges from hours upon hours of reflection, analysis, reading, and listening. It is a confirmation, a final symbolic acting-out of a carefully planned choice. In the other case, individuals struggle to remember advice about who to vote for. The unsophisticated and uninformed citizens who find themselves in a voting booth by dint of social or other pressures may vainly stare at their shoes in hope of finding inspiration. These voters are likely to use political parties or the perceived ethnicity of the names of candidates they have not seen before as a cue. The unsophisticated voters may feel ambivalent—proud of having made it to the polls to complete their civic duty, yet frustrated and confused by the many choices of candidates and referenda before them.

The final vote tally is a composite vote, summed across all strata of voters from the least to the most informed. This leads to an interesting series of questions. What, for example, is the direction of the vote moving from the least to the best informed strata? How would the aggregate vote decision change if the proportion of well-informed voters rises or falls over time? What kind of campaign appeals tend to mobilize the less-informed voters and get them to the polls?

The relationship of sophistication to voting behavior is fundamental to the theory of mass politics and stratified pluralism. The character of the correlation between these two variables tells a great deal about the nature of the voting act itself. To the extent that less sophisticated voters vote as frequently as more sophisticated voters, one confronts evidence that voting is primarily a symbolic act, an expressive civic duty rather than an instrumental, goal-oriented action. Further, if less-sophisticated individuals vote only sporadically, the question arises as to what stimulates these half-attentive citizens to make an appearance at the voting booth.

It is not evident, for example, that the most active campaign participants are in fact thoughtful, sophisticated analysts of the political scene, attentive to every nuance in political speech making, and walking reference books of political knowledge. They may be simply patronage seekers, marginally intelligent political soldiers unable to get a job in the private sector and anxious to find a political sinecure of some sort. This stereotype of political hangers-on was part of the historical motivation to establish the civil service. The picture conveyed by television of convention delegates as drum-banging, horn-blowing, sign-waving, overweight, middle-age Americans does not reinforce the image of sophisticated political activists.

These stereotypes of uniformed voters staring at their shoes and fat convention delegates blowing on horns frame the issue. The fact of the matter is that political sophistication is strongly correlated with political activity. The better informed are more likely to vote and more likely to participate in politics beyond the act of voting. This critical aspect of the theory of stratification is confirmed by the data.

To put these findings in perspective, however, it is necessary to examine this correlation more closely. The relationship, for example, turns out to be nonlinear. There is a steep increase in the likelihood of voting moving through the lower half of the sophistication continuum, but it levels off to more modest increases within the upper half. For participation beyond voting, the correlation is also nonlinear, but the shape of the curve is just the reverse, with sharp increases in participation only for the highest sophistication strata. Such findings prove to be critical elements of a reformulated theory of political stratification.

Furthermore, it is important to examine the basic sophistication-participation correlation in the context of other critical variables such as party identification and issue voting. A fundamental interaction effect becomes evident. Not all of the effects of sophistication are direct. At times it proves to be a critical intervening factor that connects two other variables. An example of this phenomenon is that the relationship between strong party affiliation and campaign participation is found only among the more sophisticated voters. The entire analysis, however, is guided by a single concern derived from the theory of stratified pluralism, namely the extent to which the more sophisticated citizens hold the balance of power in the electoral process.

Voting and Nonvoting

The respondents who reported voting in the presidential election were averaged at each level of sophistication, from the lowest to the highest decile (Figure 4.1). Only 38 percent of the least sophisticated decile vote, while 96 percent of the highest do so. This is as high a difference as is likely to occur in attitude-behavior linkages. It translates into a tau beta correlation of about .40.[1] Over the whole range of the sophistication continuum one finds a .75 percent increase in the likelihood of voting for each 1 percent increment in sophistication. As before, the differences are most distinct for the lowest sophistication decile. The effect of sophistication on voting is less dramatic in the upper ranges of the sophistication curve. The slope for the upper half of the sophistication distribution is only about a .2 percent increase in the likelihood of voting for each 1 percent increase in sophistication.

The nonlinearity of the relationship, namely the asymptotic leveling-off of increases in electoral voting for each unit of increase in sophistication, leads to speculation on the nature of the sophistication phenomenon itself. If the real differentiation is at the lower end of the scale, perhaps the real phenomenon that makes a difference is political ignorance rather than sophistication. Increasing political ignorance seems to lead to increasingly dramatic effects, while increasing sophistication seems to hit a critical threshold of some sort beyond which further

1. Because the dependent variable is dichotomous, one must take care not to misrepresent the nature of the covariation by using parametric correlational or regression statistics. Additionally, the relationship seems to be asymptotic, suggesting a ceiling effect of some sort. The strength of the relationship is perhaps best indicated by computing a least-square linear slope and summarizing the percentage increase of the likelihood of voting that corresponds to each increment in sophistication.

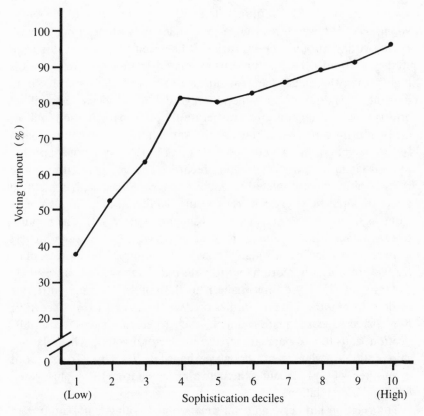

Figure 4.1. Sophistication and Voting. *Source:* NES 1956–1980.

interest, knowledge, and conceptual sophistication do not make much of a difference.

The repeated finding of a nonlinear effect confirms the notion that voting is subject to threshold effects because it identifies a critical minimum of participation in the political system. Political participation has the additive characteristics of a Guttman scale, since a substantial number of people vote but participate no further in politics, while almost everyone who is active in political campaigning and fund raising votes. This can be understood as a ceiling effect, to borrow the educational testing notion of a criterion which is so easily met that it does not differentiate among the brighter students.

The overall estimates between sophistication and voting, however, must be corrected downward. The 1980 National Election Study provides a test of the validity of reported voting. Examination of the public voting records for each respondent, regardless of whether or not they reported voting, produced no surprise. It has been known for years from studies and polls that the turnout estimated from survey responses is higher than the actual national turnout each year by about 10 to 15 percent. This difference is generally regarded as a "social desirability" effect, a natural tendency to exaggerate reported participation in a socially approved behavior. Indeed, the validation study confirms that a full 15 percent of those who reported voting in 1980 were not supported in their claim by the official voting records. The exaggerated response is itself differentially related to sophistication. As a result, the actual effect of sophistication on increasing the likelihood of voting is not as stong as the raw survey results would suggest (Figure 4.2). The impulse to exaggerate voting behavior is twice as prevalent among the highest sophistication deciles, a roughly linear relationship. The more sophisticated are not only more likely to vote but demonstrably more likely to feel guilty if they do not make it to the polls. The same pattern is evident from the validation studies of 1964, 1972, and 1976. According to a corrected least-square estimate, each 1 percent increase in sophistication leads to a .6 percent increase in electoral voting. This relationship is still very significant, though perhaps less dramatic. To express it in another way, 64 percent of actual voters come from the sophisticated half of the population.

The relationship between sophistication and voting is not an artifact or a statistical fluke, resulting from the fact that better-educated people know more about politics but are more likely to vote for other reasons connected with the educationally linked socialization process. Social pressures or differences in economic conditions do not explain the increase in levels of voting. A relatively straightforward empirical test shows that there are significant effects of sophistication on voting over and above the effects of such relevant sociodemographic variables as education (Figure 4.3). Sophistication does make a difference.

It is also clear that the sophistication-voting linkage is not simply a tautological correlation between voting and expressed interest in politics. The potential difficulty of such attitude-behavior tautologies has been highlighted by Bem (1965). He uses the example of brown bread. When asked their opinion of brown bread, most respondents pause for a moment. They have not really developed an "opinion" about brown bread, so they review and judge their own behavior. As the logic goes: "I eat brown bread a lot, so I must like it." In turn, with regard to

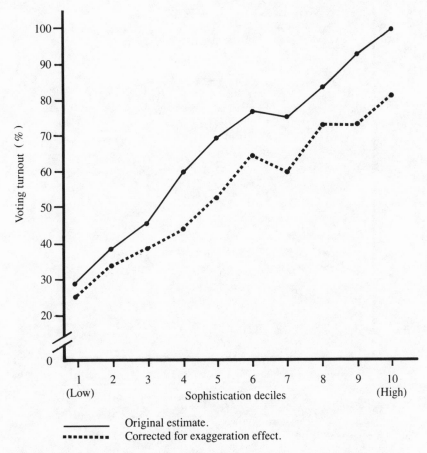

Figure 4.2. Sophistication and Voting Corrected for Exaggeration Effect. *Source:* NES 1980.

voting, the measure of interest in politics might represent a person's observation: "I vote every year like clockwork, so I am probably more interested in politics than the average guy." The measurement of knowledge and conceptual sophistication are veridical rather than self-reported and self-descriptive, so the tautology is much less of an issue there.

The independent effects of knowledge and conceptual sophistication on voting are curious (Figure 4.4). Salience and knowledge are strongly correlated. The puzzle is the low independent effect of conceptual sophistication on voting. Perhaps this component is more central to par-

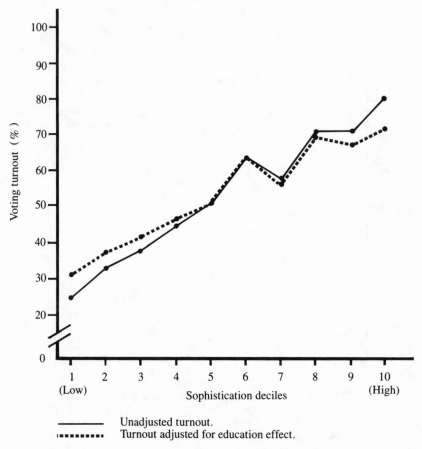

Figure 4.3. Sophistication and Voting Controlled for Education Effect. *Source:* NES 1980.

ticipation beyond voting, the rarer political acts. It appears that a citizen is likely to become interested in politics through a spiraling process of interest leading to political activity and participation, which in turn stimulate further interest. This spirial process may be more subtle or delayed until later stages of political involvement for conceptualization, thus lowering the apparent correlation.

Thus, the fundamental relationship between sophistication and voting has proven to be robust and significant. However, especially in consideration of the changing American voter thesis, an interesting question remains about potential trends in this relationship over time. Perhaps speculations on increased issue voting do not reflect an increase in the knowledge base or issue-orientation of the whole electorate but rather reflect a more subtle shift, an increased correlation between sophistication and voting behavior. That turns out, however, not to be the case. The pattern is quite puzzling (Figure 4.5). There have been some shifts, creating a curious curvilinear pattern since the 1950s. This is evidence that shifting electoral conditions do influence the character of the voting population. One interpretation could be that such correlations are a function of turnout: when interest and turnout are low, the more sophisticated are more likely to abide by their sense of citizen duty and vote, while the less sophisticated do not. Turnout, however, has declined throughout this period. There is no relationship between overall turnout level and the proportion of sophisticated voters. The mystery remains. The circumstances of particular elections do influence the behavior of the more sophisticated strata of the citizenry differentially, but no one has yet identified the conditions that spell the difference.

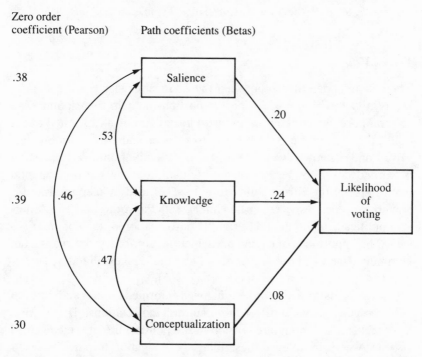

Figure 4.4. Sophistication Components and Voting. *Source:* NES 1956–1980.

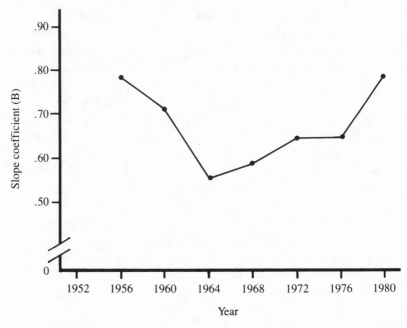

Figure 4.5. Sophistication-Voting Correlation Trend. *Source:* NES 1956–1980.

Proxy Voting

There is an apparent gap between the political expectations of the citizenry and the ability of at least a portion of them to respond. The cultural norm which requires adults to keep themselves informed about political events and candidates and to register and vote is widely perceived and acknowledged. On average, depending on how a question is worded, 90 to 99 percent of the population affirm the fundamental importance of the citizen's duty to vote. The need to keep informed is equally universal, especially when linked with the voting act. The American political tradition emphasizes the participation of the common citizen. The importance of citizen participation, according to surveys from Germany, Italy, and Mexico, is about half the level exhibited by American respondents (Almond and Verba, 1965).

But the actual practice of keeping well-informed about candidates in public issues falls far short of these cultural expectations. There exists a generalized and moderate tension in the political life of the citizenry. As one American noted in describing the obligation to participate, "I am saying what he [the citizen] ought to do, not what I do" (Almond and Verba, 1965, p. 133). In some cases, this generalized guiltiness leads to a withdrawal from politics. More often, the coping strategy is to make political decisions on limited information. This phenomenon provides a clue to the paradox of mass politics and to the working of the electoral system in aggregate.

The primary theory explaining the behavioral strategy for low-information voters is the notion of proxy voting. This theory is straightforward enough. It is based on the expectation of what people would do if, for example, the inner workings of automobiles had always been a profound mystery to them but they were in the position of having to decide whether to fix an old car or buy a new one. They would be likely to ask a friend, co-worker, or relative—someone who in all likelihood they had found before and come to rely on for car advice. Their confidant would probably be a friend or associate rather than a professional advice-giver. Their garage mechanic, for example, though well qualified to give advice, is liable to have strong biases of self-interest, as is a new-car salesman. They are not likely to put themselves in the position of asking twenty experts and weighing the conflicting evidence to derive their own conclusions. That would be a time-consuming strategy and would require them to become an expert themselves. So decisionmaking under conditions of both low information and relatively low motivation personally to evaluate and collect information is not unique. In various domains most people follow that strategy several times a week. With a pronounced lack of interest in understanding the details, they simply follow the advice of a trusted source.

The phenomenon of opinion leadership works the same in political life (Lazarsfeld et al., 1944; Berelson et al., 1954; Katz and Lazarsfeld, 1955). People seek out political advice from friends and colleagues of a similar social or educational level or from a higher educational level. The advice givers are demonstrably better informed, and the flow of information tends to move from higher to lower levels of educational attainment.

There are two distinct types of political discussion and consultation. In the first type, the discussion is primarily among equals: "The social contact need not 'tell' the voter what to do. The voter tells himself, simply by talking it out. For example, a voter who changed some of his ideas on the Taft-Hartley Law said: 'I just figured it out. I talked to the fellas about it. We discussed it. Some agreed and some disagreed. We were just talking and I thought of it.'" The second type of political discussion approaches voting by proxy: "Sometimes it is practically an order to change votes. As one woman reported, 'My brother sent word to me to vote for him [Truman]. We just talked about what is going on. I usually take his advice because he knows' " (Berelson et al., 1954, pp. 292–293).

The proportion of proxy voting—the frequency with which spouses, union workers, and friends of friends are in effect sent off to the polls with an assignment to complete—is hard to estimate. In the low sophistication quartile, for example, union members are 14 percent more likely to vote than nonmembers. At higher levels of sophistication there is no difference. But that is incomplete evidence. Strict proxy voting is particularly difficult to estimate because it so clearly violates the principles of citizen duty. Proxy voting is not likely to be an unself-consciously described behavior. Proxy voters probably see their behavior in a somewhat different light, perhaps appropriately so. They want to do their duty as citizens, have a vague preference among the candidates, and voluntarily seek out advice. As a result, it is impossible to label the exact proportion of proxy voting and estimate its net contribution to the vote.

But the data do allow some estimate of the phenomenon and its relationship to political sophistication. The clue is in the steep rise in the proportion of people voting even at the lowest levels of the sophistication curve. In effect, voting behavior rises faster than sophistication as one moves from the least to the most sophisticated members of the citizenry. This is an empirical demonstration of the gap between the norm of civic duty and the hard work of political information-processing. The gap is even more evident when the level of generalized civic norms is compared to the sophistication continuum (Figure 4.6). The breadth of acceptance of civic duty is wide, with a significant falloff only in the bottom two deciles. There is a corresponding behavioral falloff in the bottom deciles. There is also a correspondence of civic norms and behavior at the other end of the continuum as the highest levels of voting duty come in line with the highest probability of voting and the highest levels of political information. The key lies in the middle of the continuum, where the largest gap would be anticipated between the norm and the behavior of political duty (Figure 4.7). Proxy voting should be most prevalent in the middle levels of the sophistication continuum.

This knowledge gap hypothesis was tested by means of a series of survey questions in the National Election Studies that require respondents, if they discuss politics at all, to distinguish between those political

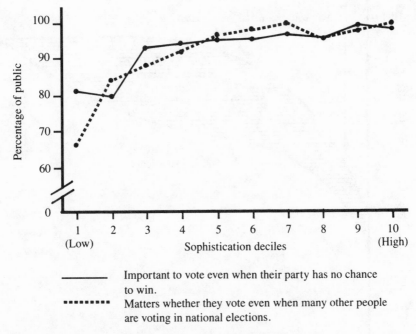

Figure 4.6. Norms of Citizen Duty. *Source:* NES 1976.

discussions in which they play the role of political influential and those in which they primarily seek out advice. The percentage of the population who seek out advice but do not feel in a position to give it was arrayed across the sophistication continuum (Table 4.1). As expected, the behavior of participation in political discussion is strongly, positively, and linearly associated with levels of sophistication. And the curvilinear function of proxy voting is revealed as predicted. The potential for proxy voting exists in roughly one voter out of five. The potential for proxy voting is about twice as high at the middle levels of the sophistication continuum.

Thus, although it is impossible to make precise estimates of the net effect of proxy voting on the aggregate vote decision, these are clues to how the shape of the curves of sophistication and participation may lead to a knowledge gap and a corresponding coping behavior of proxy voting. In any case, the net effect of the cues provided by friends and associates is not likely to be as significant as those of the most fundamental organizing symbols of American politics, the political parties.

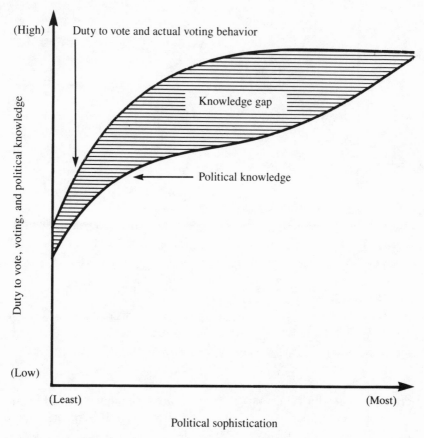

Figure 4.7. Model of Knowledge Gap.

Party Identification and the Swing Voter Theory

Political parties and partisanship are central facts of American political behavior. Partisanship is "the most important single influence on political opinions and voting behavior. Many other influences are at work on voters in our society, but none compare in significance with partisanship" (Flanigan, 1972, p. 37). Voters do not confront each election and set of candidates anew. They are likely to rely on their "standing decision," their political party (Key, 1961). Political parties "created democracy and . . . modern democracy is unthinkable save in terms of the parties" (Schattschneider, 1960). And empirical research by political scientists which follows from Schattschneider, most notably the group at the University of Michigan, heavily emphasizes the phenomenon of party identification. Thus, in a critical evaluation of the Michigan tradition, Rusk noted that "the entire Michigan theory rises or falls with the concept of party identification and its utility" (1981, p. 4).

Ironically, partisanship has been viewed both as a part of the indictment of the competence of the average voter and as the savior of the political system. All voting studies note the strong inheritance factor of party identification. Seventy-four percent of Americans describe themselves as inclined toward the same political party as their parents. Indeed, inherited party identification is equally as prevalent among people whose parents are and are not politically active (Campbell et al., 1960).

The studies are less explicit in characterizing the reliance of voters on party cues. One study uses such language as a "psychological force," a "sense of attachment," "loyalty," or "identification" in describing the role of party cues and decisionmaking (Campbell et al., 1960). The classical caricature is the experience of Republican President Theodore Roosevelt campaigning in the erstwhile Democratic South: "As this Republican president was speaking, he became disturbed by a member of the audience who turned aside all of Roosevelt's arguments with the incantation, 'My granddaddy was a Democrat, my Daddy was a Democrat, and I'm a Democrat.' Ultimately enraged by this display of blind loyalty, Roosevelt confronted the voter: 'Well, if your Grandfather were

Table 4.1. Knowledge Gap and Proxy Voting (%)

Information-seeking pattern	Sophistication deciles									
	1	2	3	4	5	6	7	8	9	10
Proxy voters (discuss politics, vote influenced by others)	15	15	18	23	24	21	15	18	14	10
Active voters (discuss politics, share information)	8	15	19	29	26	37	43	48	55	69
Apathetic voters (infrequent discussion of politics)	77	70	63	48	50	42	42	34	31	21

Source: NES 1968, 1976, 1980.

a Republican, and your Father were a Republican, what would you be?' The answer was quick, 'Why I'd be a damn fool, of course' " (Pomper, 1975, p. 19).

The unthinking reliance on party cues and party-linked clichés is just as forcefully, if less dramatically, revealed in open-ended survey evaluations of the two parties. Take the responses of one Republican voter, for example: "(Is there anything you like about the Republican party?) I just lean more toward their view. I don't know anything specific except when I hear representatives of the party I like what the Republicans stand for. (What sort of thing is that?) I don't know, I am not qualified to go into that. I'd make a statement and it would sound stupid" (NES interview transcripts).

Yet equally prominent in the literature is evidence that strong party identifiers are more active and involved in political life than weak party identifiers. Part of the paradox of mass politics is the existence of swing voters, less involved voters who are not affiliated with either political party and who may influence the critical electoral balance in swinging back and forth between the candidates of one party or another from election to election (Shanks, 1969). Political sophistication does vary across the seven traditional categories of party identification based on the strength and direction of the affiliation (Table 4.2). Republicans are in general more sophisticated than Democrats, although there are fewer Republicans. This is true at each level of strength of identification. True independents are the least sophisticated of all, with only 15 percent of their number falling in the high sophistication quartile.

Stronger identifiers are generally more sophisticated, although this is considerably more complicated. Part of the difficulty results from the awkward way in which party identification has traditionally been operationalized in the National Election Studies. Respondents are asked first, "Generally speaking do you think of yourself as a Republican, a Democrat, an Independent, or what?" If they describe themselves as a Democrat or Republican, they are asked if they would describe themselves as a strong or a not very strong Democrat or Republican. Then the Independents are queried further, "Do you think of yourself as closer to the Republican or Democratic party?" These self-identified leaning independents complicate the otherwise linear increase of sophistication with strong party identification. In some ways the leaning Democrats are more like the strong Democrats. The same is true with the leaning Republicans. These voters are thoughtful and active but prefer to define themselves as independents leaning toward the Dem-

Table 4.2. Sophistication and Party
Identification (%) ª

Party identification	Sophistication		
	Low	Medium	High
Strong Democrats	19	54	27
Democrats	30	50	20
Leaning Democrats	21	52	27
Independents	34	51	15
Leaning Republicans	17	48	35
Republicans	22	51	27
Strong Republicans	14	45	41
Overall	25	50	25

Source: NES 1956–1980.
a. Excludes respondents who had missing data or
declined to be classified in terms of party affiliation.

ocratic or Republican party. The problem is that each level of party
identification has its component of thoughtful, issue-sensitive voters,
and the relationship between sophistication and party identification is
complex. Thus, low-sophistication strong Democrats look more like low-
sophistication strong Republicans than high-sophistication Democrats
(Table 4.3). Strong Democratic and strong Republican identifiers generally assert that they "always vote for the same party." But such as-
sertions of unquestioned loyalty decline as sophistication rises for both
parties. On another dimension, the fundamental sense of how responsive
the government is to "people like me," the high-sophistication Democrats and Republicans are again more like each other than the low-
sophistication identifiers in the same parties.

Thus, there are complex interactions between party identification and
political sophistication. There is a great diversity of fundamental beliefs
about government and cognitive styles within each level of party identification. Some highly sophisticated issue-sensitive voters feel comfortable identifying themselves as strong Republicans "who always vote for
the same party," while other equally sophisticated voters of similar
demographic background prefer to identify themselves as independents
leaning toward the Republican party.

Table 4.3. Sophistication, Party Identification, and
Political Beliefs (%)

Political belief	Sophistication	Strong Democrats	Strong Republicans
Always vote for	Low	74	70
the same party	Medium	72	64
	High	68	60
Agree that	Low	54	56
people like	Medium	35	30
them don't	High	18	13
have any say			
about			
government			

Source: NES 1956–1980.

The swing voters present a critical problem: "Not only is the electorate as a whole quite uninformed, but it is the least informed members within the electorate who seem to hold the critical balance of power, in the sense that alternations in governing party depend disproportionately on shifts in their sentiment" (Converse, 1962, p. 578). Is the unintended consequence of the American tradition of party identification to hand over the balance of power and electoral decisionmaking to the whimsies of the less attentive and sometime-voting stratum of political independents? Yet the problem may not be as serious as it seems. Although the floating voters show a high susceptibility to short-term change, they are relatively less exposed to the flow of information during a campaign and thus, despite low levels of party affiliation, are least likely to show changes in patterns of behavior (Converse, 1962). The contribution of various strata of the electorate to the vote shows that, although there is a less-informed and highly variable independent stratum, the likelihood of voting in this stratum is so low that its net contribution to the aggregate vote is not very significant (Shanks, 1969).

Separate measures of sophistication and party identification also show that two-thirds of those who initially identify themselves as independents actually lean toward one party or the other, and these independent leaners are almost as highly sophisticated and active as the strong party identifiers. Patterns of defection and protest voting indicate that, although those who define themselves as true independents fall predominantly in the lower levels of sophistication, swing voters show typical levels of political sophistication (Table 4.4). Those citizens voting for John Anderson as a protest vote in 1980, for example, had relatively high levels of political sophistication. And although the Wallace protest voters in 1968 did not have sophistication levels as high as Anderson's, they did not fit the unsophisticated stereotype.

Participation beyond Voting

Participation in the political world beyond the act of voting is cut from very different psychological cloth. Such activities as attending campaign meetings, contributing to political organizations, writing letters to officials, and signing petitions are, all things considered, rare phenomena. While roughly two-thirds of the population are likely to vote in a presidential election and over 90 percent feel they at least ought to vote, active participation in the day-to-day workings of the political system for "extra credit" are, by general definition, over and above the accepted norms of citizen duty. Roughly speaking, only one in twenty Americans can confidently be described as actively involved. That parameter has remained relatively constant since the 1950s, although the critical threshold might fall a little below or above the figure. For example, 3 percent of the population report being members of political clubs or organizations, 5 percent describe themselves as actively working for candidates, 8 percent report attending political rallies or meetings, and about 10 percent claim to have given voluntary contributions to a political party or candidate. In the domain outside of campaign politics, 4 percent

Table 4.4. Swing Vote (%)

	Sophistication		
Voting behavior	Low	Medium	High
True Independents	33	51	16
Swing voters	19	54	27
Protest voters	18	55	29
Party voters	15	51	34
Nonvoters	42	47	11

Source: NES 1956–1980.

describe themselves as having written a letter to an editor on an issue of national political concern, and 8 percent report having organized and worked with others to respond to a national problem (NES).

Most participants in the political scene probably have a somewhat distorted sense of the level of public participation. Being actively involved themselves, they have many friends and colleagues who are equally active and probably equally interested in discussing the latest details of campaign strategy. But the mathematics of random survey sampling generate a very different picture. At campaign time it might appear that almost everyone is politicized, because banners, bumper stickers, and buttons seem to be everywhere. But in fact only 7 percent of the mass public report displaying bumper stickers or wearing buttons. Since active participation in campaigns and political activities costs time and money, most people are no doubt too caught up in the day-to-day pressures of their lives to contribute much of either. That is an important element in the dynamics of the working political system. But beyond that, even minimal political involvement appears to be avoided by the great majority of the public. For example, the federal income tax form allows citizens to check off a one-dollar contribution for the political campaign fund. It is clearly stated that the designation of this contribution neither adds to their tax nor diminishes their potential refund. Yet only 30 percent of the public opt for the check-off.

Participation in political activities beyond voting is highly correlated with political sophistication, but the nature of that correlation is different from the correlation between sophistication and voting, and this difference, coupled with the rarity of the participatory act, provides another clue to the paradox of mass politics. At first glance, the relationship between sophistication and voting looks roughly similar to the correlation between sophistication and political participation beyond voting. In both cases there is a moderately strong positive correlation in the range of .30. But the data on the number of campaign activities (out of a possible list of twelve) and of noncampaign political activities (out of a possible list of nine) for each of the ten strata of sophistication have a nonlinearity for the most sophisticated strata at the upper end of the continuum (Figure 4.8). The relationship between sophistication and voting is nonlinear at the other end of the continuum. Thus, variation in sophistication makes its most significant diffference in voting at the very lowest levels of sophistication, while the reverse is true for the effect of sophistication on political participation. The two highest strata of sophistication participate at levels two or three times the overall

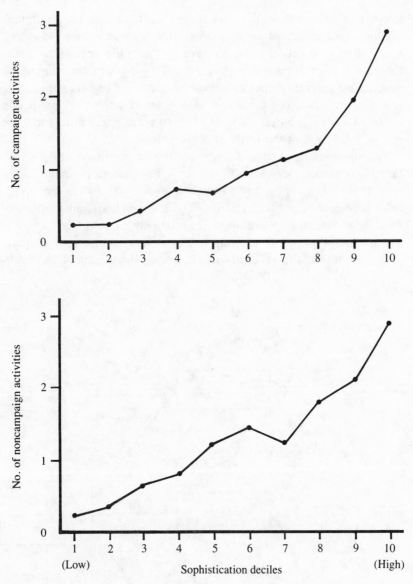

Figure 4.8. Participation Beyond Voting. *Source:* NES 1972–1976.

average and fifteen times the level of the lowest stratum. Thus, although the linear correlation of the relationship looks roughly the same as that with voting, in practical terms it makes a bigger difference. Thus, while the most sophisticated half of the population generate 64 percent of the votes, they generate 80 percent of the political acts beyond voting. The top stratum is between ten and fifteen times as active in participation beyond voting but barely twice as likely to vote. These differences are in part a function of the rarity of participatory acts.

The components of sophistication are linked in various degrees with individual participatory acts (Figure 4.9). The pattern is similar to the correlations with voting. In this case, salience is clearly the most powerful predictor of political activity. The independent contributions of knowledge and conceptualization are relatively modest. This is an important and appropriate warning to those who might casually equate political interest with political knowledge in thinking about the strati-

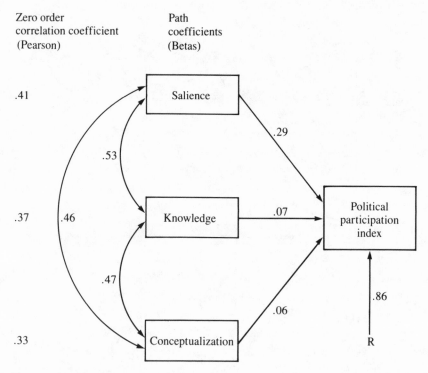

Figure 4.9. Components of Sophistication and Participation Beyond Voting. *Source:* NES 1956–1980.

fication of the electorate and the role of political activists in the overall working of the system.

The analysis of the correlation of sophistication with specific political activities confirms the overall pattern. On the whole, the nonlinear correlation between sophistication and participatory acts is reflected in each of the individual behaviors, such as contributing funds or attending rallies. Such common and casual behaviors as displaying bumper stickers or wearing buttons have a somewhat lower correlation with sophistication. The one exception is political protest. The relatively rare behavior of signing petitions or participating in a sit-in is more highly correlated with conceptual sophistication than with political knowledge or salience. Such a finding makes theoretical sense. The ideological orientation tapped by the conceptualization measure ought to be tied most clearly to protest-oriented behavior.

The sophistication-behavior linkage does not mean that there are behavioral specialists, such that wearing a button one year is more highly correlated with wearing a button another year than with some other activity. If this were the case, it would indicate habitual patterns of political activity. Each of the political activities, however, is correlated about as strongly with the other activities as with sophistication. There is no strong evidence of habitual specialization. This moderate and consistent pattern of intercorrelation is another clue to the paradox of mass politics.

Sophistication as an Intervening Variable

The absence of either behavioral specialization or unique patterns of correlation of sophistication with particular participatory acts tells something about both the nature of political participation and the nature of political sophistication. Sophistication is a generalized propensity to participate in political activities, that is, an inclination to respond to political stimuli. Strong political stimuli, however, even in the environment of the politically sophisticated, are quite rare. Thus, under the relatively infrequent circumstance of an explicit invitation to citizens to attend a political meeting at a neighbor's home, the most sophisticated strata of the population are more likely to attend. But in the absence of such a stimulus, the more sophisticated, like everyone else, are more likely to go with their day-to-day activities. Thus, the loose linkage between sophistication and political behavior of various sorts means that sophistication does not "cause" participation. It functions instead as an intervening variable. Among the more sophisticated strata, there is a stronger connection between a political stimulus and actual political behavior. Thus, if in the world at large random political stimuli are impinging on everyone, the higher levels of attentiveness and knowledge of the more politically sophisticated will make them more responsive, that is, make them interpret political stimuli in political terms.

Political behavior is usually analyzed in terms of direct causal relationships, such as higher-status people being more likely to vote Republican or older people having a stronger sense of party affiliation. The sophistication-behavior linkage has a somewhat different character. It parallels the phenomenon of political empathy whereby, in order for regional and national democratic institutions to thrive in developing nations, substantial portions of the population need to be open to new ideas beyond the parochial and traditional cultural norms that are likely to dominate the village setting (Lerner, 1958). An example is the storekeeper in Turkey whose ownership of a radio and relative possession of political and economic sophistication gave him a broader political horizon than most of his fellow villagers. Sophistication operates much like this kind of political empathy. Sophistication does not cause opinions, in the sense of inclining individuals toward either conservative or liberal positions on political issues. Yet in a political environment that strongly reinforces liberal or conservative beliefs, a more sophisticated individual is more likely to respond. Politically mobilizing stimuli also lead more directly to actual political behavior among the more sophisticated.

Sophistication plays this critical intervening role with other demographic variables traditionally associated with political participation. For example, sophistication strengthens the effects of economic status and party affiliation on campaign participation. The observation that the upper economic strata are more active in political life has become a political truism. It is central to the historical analyses of Marx and Weber, and it remains a focus of behavioral analyses of participation (Milbrath, 1965; Verba and Nie, 1972). The correlation between economic stratification and political participation, whereby the wealthier strata are more active politically, has been found in various nations and is especially characteristic of the United States (Verba et al., 1978). It appears to be a basic parameter of political life.

One way of interpreting this linkage between income level and political participation is in terms of the relative likelihood of being exposed to political stimuli. The more involved people are in economic activities, the more likely they are to encounter regulatory or other political sanctions that might require a political response. To explore this potential interactive effect of sophistication, the analysis must report the correlation between income and participation separately for low-sophistication and high-sophistication quartiles (Figure 4.10). As expected, the average level of participation for the high-sophistication group is significantly higher than for the low-sophistication group. The relationship between income and participation is much stronger for the high-sophistication group. Indeed, there appears to be no meaningful connection at all between income level and participation for the low-sophistication group, yet within the high-sophistication group, the upper economic strata are almost three times as politically active. Thus the strongest predictor of high participation is high income, with a correspondingly increased exposure to political stimuli reinforced by high sophistication, which increases the likelihood of interpreting those stimuli in political terms.

When the analysis is repeated with party identification, the connection between being a strong Republican or Democrat and behaving like one varies tremendously between the lower and upper levels of the sophistication continuum (Figure 4.11). Although substantial numbers of low-

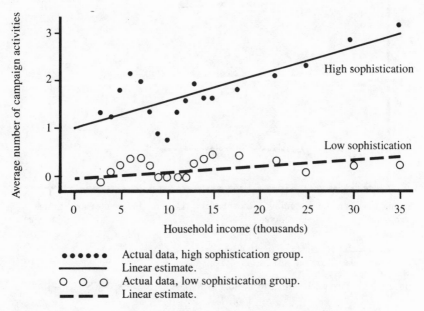

Figure 4.10. Income and Participation. *Source:* NES 1972–1976.

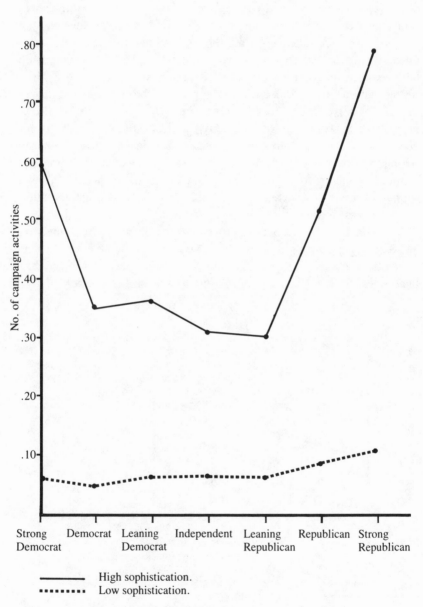

Figure 4.11. Party Identification and Participation. *Source:* NES 1956–1980.

sophistication individuals might identify themselves as strong Republicans or strong Democrats, such self-identifications do not mean much behaviorally. Only for the high-sophistication strata does such a political vocabulary translate into meaningfully differentiated political actions. Thus, the character of the sophistication variable is such that its most important effects may be indirect and catalytic, providing a connection between two other variables. Statistically, that calls for attention to interactive as well as direct effects.

Issue Voting

The critical role of sophistication in making the connection between political stimuli and political participation beyond voting demonstrates a parallel in the phenomenon of issue voting, that is, in making the connection between political opinions, such as they are, and the ultimate vote decision. Issue voting presents tremendously complex methodological problems in attempting to assess the relative importance of specific political issues versus other factors in the vote decision. Part of the difficulty stems from the naiveté of the original research on issue voting, which required respondents to place themselves and a variety of candidates on a battery of policy issues in order to compute their "distance" from the perceived candidate position on each issue. Sophistication, it turns out, plays an important intervening role in such a process.

A study of the interests of businessmen, for example, might focus on a cluster of attitudes toward the ideology of free enterprise, the importance of a healthy business climate, the disadvantage of regulating business profits, and the threat of union shops and minimum wage laws to the economy. If this issue area is not atypical, a survey would find 90 percent of the general population offering opinions in response to such questions. The study might thus determine that bourgeois ideology, defined as the tendency to favor business interests, explains 40 percent of the variance in voting Republican and that, over and above the influence affiliation, it still explains a healthy 10 percent of the variance, which would represent a unique issue-voting effect. If such figures are approximately correct, the study would appear to have located and demonstrated the existence of an important belief cluster. All of this is entirely legitimate, as far as it goes, but such a belief cluster is not necessarily meaningful or salient for the whole sample. For some citizens such a belief cluster might be a dominant consideration in voting, yet for the rest of the citizenry the issues are not particularly salient or relevant to behavior because their belief systems are for the most part organized around other economic or social issues. Thus, the overall variance explained, namely 10 percent, is in a way misleading, because it represents the average of two groups—one group for which it explains no variance at all, and the other, smaller group for which it is extremely salient, explaining perhaps 50 percent of the variance over and above party affiliation.

Each of the three components of sophistication in the linkage between attitudes and behavior might even have a unique role (Figure 4.12). Presumably, there is a group within the population—perhaps comprised of people who grew up in families that stressed entrepreneurial ethics but who are no longer tied to the economic interests of the business community—for whom support for business interests is clear and consistent but simply not very salient in voting. There might be another group for whom business interests are salient, and these interests would influence voting were it not for the fact that these individuals are unaware of or confused about which party or candidate supports these positions. In such a case, the belief cluster would fail to exert an influence on voting, but not because of a lack of perceived salience. Yet another group might hold clear and consistent beliefs on business interest issues, see them as important, and be aware that Republicans tend to favor business interests, yet organize their overall belief system in such a way as to preclude these opinions from influencing behavior. People might, for various reasons, put a heavier emphasis on other considerations,

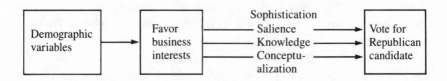

Salience	Is the individual's attitude toward business interests particularly important in the vote decision compared with other issues?
Knowledge	Is the individual aware that the Republican party has generally favored business interests in its platforms and policies?
Conceptualization	Is the individual inclined to vote on the basis of issues at all, or is the vote decision seen rather as a vote for the most capable candidate regardless of issue stands?

Figure 4.12. Example of Issue Voting: "Bourgeois Ideology."

such as the personality or perceived competence of candidates, or on an entirely different set of issues. Thus, though they describe business interests as important in the abstract sense, their behavior reflects a more marked concern with other political objects.

Such a scenario assumes issue salience is the necessary intervening variable between having policy positions and policy-oriented voting (Shapiro, 1969). It also resonates with the three conditions of issue voting. For an issue to influence voting decision: the issue must be recognized as such, it must arouse a minimum of feeling, and it must be accompanied by the perception that one political party favors the person's own position more than the other party does (Campbell et al., 1960). The methodological lesson for research is to include independent measures of the respondents' knowledge of a particular issue area and their perceived sense of the issue's relevance to the vote decision. Such an approach would make it possible to explore the persisting theory of pluralism and issue publics by direct measurement.

The data at hand provide clues to the puzzle of issue voting and sophistication for each of the presidential elections since 1948, except 1952, for which data are unavailable. The distance between the respondents and the major party presidential candidates was computed for each election for all available issues.[2] The analysis was done separately for low, medium, and high levels of sophistication, so as automatically to remove the effect of any differences between the sophistication groups, numbers of expressed opinions, or perceived candidate positions (Table 4.5). The pattern is clear. Political sophistication provides the critical link between opinion and behavior, for the more sophisticated citizens rely more heavily on the position of a candidate in their electoral calculus. Even in the election with the lowest overall levels of issue voting, the Kennedy-Nixon election of 1960, the variance in voting was four times as high for the sophisticated subgroup. In one of the most ideologically distinct of these presidential contests, Johnson versus Goldwater in 1964, the explanatory power of issues in the vote decision (in terms of explained variance, traditionally measured by the square of the correlation coefficient) was 21 times higher for the sophisticated respondents. The

2. To calculate the relative agreement on issues between potential voters and the alternative presidential candidates, respondents were asked to estimate the candidates' positions as well as their own position on a series of four to eight specific policy questions. The absolute values of the distances between candidates and voters on these issues were aggregated into an index which in turn was correlated with voting behavior. Individuals who are unsure of a candidate's or of their own position on a particular issue are regarded as having no issue distance rather than being removed from the calculations.

Table 4.5. Issue Voting and Sophistication

	Correlation between issue agreement with candidate and vote decision		
	Sophistication		
Study	Low	Medium	High
Elmira 1948 Truman v. Dewey	.40	.42	.62
NES 1956 Stevenson v. Eisenhower	.24	.58	.76
NES 1960 Kennedy v. Nixon	.26	.47	.53
NES 1964 Johnson v. Goldwater	.16	.55	.73
NES 1968 Humphrey v. Nixon	.38	.59	.68
NES 1972 McGovern v. Nixon	.49	.55	.76
NES 1976 Carter v. Ford	.20	.49	.64
NES 1980 Carter v. Reagan	.43	.55	.76

same patterns appear when the effects of party identification and the perceived personal qualities of the candidates are controlled for statistically.

These data provide a picture of how the mass public reacts to election campaigns. It is a model, in effect, of political communication between elites and mass publics. As candidates are seen on television shaking hands and making speeches, two types of messages are being communicated. At the symbolic level, the candidates' personal style and demeanor are appraised by people in the audience at all levels of sophistication. Perhaps the public perceives the contrasting styles between the young and aggressive challenger versus the older, more cautious, and more experienced incumbent. Such perceptions may or may not resonate with the personal preferences of the voters and, in turn, influence voting behavior. At another level of communication, there is political content in the speeches and position papers of candidates and in the commentaries of journalists. But the abstract political concepts at this level of communication are not perceived or interpreted by a substantial portion of the audience. Only the more sophisticated strata are much inclined or easily able to make sense of such abstractions, match them against their ideological predispositions, and utilize such information in voting decisions. The political rhetoric of abstractions is vaguely familiar to less sophisticated voters. Perhaps this is one reason that they so often feel obligated to have an opinion on such issues. But their expressed attitudes on these topics have little bearing on their thinking and their voting decision as the election draws near.

5 | Political Socialization

> The uneducated man or the man with limited education is a
> different political actor from the man who has achieved a
> higher level of education.
>
> Gabriel Almond and Sidney Verba

SOME INDIVIDUALS are thoughtfully attentive to the political world around them, while others seem to be completely oblivious. An understanding of the roots of political sophistication leads to an understanding of the phenomenon itself. It appears that sophistication is an enduring personal trait rather than an episodic product of circumstance or mood. But such premises should be carefully explored. Most importantly, the data at hand allow for an analysis of which underlying factors, such as education, family socialization, intelligence, personality, and social roles, prove to be most important in explaining the development of political sophistication. If the link between civic duty and political knowledge proves to be particularly strong, then efforts might realistically be taken to raise the overall level of sophistication in the electorate. If sophistication proves to be primarily a product of IQ and the innate ability to process abstract political symbols and concepts then the ramifications for policy would be very different.

The Causal Model

The relevant variables are drawn from the familiar cluster of social status and demographic traits. Education is a critical determinant of sophistication. Education is also positively correlated with occupational status and income, inversely correlated with being nonwhite, and because younger citizens are more likely to have attended school for a longer period of time, inversely correlated with age. Politics for many years was defined as outside the realm of proper interest for women in American political culture. One might expect that some residue of that tradition is still in evidence.

The traditional technique of multiple regression displays the net effect of each causal factor on political sophistication. The causal pattern proved to be quite consistent across the nine core data sets, so the findings have been averaged together to provide an overall model (Table 5.1). The social-status variables, especially education, prove to be the central causal factors. Blacks are less sophisticated than whites, but this is explained primarily by the lower level of formal education among black Americans. Women are less sophisticated, and this effect is not diminished significantly by the effects of other factors.

There is no evident correlation between age and sophistication. But after controlling for the fact that older Americans have on average spent less time in school, the suppressed age effect becomes evident. Indeed, older Americans are more politically sophisticated than younger ones.

Table 5.1. Roots of Sophistication

Source	Correlation with sophistication	Beta coefficients from multiple regression
Status		
Education	.44	.36
Occupation	.30	.06
Income	.32	.12
Demography		
Race (black)	−.15	−.05
Age	.02	.17
Sex (female)	−.18	−.17
Context		
Non-South	.08	.01
Urban	.11	.03
Group participation	.29	.13
Psychology		
Self-esteem	.19	.07
Interpersonal trust	.27	.09
Early socialization		
Parents' interest	.22	.15
Parents' socioeconomic status	.20	.02
Urban upbringing	.15	.04
Multiple correlation		.58

Source: Nine core data sets.

Geography and social context do not make much of a difference. But participating in social group activities is a surprisingly strong predictor of sophistication, and the effect persists even when adjusting for the fact that education and group participation are correlated. This suggests that there may be alternative paths to sophistication, other mechanisms than formal education. Such a possibility might require a rethinking of the nature of sophistication itself and its ramifications for the quality of political life. Finally, the effects of parental political involvement are important. Parental views on the significance of politics are passed on across generations in parallel with the heritage of political party affiliations.

In short, geographic and contextual factors shrink to practical and statistical insignificance in the face of other casual factors. Without question, the key casual factor is education. It explains four times as much of the variance as the next most influential factor. Another small cluster of factors with regression coefficients in the range of .13 to .17 have only a modest independent effect on the acquisition of political sophistication. Setting aside those variables that do not have a significant independent effect on sophistication, the remaining factors form a time line of life stages (Figure 5.1). Formal schooling is the central factor. The discussion of politics in the home and other cues and values communicated by politically active parents represent a significant independent effect. Later in adult life, participation in voluntary groups and career environments associated with higher income levels exert influence. Age itself, or simply growing older, allows for a gradual political learning. A lessening of the competing demands on time from family rearing and career development in early adulthood may also lead to increased political involvement among older citizens. The one independent negative effect in the acquisition of political sophistication is socialization as a woman.

The roots of each of the components of the sophistication index are fundamentally the same (Table 5.2). Education is the most prominent causal factor in each case. In a few cases there are unique patterns. For example, participation in voluntary social groups has a principal effect on interest in politics and only a minimal effect on knowledge or conceptualization. A similar pattern characterizes parental interest in politics, which leads to increased interest but not knowledge among younger family members. Several alternative theories explain the central importance of education and the role of other social-status variables in the acquisition of political sophistication.

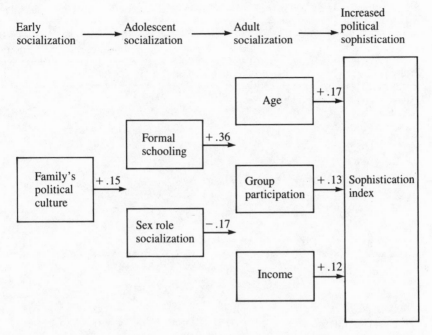

Figure 5.1. Life Stages and Acquisition of Sophistication. *Source:* Table 5.1.

Sorting Out Socialization Effects

There are three theories on the origins of sophistication. They are the class culture, economic interest, and cognitive ability theories of political involvement. Class culture refers not to subjective class identification, which has never proven to be a powerful explanatory factor in American political behavior, but rather to class-differentiated value systems (Rodman, 1963). The dominant symbols and rhetoric of American politics reinforce not only the legitimacy of mass participation but the obligation of citizens to vote and keep themselves informed on public issues. Americans exhibit an unusually outgoing civic-mindedness, but this participatory norm is highly class-differentiated. The process by which some individuals acquire sophistication involves more than the simple failure of the less educated in America to become socialized into the dominant political culture. They may have been socialized into a self-reinforcing lower-class subculture that is dominated by a cynicism about politics and politicians. In this case the lack of a socially reinforced model of good citizenship among lower-class subcultures will affect their levels

Table 5.2. Roots of Sophistication Components (beta coefficients from multiple regression)

Source	Political salience	Political knowledge	Political conceptualization	
			Differentiation	Integration
Status				
Education	.28	.30	.28	.27
Occupation	.12	.06	.07	.00
Income	.03	.12	.10	.13
Demography				
Race (black)	.00	−.06	−.09	.00
Age	.13	.05	.13	.08
Sex (female)	−.11	−.13	−.09	−.14
Context				
Nonsouth	.00	.00	.00	.00
Urban	.00	.00	.12	.09
Group participation	.19	.12	.00	.00
Psychology				
Self-esteem	.16	.07	.00	.00
Interpersonal trust	.00	.10	.00	.00
Socialization				
Parents' interest	.19	.11	.10	.12
Parents' socioeconomic status	.00	.04	.00	.00
Urban upbringing	.00	.00	.04	.00

Source: Nine core data sets.

of sophistication independently of the other factors associated with socioeconomic status.

The second theory on the origins of sophistication sees it simply as a matter of economic interest. Higher-status individuals are likely to be more involved in and tied to the functioning of the economic system, to be more alert to government regulation of business and the stock market, and to have more to lose if tax regulations are changed. The propertied citizenry have a "greater stake in society" and accordingly are more responsible in their decisionmaking (Lane, 1959, p. 225).

The third theory focuses on an entirely different explanation of the correlation between socioeconomic status and sophistication. It in fact suggests that the relationship is to some extent spurious, as both educational achievement and political sophistication are natural outgrowths of cognitive ability. The pattern of causation here is complex. On the one hand, a higher innate IQ increases the chance that an individual will be admitted to, or receive the financial aid necessary for, a college education. So the causal direction runs from IQ to education. On the other hand, a college education refines the very verbal and cognitive skills that are primarily what the IQ tests measure. So an important causal path might run from education to IQ. It is, no doubt, a two-way causal process.

These three theories are not mutually exclusive. All three phenomena are likely to be at work simultaneously. To assess the evidence in support of each theory, however, requires an examination of different sets of variables. The task would be simplified if each of the three traditional components of socioeconomic status—education, occupational status, and income—corresponded to one of the three theories. Unfortunately the structure of the unmeasured and measured variables is somewhat complex (Figure 5.2). Education reflects both cognitive ability and the socialization of participatory norms. Occupational status probably reflects all three unmeasured variables. Only income is primarily associated with only one of the unmeasured constructs.

Other measures in the various data sets may help in identifying these underlying causal processes. Clearly, a class-culture model of sophistication might be tested by measuring perceived civic duty independently of sophistication and exploring its role as an intervening variable. Such an index and a path analysis of its intervening role for the national elections of 1956–1960 indeed support the social obligation hypothesis, but surprisingly, the mediated effect of education through civic duty is rather small (Figure 5.3). It would seem that a sense of civic duty is not so much learned at school as reinforced by working and associating with individuals of high occupational status and income.

There is no data bearing directly on cognitive ability. However, the BAS Study (Appendix C) included a brief vocabulary test which gives some purchase on the question. Perhaps what is measured by tests such as these might be better identified as verbal ability than as IQ. The scale is highly correlated with education. Both education and the vocabulary IQ test had identical zero-order correlations with political sophistication ($r = .33$). Education appears to be a somewhat stronger factor in multiple regression (Figure 5.4). Nevertheless, the evidence supports the idea of an independent cognitive-ability effect.

The fact that income appears to contribute independently to level of

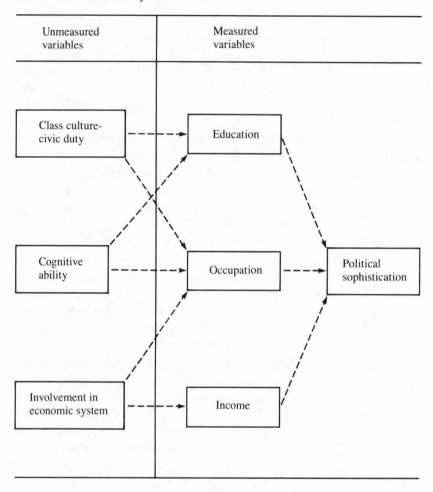

Figure 5.2. Sources of Sophistication: Measured and Unmeasured Variables.

sophistication offers support for the economic involvement hypothesis. To explore this matter further, however, it would be necessary to derive an improved measure of economic involvement. It could perhaps be developed from a careful recoding of reported occupational titles and industries and, where applicable, information on respondents' investments.

The lack of direct correspondence between the three traditional measures of socioeconomic status and the more interesting theories that underlie the general model limit the ability to do anything more than outline broad causal patterns. There is some evidence in the data to support each of the three theoretical models. A more refined analysis of the causal nexus is possible, however, with respect to the differential effects on the three sophistication components (Table 5.2).

There are three distinct causal patterns for education, occupation, and income. Education is clearly the dominant causal factor, and it has a consistently strong influence on each aspect of sophistication measured. A higher-status occupation, however, seems to lead to a subjective sense that politics is important, but only marginally to political knowledge, and not at all to the use of abstract integrating concepts. Conversely, a higher level of income leads not to interest in politics but to knowledge and conceptual sophistication.

Such a pattern suggests that political salience parallels the class culture–civic duty theory most closely. What is measured in this case is an expressed cultural value, namely that politics is important to the indi-

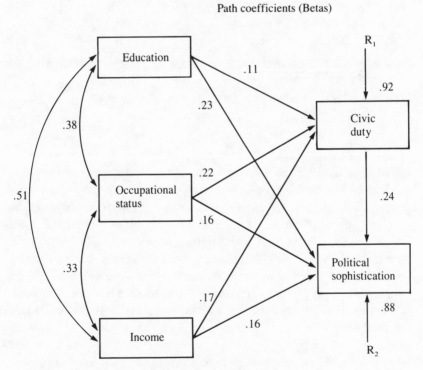

Figure 5.3. Model of Civic Duty. *Source:* NES 1956–1980.

Path coefficients (Betas)

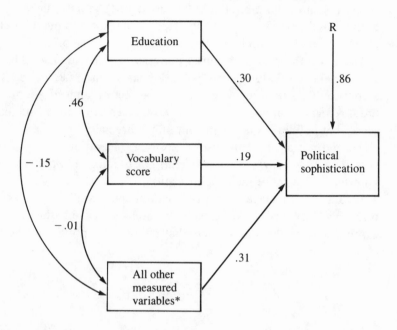

*Occupation, income, race, age, sex, social integration, self-esteem, and parents' socioeconomic status.

Figure 5.4. Cognitive Ability and Sophistication. *Source:* BAS.

vidual. Conceptualization, in contrast, refers not to a cultural value but to intellectual skills in use—the practice of differentiating and organizing political objects and issues—a notion more akin to the cognitive ability theory. Education apparently reflects both the cognitive ability and the civic duty phenomena. Occupational status, reflecting increased social interaction with other high social-status individuals, leads primarily to an increased salience of politics. Such social interaction seems to foster the communication of basic values much more than specific political information. This pattern corresponds closely to the data on civic duty.

The possible effects of income and the associated notion of economic involvement are less clear-cut. One might expect income to be equally related to all subcomponents. It seems, however, that an increased involvement in the economic sphere leads to political knowledge and to a familiarity with abstract political and presumably economic constructs, but not necessarily to an increased salience of politics. Apparently, economic interest leads more readily to cognitive than cultural effects. The overall pattern is one of three conjoint reinforcing influences, with a social status index being a better predictor of overall sophistication than any of the three components taken singly. Education is clearly the dominant factor, however, and is equally influential on each of the subcomponents of political sophistication.[1]

The summary statistics, such as those from the regression equations, give a crude estimate of what kind of difference being old, being black, or being female makes in terms of exposure to current events and political ideas. The negative zero-order correlation of − .15 reveals that blacks are generally less involved in politics. The smaller beta of − .05 indicates that much of the original difference is explained by other variables, primarily the lower average level of education of blacks. The very old and the very young do not pay much attention to politics. But the inverse correlation of age and education hides this relationship. Women think of themselves as less interested in politics, and are in fact less informed about politics, than men.

The pervading influence of these ascribed characteristics becomes clearest in depth interviews from the BAS study. A twenty-two-year-old black housewife from California remarks: "Well, the main thing I always worry about is having enough for my kids. I guess when you get married and you have babies you worry about things like that . . . You know, I never got interested in politics, that's why some of these questions are so hard for me to answer, because I never really thought about it as far as the government and things like that are concerned, because I just figure, if it's going to be, it's going to be . . . Everybody [in this neighborhood] is black, all I know about is black people really." A seventy-year-old retired white construction worker from California observes: "They talk about old age pensions! I went down to file for mine. They asked me how much was coming into the house, and I told them and they said it was too much coming in. That's right, I don't qualify."

1. Ironically, although research on the central role of education has been actively pursued, the role of education as a causal variable has in fact been minimized. Verba and Nie (1972), for example, use the phrase, "the general socioeconomic model" and, with a minimum of discussion, illustrate the education-participation correlation in their data. They refer to this as a causal baseline, which they then proceed to remove statistically from the data in the tables in order to demonstrate the independent effects of other variables with greater clarity. Perhaps the familiarity of the basic finding has obscured its theoretical origins, indeed, the reason researchers became interested in these patterns in the first place (Lane, 1959; Lipset, 1960).

You're supposed to be 'dead and dozed' before you qualify for these things . . . I vote but I don't think my vote is important as I did once . . . It has disturbed me, I look back to the changes made in the last ten years and to think about how it will be in the next ten years. It kinda makes me glad I won't be around to see it."

These interviews frequently manifest a central theme, salient issue or cluster of issues the respondent keeps coming back to. For older people, the theme often revolves around the difficult economic pressures of retirement on a fixed income in an inflationary economy. The retired construction worker has limitless stories about the frustrations of his life situation. Racial issues dominate the direction of the interview for many of the black and Chicano respondents, especially the younger ones. For most female respondents, their status as a woman is not a focal point around which issues and political conceptions are organized, although that may change in time. But the demands of their roles as wives and mothers pervade the interviews. One young woman who was deeply involved in the student protests describes herself as having other obligations now. She reports having no time for politics, hardly even following national events in the media. The flow of these interviews consists of an interviewer probing with abstract questions about the overall functioning of the American political system and the respondents attempting to interpret these abstractions in terms of the concrete experiences and pressures of their own life space. It is no surprise, therefore, that such factors as being old or being black define the dominant patterns of response.

The underlying theories that attempt to explain these phenomena are straightforward enough. There exists in this country vestigial social roles for blacks and women which reflect the recent past when their involvement in the political process was much more overtly constrained. An interesting aspect of race and sex is the diminishing correlation of each variable with sophistication over time. The situation regarding race is especially complex. The period just following the Civil Rights Act of 1964 marked a high point of rising political interest and expectations among American blacks. But by 1968 and continuing into the 1970s, the slow pace of change in race relations fostered a renewed cynicism and distrust of government. The political enfranchisement of women was a somewhat more sudden and dramatic historical event. Although women had won the vote in some states by the turn of the century, full women's suffrage was not guaranteed by federal law until 1920. So the majority of the women respondents in the studies were socialized in a period in which there at least were no legal restrictions on political participation. But there appears to be a pattern of a cultural lag, a vestigial sex role reinforcing the notion that politics is men's business. The negative beta of $-.17$ for women represents one of the strongest factors in the multiple regression on political sophistication. A 1950 study, which involved an extensive and carefully developed measure of the knowledge of current issues, found sex to be the single most significant predictor of knowledge, more powerful than either IQ or education (Swanson, 1950).

Although not all of the samples are strictly equivalent and the measurement of sophistication varies from study to study, it is possible to plot the shifts in correlation over time (Figure 5.5). There has been a modest decline in the correlation of being a woman and being less politically sophisticated. Less than half of the women in the 1948 sample grew up in a period of women's suffrage, whereas by 1968 only a small minority could remember Susan B. Anthony as anything except a historical figure.

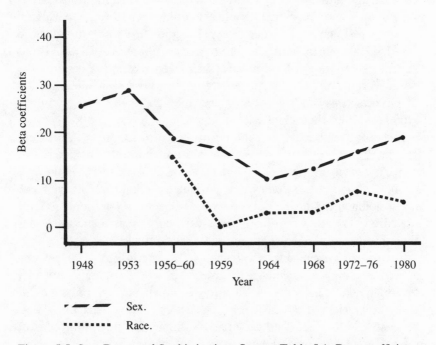

Figure 5.5. Sex, Race, and Sophistication. *Source:* Table 5.1. Beta coefficients represent the "net effect" or "partial correlation" between sex or race and sophistication controlling for the effects of other demographic variables.

Political alienation and cynicism may prove to be important mediating variables for blacks and perhaps some women as well. Thus these patterns over time may reflect political cycles and not simply a straight decline following a single historical event.

The character of the impact of age differs from that of either race or sex. It is a continuous variable, and its apparent effect is somewhat nonlinear. The pattern with regard to voting reflects a steadily increasing level of participation as individuals become more tied to the community and the economic system up to about 60 years of age, at which point life forces begin to work in the opposite direction. Because the measures of sophistication are based on current levels of interest in politics and knowledge and refer to topical issues and facts, there is an actual decline in political sophistication as individuals move into retirement and become less socially and economically engaged in the political system.

Because age and education are inversely correlated, there is a suppressor effect obscuring the true relationship between age and sophistication (Rosenberg, 1968). After a correction for the negative correlation between age and education, a somewhat more linear relationship results, with an apparent threshold of political learning around age forty (Figure 5.6). Interestingly, the decline in sophistication as a result of advanced age does not appear until the age of eighty and above. It would thus appear that although older citizens (sixty and above) may not get to the polls as frequently as younger voters, in part because of the difficulty of physical travel to the voting place, they continue to follow public affairs well into their eighties.

Psychological factors present particularly frustrating measurement problems in survey research. One would prefer to rely on clinical evidence in the case of personality and on ideographic materials in the case of socialization effects. The social psychology of political behavior was not a dominant interest of those who designed the questionnaires for the core data sets. Accordingly, measurement is sparse and the scales themselves seldom involve more than four or five items.

The research is entering as well a tangled "underbrush" of intertwined and interactive causal linkages (Greenstein, 1967). Some personality factors may influence the vote decision of individuals, but only in those cases for which political and ideological factors are especially nonsalient. A sense of self-esteem and personal worth may be an important factor in explaining why some individuals and not others achieve higher levels of education. Because the survey data were all collected over a brief span of time, there is no way of sorting out these patterns of two-way

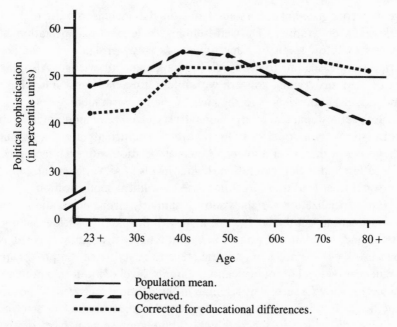

Figure 5.6. Age and Sophistication. *Source:* NES 1980.

causation. Also, the limitations of measurement constrain the ability to explore multivariate interaction of even a sampling of the potentially relevant factors of personality and socialization. Nonetheless, there are repeated measures of two related elements of personality—self-esteem and interpersonal trust—and three socialization variables—parents' interest in politics, parents' SES and parents' urban residence.

A psychological model of political sophistication that focuses on the mediating role of self-esteem and thus of interpersonal trust on social learning makes it possible to examine low self-esteem as an inhibitory mechanism in the development of political sophistication (Sniderman, 1974). While the mass media are an important initial source of political information, much of what people know about politics depends heavily on interaction with friends and colleagues. Both low self-esteem and low interpersonal trust are important elements of a potential psychological barrier to that exchange of information. The inhibitory mechanism may work as well to limit the political attentiveness and interest of individuals. This would effect exposure to information in both an interpersonal and a mass media setting. Low self-esteem is part of a general configuration of personality factors that includes a sense of pow-erlessness and futility. The self-fulfilling cycle of low expectation of success and low levels of achievement is easily translated into the po-litical sphere, leading to low levels of interest and knowledge. Also, the associated anxiety and concern with internal psychological states limit individuals' attentiveness to the cues of their environment.

Both self-esteem and interpersonal trust indeed have moderately high correlations with sophistication. The beta coefficients are lower, but they suggest that, over and above their association with such factors as education and social integration, higher levels of self-esteem and inter-personal trust lead to a direct increase in political sophistication.

Early socialization variables show a similarly strong correlation with sophistication, but the betas associated with the parents' socioeconomic status and an urban upbringing are substantively insignificant, perhaps because these variables are several steps removed from the proximate influences on level of sophistication. Parents' level of interest in politics, however, shows a surprising strength in the multiple regression. The .15 coefficient is among the highest. Apparently the level and character of political discussion in the childhood home represents a facet of the socialization process not tapped by the other status and demographic variables. Its effect is consistently strong across each of the subcom-ponents.

Group Participation and the Theory of Pluralism

The participation of citizens in voluntary associations and political party activities is an important tenet of classic pluralism. Tocqueville found America in 1835 to be a nation of "joiners," individuals ready to band together in formal or quasi-formal organizations to further their common interests, and that tendency is still in evidence (Almond and Verba, 1965). So the notion of alternative paths comes back to the theory of group pluralism.

According to this theory, group participation has three reinforcing effects which may increase the level of political sophistication. Its first effect is the psychological phenomenon whereby group participation gives individuals a sense of community, a feeling of efficacy and in-volvement in the political decisionmaking process. Group activity, even if it is not explicitly political in character, may foster a general atten-tiveness to public affairs. Uninvolved individuals, in contrast, may be socially and culturally isolated, exhibiting a diffuse dissatisfaction and sense of political futility. The second effect is cognitive. Multiple group participation, as in a union, PTA, and fraternal organization, extends the breadth of individuals' political thinking. Were people only union members, they might develop a narrowly focused group-interest orientation toward politics. Exposure to the cross-cutting ideas and perspectives of other organizations may lead them to a more balanced and thought-out approach to politics. The third and perhaps most important effect of group activity is that it extends the depth of people's political thinking. National politics in modern industrial societies involves remote issues and objects. Unattached individuals may be able to make no sense of what they read in the newspaper concerning complex wage-and-price regulations or changes in the structure of taxation on imported goods. Contact with union spokespersons, a shop steward, or even a union newsletter might translate those distant events and symbols into more meaningful and proximate concerns for the individual. Likewise, participation in local meetings may strengthen a person's understanding of such general political principles as political compromise and minority rights (Kornhauser, 1959).

Group participation includes a variety of voluntary associations, the great majority of which are not explicitly political, such as social groups, professional or farm organizations, cooperatives, fraternal or veterans groups, athletic clubs, and charitable or religious organizations. Joiners are more outgoing and more highly educated individuals, as shown by the .29 correlation between group participation and political sophistication. The beta of .13 places social integration among the strongest predictors of political sophistication and supports the alternative paths notion that group life plays an important part in the process of political socialization.

The Political Environment

There are even broader contextual variables, such as the different urban and rural environments and the distinctive character of the American South. These variables provide a further test of the environmental reinforcement element of the spiral theory. A lower level of sophistication might be expected to occur in rural areas and in the South:

The full-time farmer has been much less firmly bound up with the flow of national events than any other group in society. He has tended to work alone in an occupation which, save for the winter months, has left little leisure to attend to the world beyond the horizon. Interest grows from roots of information, and a continuing flow of information nourishes abiding interest. Even today the farmer may be less consistently exposed to political information than the urban resident . . . the currrent American farmer may bear the signs not only of some lingering remoteness from national politics, but apathy inherited from preceding eras in which the political communicaiton system was much less developed. (Campbell et al., 1960, p. 413)

The small farmer has been the keystone of rural life, though the trend now is toward large-scale, corporate agribusiness. The independent family farm plays a much reduced role in modern rural America. Still, a rural existence is characterized by a different pace if not style of life. Those who persist in their agricultural pursuits long after the economic pressures have sent their neighbors and children to the cities represent an especially self-reliant breed who manifest an even stronger resistance to involvement in abstract questions of national and international politics.

The South, in a sense parallel to that of rural life, is likewise characterized by strong local ties and remoteness from national political conflict: "In the discussion of southern politics a prominent place is given to the low levels of voting in the region . . . the one-party system both contributes to low levels of citizen-interest and in turn perhaps is perpetuated in part by citizen disinterest . . . while low popular interest in elections is commonly attributed to Negro disfranchisement, as a matter of fact, only a small proportion of the white population regularly votes" (Key, 1949, p. 489).

The impact of the distinctiveness of life in the South and in rural areas on sophistication is not strongly supported by the data. The correlations are very low. The explained variance in both cases, though based on rather crude contextual dichotomies, is less than 1 percent. This difference suggests that the stereotypes of the South and of rural communities as politically unsophisticated are overdrawn.

The Spiral Theory

It is difficult to put all of this data in perspective. There are a great many variables, and most have some modest effect. A stronger theoretical foundation is needed, if only a metaphor or analogy for better understanding the process by which some individuals come to be politically sophisticated and active and others do not.

A spiral theory of the acquisition of political sophistication is a convenient way to summarize the data. Multiple regressions by their nature define one variable as dependent, in this case political sophistication, and define the other variable as independent. This creates a problem because, over time, sophistication is both influenced by and influences these other factors of social and political position: "The more that people read about and listen to the campaign on the mass media, the more interested they become in the election and the more strongly they come to feel about their candidate. In every comparison between those higher and lower in media exposure, interest and intensity increase from August to October. Here is a finding that typifies the spiral effect of mutually influencing variables and complex human situations 'the appetite grows by what it feeds on.' Communication exposure affects some of the factors that affect it" (Berelson et al., 1954, p. 246).

Sophistication is itself a stable and fundamental variable with considerable inertia. Independently measured indices of sophistication from the National Election Studies of 1972–1976 have a correlation of .72 (Pearson), which is only slightly lower than the test-retest correlation of party identification, .78. Sophistication, like party identification or even IQ, can thus be seen as a fundamental variable of political personality. Such a variable reflects the influences of the social environment on the individual and in turn mediates their impact on future political and social behavior. Like IQ, political sophistication is heavily intertwined with an individual's educational achievement. Like party identification, it serves as a conduit of political attitudes drawn from childhood. But also like IQ and party identification, political sophistication is not a totally ascribed and unchanging attribute. If individuals find themselves in a supportive, stimulating, and active political environment, they are likely, over time, to spiral upward in political knowledge and involvement. In turn, in a politically sterile environment where there are few socially reinforced rewards for involvement and attentiveness, they are likely to turn their attention to other domains and define politics as a passion of their youth.

Education is centrally important in this spiral process. Education inculcates a sense of citizen duty, leads to occupational environments that are likely to reinforce political activity or interest, and reflects the cognitive ability necessary for understanding the abstract concepts that make up the basic vocabulary of political life. Thus, educational level is the primary determinant of the starting point of young adults in political life, and most individuals, from the natural stimuli and electoral politics, spiral gradually upward to somewhat higher levels of political sophistication.

Sophistication

	(Low)	(High)
(Low)	Predicted Low Sophistication (39% of total), Citizen duty, 83% Government trust, 47% Party loyalty, 34% Turnout, 54% Campaign participation, 3% Other political participation, 5%	Deviant case: "Alternate path" (26%), Citizen duty, 96% Government trust, 51% Party loyalty, 35% Turnout, 83% Campaign participation, 11% Other political participation, 17%
(High)	Deviant case: Apolitical (9%), Citizen duty, 95% Government trust, 60% Party loyalty, 26% Turnout, 62% Campaign participation, 6% Other political participation, 12%	Predicted high sophistication (26%), Citizen duty, 96% Government trust, 63% Party loyalty, 36% Turnout, 87% Campaign participation, 16% Other political participation, 25%

Education

Figure 5.7. Alternative Paths to Sophistication. *Source:* NES 1972–1976.

Other demographic elements suggest alternate paths of sophistication. Participation in group activities, high levels of income, and an especially politically active parental environment lead to increased sophistication independent of the effects of education. Those who have tread an alternative path to political involvement, one other than the usual educationally linked spiral, reflect a somewhat different style of sophistication. A case in point is those individuals who, without much formal education but through heavy involvement in union activities or party politics, come to be extremely active politically. Such variables as group participation lead to higher levels of political salience but not necessarily to higher levels of conceptualization involving the more abstract issues of political discourse.

Cross-classifying the citizenry by both sophistication (dividing the continuum in half) and education (separating noncollege from college educated) reveals that most people fall in the category of low education and low sophistication or high sophistication and high education. This scheme reveals as well two deviant cases: that portion of the citizenry who are politically sophisticated but not well educated, and the much smaller portion who are well-educated but apolitical. Comparison of the attributes of the alternative-path groups to those of the other groups gives some sense of the comparative impact of education and sophistication on political attitudes and behavior (Figure 5.7). For example, both education and sophistication lead to a high sense of citizen duty. But groups on the alternative paths are less likely than those with high education to trust the government. They are involved but skeptical. Despite their lower level of education, they are heavily involved in party politics—by most measures almost as heavily involved as the high-education, high-sophistication group. The small group of college-educated apoliticals shows that college has a number of political socializing effects independent of increases in sophistication. An exception is party loyalty. In general, then, regardless of whether people come to political participation via the traditional educational route or by some alternative path, their style of involvement is likely to be pretty much the same.

In summary, then, there is clear evidence that political sophistication is an enduring and fundamental variable of political life. It has roots in both early political socialization and exposure to formal education, and it is maintained through subtle reinforcing mechanisms involving interpersonal psychology, group participation, and involvement in economic life. Formal education is an especially important causal variable, but it need not function as a gatekeeper. It represents but one of several alternative paths to political involvement and sophistication.

6 | The Role of the Mass Media

> Politicians, journalists, academics and gadflies have argued frequently and passionately that television news and advertising have a wide-ranging influence on voters . . . In most accounts, television is thought to be the most powerful medium available for persuading and communicating with the electorate. Despite the certitude with which these beliefs are held, they are inaccurate . . . In almost every instance, the prevailing view of television's role in American presidential elections is wrong.
>
> Thomas E. Patterson and Robert D. McClure

THE 1978 gubernatorial race in Georgia produced what must be the ultimate television campaign commercial:

Candidate: This is Nick Belluso. In the next ten seconds you will be hit with a tremendously hypnotic force. You may wish to turn away. Without further ado let me introduce to you the hypnogenecist of mass hypnosis, the Reverend James G. Masters. Take us away, James.

Hypnotist (in strange garb, surrounded by mists): Do not be afraid. I am placing the name of Nick Belluso in your subconscious mind. You will remember this. You will vote on Election Day. You will vote Nick Belluso for governor. You will remember this. You will vote on Election Day. You will vote Nick Belluso for governor. (Sabato, 1981, p. 324)

This commercial was actually broadcast. The political consultants who designed it spurned the traditional Madison Avenue approach of emphasizing the gentle symbolism of waving fields of grain and candidates in shirtsleeves to try a more direct approach. The resulting paid political broadcast was perhaps the ultimate outgrowth of faith in the power of television to persuade.

Belief in the political power of the mass media in general and of television in particular is strong. One might cite the comment of a television producer:

Television news has changed the way America is governed.
Television news has changed the way America votes.

And television news has changed the way America thinks. (Weston, 1982, p. 1)

Or one might cite the remarks of candidates themselves. John Connally, a 1980 candidate for President, commented, "On a scale of 1 to 10 the importance of media is at least an 8, everything else is a 2." And Vice President Walter Mondale observed, "if I had to give up . . . the opportunity to get on the evening news or the veto power . . . I'd throw the veto power away. [Television news] is the President's most indispensable power" (Robinson and Sheehan, 1983).

Politics in the Television Age

The mass media have played the role of both hero and whipping boy. Among television's possible positive effects is the raising of the overall level of political sophistication by bringing political information to a broader audience not otherwise inclined to pay attention (Nie et al., 1976; Popkin et al., 1976). Both the preservation of the media system and the expansion of mass literacy are necessary to the viability of a democracy (Lerner, 1958; Pool, 1963). In the industrialized nations of the twentieth century the democratic polity cannot function as such without the institutional structure of independent mass media (Lippmann, 1922).

The media may have at the same time contributed to the ills of mass democracy. It is claimed, for example, that television has stimulated the growth of political cynicism and malaise (Robinson, 1975, 1976). The media are said to have trivialized politics, depressed voter turnout, led to the decline of the party system, caused a dramatic centralization of political power, and increased the domination of the executive branch over Congress (Marcuse, 1964; McQuail, 1969; Mendelsohn and Crespi, 1970; Minow et al., 1973; Kraus and Dennis, 1976). This is an impressive list of effects. Sometimes television journalism is told to look more like newspaper journalism (Manheim, 1976). At other times the media are advised to do a better job of getting to the underlying political issues (Boorstin, 1961; Gans, 1979).

Common to both the boosters and the critics of the mass media, however, is a shared sense of the media as the central political educator. This is an important part of the continuing paradox of mass politics. Though the media are regarded as persuasive and powerful, few people are very interested in or well-informed about politics.

The strength of media effects has itself been a subject of debate.

Responding to a growing concern about the effects of propaganda after the Second World War, studies on the persuasive effects of the mass media concluded that, despite the expectations, there is a "law of minimal effects" (Klapper, 1960). Other studies contradict this position, showing that the mass media play a vital role in contemporary politics (Clarke and Fredin, 1978; Comstock et al., 1978; Graber, 1980; Patterson, 1980; Zukin, 1981). As it turns out, the research designs favored by both positions are simply too incomplete to resolve the issue (Neuman, forthcoming). The question of strong media effects remains open.

The issue of media effects is critically important to the understanding of political communications and mass sophistication. Theoretically the media could do more to inform and educate the public politically. But in fact they cannot do much more.

Political information is available in great richness to all in the United States who wish to pay attention. Those who blame the media for the ills of the modern American polity tend to confuse the characteristics of the medium with the characteristics of its audience. The distribution of political knowledge in American society would stay pretty much the same even if the entire mass media industry agreed cooperatively to double the flow of political communications. The distribution would also probably remain the same if the flow were cut in half. The widely shared sense of the effectiveness of the media must be reconciled with the repeated finding that the media message is not getting through.

Political Content of the Mass Media

In 1961 at a convention of the nation's broadcasters, the newly appointed chairman of the Federal Communications Commission, Newton M. Minow, put forward a challenge to the assembled broadcasters that was to haunt them for decades to come: "I invite you to sit down in front of your television set when your station goes on the air and stay there without a book, magazines, newspaper, profit-and-loss sheet or rating book to distract you—and keep your eyes glued to that set until the station signs off. I can assure you that you will observe a vast wasteland" (Barnouw, 1970, p. 197).

The "vast wasteland" phrase resonated widely with media critics and industry apologists. It is now largely forgotten that a young President Kennedy was also at the convention's podium that day. He remarked: "The flow of ideas, the capacity to make informed choices, the ability to criticize, all of the assumptions on which political democracy rests, depend largely on communications. And you are the guardians of the most powerful and effective means of communication ever designed" (Barnouw, 1970, p. 196). The sharp contrast between the two speakers highlights the tension between what many believe the media could contribute to the democratic process and the mundane reality of day-to-day commercial communications.

The fact of the matter is that the American polity conducts its business on borrowed time. It is borrowed from a commercial, entertainment-oriented media system. The economics of television, and thus of political communication, is based not on the providing of programs to audiences but rather on the selling of audiences to advertisers (Owen et al., 1975). The profitability of television is a direct mathematical function of the number of heads in front of television sets as measured by the Nielsen and Arbitron audience ratings. Television news is not exempted from Nielsen economics (Barnouw, 1978). The same is true of newspapers, which derive 90 percent of their income from advertising. Their readers' subscriptions hardly pay for the paper and ink. The proportion of magazine income from reader subscription is somewhat higher, but few mass circulation magazines would be economically viable without advertising support.

One element in the production process of newspapers brings home the dominance of commercial economics. Newspapers take care of first things first. The number of pages for a daily newspaper is determined by the demand for advertising, and the advertising copy is set up first. The editorial staff of a newspaper is then confronted with what is known in the trade as a "news hole," the space left over after the advertising is in place. There is often more room for news on Wednesdays because of the traditionally heavy demand for food advertising. In general, about 40 percent of the space in the average newspaper is available for news to be fit in around the ads.

Political communication is only a small fraction of the communications flow. The public tends to think of newspapers as primarily a news rather than entertainment medium. They share the awe of most politicians for the power of broadcast journalism. Thus they would instinctively assume that there is a fair amount of political information in the flow of mass media content. But in fact the flow of political content is dwarfed by the flow of entertainment content in the American commercial system. In the newspapers, for example, where 60 percent of the content consists of advertising messages, the rest of the content consists primarily of human interest stories, horoscopes, sports scores, recipes, and movie reviews. There is relatively little hard news or political content. Roughly speaking, 10 percent of the editorial content, or 4 percent of the total newspaper content, consists of national and international news, and only a portion of that is political in nature. The percentages for television are roughly the same. Only 4 percent of television programming consists of news (Bagdikian, 1971). Among the highest-circulation magazines— *TV Guide, Reader's Digest, National Geographic, Woman's Day, Modern Maturity, McCall's, Ladies' Home Journal,* and *Good Housekeeping*—the proportions of political content are roughly the same (Compaine, 1982).

Strictly speaking, political news remains a small fraction of the overall information flow. More important, the kind of hard information about issues and events that prompted President Kennedy to comment on the media's central role in the political process represents only a fraction of political news. Campaign hoopla, for example—the description of the candidates' travel schedule, the handshaking, the crowds, the pictures of balloons and motorcades—dominates campaign coverage. Over 80 percent of campaign stories discuss the horse-race question, whereas half make no mention whatsoever of any policy questions (Robinson and Sheehan, 1983). In 1976, 51 percent of newspaper campaign coverage and 63 percent of television coverage focused on campaign events. As for the candidates themselves, 77 percent of the newspaper coverage focused on their personal qualities and general competence rather than their issue positions and the substance of their speeches. Only 4 percent of the coverage dealt with economic policy, and only 5 percent with foreign policy (Graber, 1980).

This does not represent a conspiracy of journalists to keep the public ill informed. It is a structural fact of life in the news process. Reporters focus on the "indisputable fact and the easy interest"—the factual description of events rather than the less easily communicated and perhaps less interesting underlying causes and abstract issues (Lippmann, 1922, p. 221).

A central irony of American political communications is that a rich diversity of political coverage, including in-depth analysis of issues and policy, does indeed exist, but it is only a small trickle in the broader media tide. To a large extent, only the political elite attend to the political press. For every household that receives a journal of political opinion such as the *New Republic* or *National Review,* there are 100 households that subscribe to *Good Housekeeping* and 400 that subscribe to *TV Guide.* General news magazines such as *Time* and *Newsweek* have in-depth political coverage, but each reaches only one household in 20. Television documentary programming has the largest audience potential. Most viewers, as the networks know well, prefer entertainment programming to "talking heads." Relatively little is known about the audience sizes for public affairs programming because the networks frequently schedule them for "dead weeks," the three or four weeks of the year when the Nielsen and Arbitron audience ratings are not collected. Public broadcasting covers public affairs in considerable depth but rarely attracts more than 3 percent of the viewing audience for such fare. The "McNeil Lehrer Report" covers individual political issues in depth on a nightly basis, but its ratings are so abysmally low, even for public television, that Nielsen frequently puts an asterisk next to the program, indicating that the audience is simply too small to be estimated by the usual statistical procedures.

Even when the audience does run across some political content amid the media flow, there are further barriers to communication. Despite the average level of media exposure in a given day, which probably involves over four hours of television as well as exposure to newspapers and magazines, citizens remember little of what they see and read. Viewers of network news can spontaneously recall only 5 percent of the stories they have seen, and political analysis and commentary have the lowest recall rate of all categories of news (Neuman, 1976). Furthermore, news content receives the lowest level of attention of all types of programming (Bechtel et al., 1972). Similar patterns are found for the print media (Patterson, 1980; Weaver et al., 1981).

As a general rule the higher the level of abstract, issue-oriented, political content, the smaller the audience it is likely to attract (Neuman, 1984; Figure 6.1). This might be termed the inverse law. There is no rule that nonpolitical content will reach a large audience. Numerous nonpolitical magazines and television programs, for example, reach very small audiences. But there is a strong pattern for the political content: its audiences are consistently small.

There are instructive exceptions to the rule. Regular programs, such as "Sixty Minutes," and special events, such as presidential debates and the Watergate hearings, do attract a relatively large and attentive audience. But this may be in spite of rather than because of the political content involved. In each of these cases there is a dramatic confrontation, in which someone will presumably win and someone will lose. The excitement generated in these circumstances, as television writers have known for years, helps to keep heads in front of television sets.

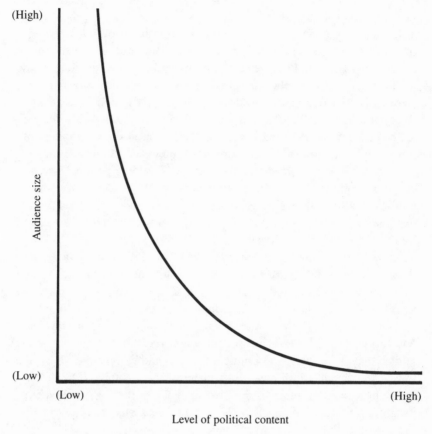

Figure 6.1. The Inverse Law.

Another exception to the rule evolved in the television industry in the late 1960s when, in response to the campus political upheavals and the urban unrest, the programming staffs concluded that new programs confronting these issues would be popular. It was known as the "Year of Political Relevance." One program, for example, featured young and idealistic lawyers atempting to fight the system and bring legal rights to poor people. Another program, a situation comedy entitled "Ivan the Terrible," attempted to portray day-to-day life in the USSR. These shows performed dismally in the ratings, and the new trend was quickly aborted (Barnouw, 1975).

There is a lesson here for those who would like to reform the media. Federal Communications Commission guidelines or other well-intended incentives to increase the flow of political information are likely to have limited effects. The media environment is already rich. As long as entertainment options are available, the bulk of of the audience will simply not stay tuned to political commentary for long.

The growth of political communications through cable television is a case in point. A cable news service does indeed provide news and news headlines twenty-four hours a day. Another cable channel provides in-depth coverage of congressional floor debate and committee sessions. These are important, positive contributions to the media environment. But the combined viewing of all news and public affairs channels in cable homes seldom exceeds 1 percent of the audience (Lemieux, 1983). In terms of the flow of communications to the average home, the impact of cable has been primarily to increase the viewing of movies, sports, and reruns. Before cable was introduced, in many cities news was simultaneously broadcast on all available channels at certain times of the day. With more options available on cable, the proportion of news viewing will actually go down.

The Medium and the Message

Such phrases as "the politics of the television era" have become commonplace, labeling the era by its most preeminent and visible mass medium. They are based on the premise that television has had a significant effect on the political process: "The public has fairly well stopped following national politics through print, traditional or otherwise. Television is the preeminent link between national affairs and the national public" (Robinson and Sheehan, 1983, p. 280). According to this hypothesis, television is a fundamentally different political medium, which requires a new understanding of mass political learning:

[Television] is diluting the experiential and informational base of the American culture and . . . altering the nature and effectiveness of American democracy. Indeed . . . as the reliance on television as a teaching/learning device (in the largest sense) increases, many interpretive and interactive skills may fall into misuse and decay. And since human interaction is the very heart and soul of the political process, a general decline in analytic and expressive skills which characterize that interaction in society as a whole cannot help be reflected in the polity as well.   (Manheim, 1976, p. 85)

Is it possible that television has such debilitating and corrosive effects? Politically speaking, does the medium make a difference? The answer is no. It is based on three points.

The first point concerns whether the political content of broadcast journalism is actually different from its print counterpart. The coverage of politics in television is seen as more interpretive and negative, emphasizing conflict and neglecting abstract policy issues. Television news is regarded as structurally distinctive, requiring a continuous narrative theme which can sustain viewer interest throughout the story. Television emphasizes violence, conflict, and a general anti-institutional negativism, trivializing or ignoring policy issues (Robinson, 1976). The full network newscast would not even generate enough text to fill the front page of a daily newspaper.

Comparative analyses of political coverage, however, have shown that television's content is not actually unique (Tables 6.1–6.3). Some differences exist, but for the most part, strong similarities characterize the political coverage of all media:

The public's acceptance of the press's version of the campaign is facilitated by the consistency of coverage by the various news outlets. Although the press is not monolithic in how events are reported, it is in which events are covered. Print and television journalists alike are mostly concerned with the campaign activity and the game, and their shared news values make the same events and subjects the focus of each medium's coverage. Consequently, there are not large

Table 6.1. Campaign Coverage in 1976 (%)

Coverage	Television network news	Newspapers	News magazines
Substance			
Horserace and hoopla	58	56	54
Issue and policy	29	28	32
Other	13	12	14
Interpretation			
Descriptive	31	71	23
Mixed	12	15	24
Interpretive	57	14	53
Issue type			
Clear-cut	67	49	46
Mixed	14	23	19
Diffuse	19	28	35

Source: Patterson, 1980.

Table 6.2. Campaign Coverage in 1968, 1972, and 1976 (%)

Coverage	Television news[a]	Newspapers[b]
Issues		
Campaign	50	37
Domestic	17	21
Economic	8	11
Foreign affairs	20	21
Social problems	6	11
Candidates[c]		
Favorable	58	37
Normative[d]	4	6
Unfavorable	39	57

Source: Graber, 1980.

a. Sample of national and local television newscasts for the last 30 days of presidential campaign each election year.

b. Sample of 20 newspapers from communities of different sizes and political orientations in all parts of the country, representative of American press.

c. 1972 only.

d. References to the qualities candidates ought to have.

Table 6.3. Campaign Coverage in 1972 (%)

Coverage	Television network news	Newspapers and AP wire
Overall		
Candidates	36	36
Parties	36	31
Issues	28	33
Candidates		
Favorable	15	24
Neutral	73	54
Unfavorable	12	22

Source: Hofstetter, 1975.

differences in the judgments of television and newspaper audiences concerning the election's significant aspects. (Patterson, 1980, p. 100)

A strong consensus is developed among all reporters in covering complex political events (Crouse, 1973). Television news does tend to be more interpretive than newspapers (Robinson and Sheehan, 1983). But the medium of news magazines also tends to emphasize interpretation, and it is not clear that such a difference would be tied to malaise, apathy, or ignorance on the part of the viewing audience (Patterson, 1980). Television also emphasizes the competitive, horse-race aspects and hoopla of campaign events, but so do the other media. As for negativism, newspapers tend to be more negative than television in their election coverage (Hofstetter, 1975; Graber, 1980). Finally, none of the media apparently devotes a great deal of attention to abstract policy issues. There are thus broad similarities in the political content of the various mass media (Meadow, 1973).

The second point concerns the hypothesis that television is a technologically unique medium. This might be termed the McLuhan approach. Because television is visual, colorful, and full of motion, even the same information is likely to have different effects on the audience when conveyed through this medium as compared to a print medium. Television is said to be more credible, persuasive, and memorable than corresponding print media (Paletz and Entman, 1981).

Experiments show, however, that the message is the message. When the same content is transmitted through different media, the effects are similar. In one study a variety of video programs, including political and nonpolitical content, along with corresponding audio and print versions, were presented to experimental subjects, and only trivial differences were found in the patterns of audience interest and learning (Trenaman, 1967). A study in Japan substantiated these findings (Tsuneki, 1979). In a study of the 1976 presidential debates, subjects were randomly assigned to watch the debate on television, read a transcript, or listen to an audio-only version of the debate. This experiment focused on precisely the type of persuasive campaign communication that had motivated the television hypothesis in the first place. But again the responses for all three experimental groups were nearly identical (Neuman, 1977). These findings on the lack of a unique television effect parallel the findings on instructional television (Dubin and Hedley, 1969). If television has a unique effect, it may be too subtle to be identified by traditional experimental designs.

The third point about the television hypothesis is its emphasis on the unique characteristics of the television audience. Television audiences tend to be very large. The pattern of viewing tends to be casual and inadvertent, so that many of the individuals who pick up political information from television news stories or spot advertising are not the type to seek out such information actively in reading newspapers or magazines (Robinson, 1976). There is a dramatic trend toward the increasing reliance on television for news (Roper, 1983). As a result, the trends toward cynicism, ticket splitting, political apathy, and similar developments are attributed to the growth of reliance on television for news.

This notion of media dependence is reinforced by an implicit scenario about what would happen if all the mass media ceased to function: "No news about events from home and abroad, no explanations about shortages or failures of public services, no announcements of new programs and facilities. Presidents, governors and mayors and legislatures at all levels would be slowed or immobilized by lack of information and interpretation . . . Indeed, media are vital for public and private life: the image of a modern world without them is eerie and frightening" (Graber, 1980, p. ix). This is a powerful and persuasive scenario. The citizenry has come to rely heavily on the mass media, and it is difficult to imagine how else we would follow political life.

But such scenarios are misleading. One can make inferences about media dependence from historical trends and such phenomena as newspaper strikes as well as survey data. These data provide a different picture. All citizens spend a varying amount of their energy keeping track of the world around them. When one medium suspends activity, the public shifts its attention to other media and to interpersonal information sources (Berelson, 1949). According to studies of the flow of information in Germany under Hitler, Eastern Europe, and the Soviet Union, if all of the media constrain their activity they will lose the public's trust, and citizens will seek out other sources, including international broadcasting, interpersonal information networks, and ad-hoc substitute media such as samzidat, underground news letters, and journals (Shibutani, 1966; Mickiewicz, 1981).

These issues are relevant to the television hypothesis, which argues that an increasing proportion of the electorate rely primarily on television for political news. Reliance on television for news has indeed been trending slightly upward (Figure 6.2). But this is hardly a clearcut explanation for political cynicism or the increasing number of citizens

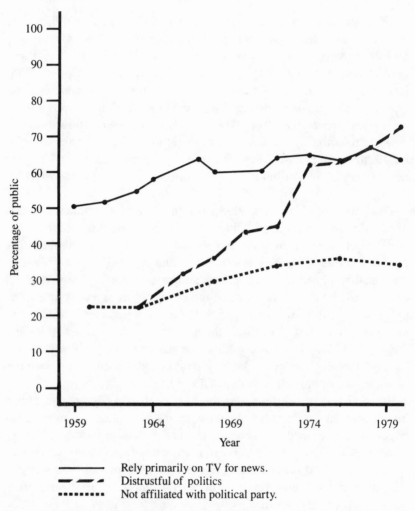

Figure 6.2. Television Dependence, Political Cynicism, and Nonaffiliation with Parties. *Source:* Roper, 1983; NES.

identifying themselves as independents rather than party supporters (Converse, 1976; Miller, 1983).

Over the years, in fact, newspapers have remained dominant in terms of the primary flow of political communications. A two-week study of news habits found that only 50 percent of adults see any national network news program at all, while 90 percent are exposed to newspapers. In a single day, only 23 percent of the adult population see a network newscast, while 69 percent see a newspaper (Robinson, 1971; Bogart, 1977). The notion that the television news audience is larger and different from that of the newspapers is simply a myth. Data from the 1976 election confirm that the electorate is more likely to have read a newspaper than to have seen a network newscast. Furthermore, politically active individuals are more likely both to see network news and to follow events in the newspaper. Popular stereotypes to the contrary, television does not appeal only to individuals of lower educational or occupational status (Patterson, 1980).

According to the television hypothesis, those citizens who depend on television for political information have an increasingly impoverished sense of the political world around them as well as a growing ignorance, apathy, and cynicism. The studies which follow this analytic line are legion (Robinson, 1975, 1976; Gerbner and Gross, 1976a, 1976b; Gerbner et al., 1977, 1978, 1979, 1980, 1981; Clarke and Fredin, 1978; O'Keefe and Mendelsohn, 1978; Becker et al., 1979; Becker and Fruit, 1979; Miller et al., 1979; Becker and Whitney, 1980; Erbring et al., 1980; O'Keefe, 1980; Reese and Miller, 1981; Miller and Reese, 1982; McDonald, 1983; Miyo, 1983; Robinson and Sheehan, 1983). But such an approach confuses the characteristics of the audience with those of the medium. Take, for example, the continuum running from the least interested and sophisticated citizens to the most. Those at the low end of the continuum do not pay attention to the political content in any of the mass media. Television is, by its nature, more intrusive than the newspaper. So if the television set is on at the dinner hour or late evening when most television stations carry news, viewers at all levels of political interest are likely to be exposed. This is inadvertent viewing. It is not as easy in television news to read only the comics and sports. Thus, by definition, the less interested will appear to rely on television for news. But it is hardly appropriate to turn around and conclude that television "causes" disinterest or any of a number of related attitudes (Doob and MacDonald, 1979; Hughes, 1980; Hirsch, 1980, 1981). The television reliance notion may in fact be more harmful than helpful in coming to grips with these issues.

Theories of Communication Effects

American business spends $50 billion a year on advertising its products through the various mass media. Given an investment of that magnitude, the advertising community ought to have a precise measure of advertising effectiveness and be able to predict in advance whether an advertising appeal is likely to succeed. The irony is that advertising researchers, like political communications researchers, have a difficult time demonstrating a clear-cut communications effect (Comstock et al., 1978; Naples, 1979). The success of the communication process in eluding empirical analysis is another side of the paradox of mass politics.

Three theories have emerged to try to explain how this complex process works. The first and most clearly relevant theory focuses on the concept of the knowledge gap: "As the infusion of mass media information into a social system increases, segments of the population with higher socio-economic status tend to acquire this information at a faster rate than the lower status segments, so that the gap in knowledge between these segments tends to increase rather than decrease" (Tichenor et al., 1970).

Studies on knowledge gaps provide evidence that individuals with higher levels of education tend to be better informed, but the findings conflict on whether there is an increasing gap over time (Gaziano, 1983). Part of the problem is a weak assumption in the original formulation of the theory, which posited that the knowledge gap would grow because political events were becoming more complex. Modern economic and technical problems are indeed complex, but so were the problems faced by the citizens of the 1940s or those of the nineteenth century. The factual details of foreign affairs and domestic policy severely tax the abilities of even the most brilliant public servant, let alone the private citizen who tries to follow these affairs through the media. It is impractical for citizens to attempt to monitor all of the available details (Lippmann, 1922). There are some issues on which knowledge gaps are increasing and others on which they are decreasing. But the consensus is clear that, when a gap exists, it correlates with education. An underlying mechanism allows the knowledge gap to reproduce itself again and again as new issues and new information enter the public arena.

The second theory that addresses the paradoxical character of political communications focuses on the agenda-setting effect (McCoombs and Shaw, 1972; Shaw and McCoombs, 1976; Weaver et al., 1981). The premise of this theory is that, if the mass media are not tremendously successful in persuading the public in what they ought to believe, the media may be successful in setting the agenda, that is, persuading the public in what they ought to consider. This distinction is viewed as a key to resolving the tension between theories of powerful versus minimal communications effects.

Unfortunately, however, the agenda-setting theory needs to be reformulated. One problem is the key assumption that, if the content of the mass media corresponds with the individual's reported list of important problems facing the country, the causal process must take the form of the media influencing the individual. Time-series studies reveal, however, that the public often responds to real-world cues independently of media coverage and may choose to ignore extensive media coverage of new issues (Miller et al., 1980; Erbring et al., 1981; Neuman and Fryling, 1985). Another challenge to the theory comes from the difference between the shared public agenda and "private" or "personal" political agendas (Noelle-Neumann, 1974). Agenda-setting surveys may actually be tapping the ability of individuals to tick off a list of "important public issues." Many individuals may simply equate this list with media coverage rather than with their own sense of what is politically important. The irony is that this awareness of the public agenda exists without much detailed learning to back it up: "Agenda-setting does not equal understanding of issues . . . most learning from the media is confined to awareness—the ability to recognize both issues and images without the ability to recall related facts spontaneously" (Weaver et al., 1981, p. 198).

The third theory that addresses the paradoxical nature of political communications is the two-step flow theory. According to this theory, the process of learning from the media is indirect (Katz and Lazarsfeld, 1955). A smaller elite of highly interested individuals learn from the media and explain their knowledge and political evaluations to friends and colleagues who have less interest and may lack the cognitive skills to interpret the media directly.

Again, however, the process appears to be more complex than anticipated, and the study results are mixed (Troldahl, 1965; Rogers, 1973, 1983; Patterson, 1980). The evidence of stratification is clear; that is, the more sophisticated respondents are more likely to attend to the media and more likely to discuss politics. But two critical elements of the theory fail the empirical test. First and more important, those who engage in political discussion tend to discuss issues with individuals of equivalent levels of information and knowledge. There is only weak evidence of a trickle-down flow of political information. Those who are interested in political information follow the media and talk with each other. Those at the lower levels of the sophistication continuum neither attend to the media nor discuss politics very much. Although interpersonal political discussion may well turn out to be an important element of interpreting complex political ideas, the two-step flow formulation is simplistic and distracts attention from the persisting issue of public political knowledge.

The Theory of Low-Salience Learning

American civic culture provides a clear-cut model of the good citizen. This is the citizen portrayed in civics classes. Whenever possible, the good citizen earnestly attends the public speeches and rallies of all major candidates for local, state, and national office, dutifully reads all news coverage of the campaign, discusses domestic and international policy issues with friends and colleagues, attentively reads any campaign literature that comes to hand, and participates in nonpartisan forums such as those sponsored by the League of Women Voters or other civic groups. The good citizen might even bring along a pad and several sharpened pencils to take notes. Such a formulation, of course, is extremely naive. The voter is expected to study the issues and candidates as if to prepare for a major examination.

A more realistic model of the typical citizen acknowledges that most political learning is fragmentary, haphazard, and incidental. The citizen does not "study" the candidates but rather picks up bits and pieces of information over time, gradually accumulating a composite picture of the prominent issues and candidates. This is a process of low-salience learning. The key distinction is between information seeking and information acceptance. The viewer of political television is "prepared to tolerate political messages without being keen to receive them" (Blumler and McQuail, 1969, p. 206). This description of political learning no doubt applies to most other media as well.

Confirming data on the low-salience theory come from the content analysis of responses to the question, "What are the most important reasons for watching television news?" (Table 6.4). The generalized sense of keeping informed about most recent events is clearly dominant. Only about one response in seven makes a specific reference to politics. This proportion may be judged to be a maximal estimate, because the question appears in the middle of a political questionnaire in a study conducted during a presidential campaign.

The basic mechanism of political learning is a spiral process. Information stimulates interest which stimulates the accumulation of further information. A study of the 1976 presidential election suggested that a "critical mass" of news coverage may well be required before the interest

Table 6.4. Reasons for Watching Television News[a]

Primary factors	Percentage of audience
General surveillance of things (politics not mentioned)	45.6
See what's new	33.3
General surveillance of politics	6.7
No particular reason	4.6
Intellectual satisfaction, as from political arguments	3.8
Follow sports	1.4
Judge what political leaders are like	1.2
Follow specific nonpolitical issues other than sports	0.9
Help make up mind how to vote	0.9
Information for discussion with others	0.8
Information about party goals	0.3
Compare promises with later performance	0.1
Enjoy excitement of election	0.1
Remind self of opposition party's weak points	0.1
Remind self of own party's strong points	0.1

Source: Hofstetter, 1975.
a. Based on up to three responses for each respondent, excluding don't know and inapplicable responses.

and learning spiral is catalyzed (Patterson, 1980). This study, unlike most voting studies that preceded it, examined the early stages of the presidential primary campaign, when the number of candidates is large and the citizen information-base is low. During this period many voters simply ignore the pack of candidates until the first primaries identify a few recognizable front-runners. This finding suggests a "perceptual floor" of some sort under which minor candidates and minor news stories are routinely ignored. This phenomenon may help to explain the dramatic movement of candidates Jimmy Carter in 1976 and Gary Hart in 1984 into the headlines and into serious contention for the nomination as a result of the early primaries.

The notion of a critical mass or perceptual floor may work not just for political communications during a national campaign but for general political communications. Again, the concept of political empathy found in developing countries, defined as an interest in and willingness to attend to information and events outside of one's immediate village environment, has relevance for the rich "media environment" of the modern American polity (Lerner, 1958). Most Americans concentrate on concrete and immediate personal concerns. They still live in villages of their own making. Generally speaking, the farther away the event, either politically or geographically, the less attention Americans pay to it. The critical fact of political stratification is that some citizens have much broader political horizons than others.

Another element in this process is the phenomenon of "the more, the more" (Hyman and Sheatsley, 1947; Star and Hughes, 1950; Patterson, 1980; Weaver et al., 1981; Gollin and Bloom, 1985). According to this theory, the more political information that citizens already have, the more likely they are to attend to and internalize any new political information in the communications flow. The theory is a corollary of the spiral theory of acquiring political sophistication. Another corollary is the theory that the larger the information base of the citizens, the sooner they are likely to be aware of a significant new political event.

Issue Publics

Another question central to the role of the mass media is whether the media inhibit or enhance political pluralism. There are three related issues here. The first deals with the content of the media themselves. By definition, mass media are concerned with mass interests and common concerns, but there is variation in the kinds of issues and opinions that the different media cover. The second question focuses on the variety of audience interests and the selective concerns of individual citizens. In a sense, the question is whether issue publics are a meaningful force in public opinion. The third question concerns the phenomenon of selective perception. This is the interaction between the diversity of media content and the diversity of public interests. Since research on pluralism and issue publics is sparse, the conclusions here must be tentative.

There are three categories of media pluralism. The first category includes the broadcast media, television, and radio. Unlike the print audience, the broadcast audience is not able to skim and skip through the content but gets basically the same message. Accordingly, the broadcast media feature the political themes of broadest interests and the news headlines. There is relatively little room for specialized or detailed coverage of issues which concern only a small fraction of the audience. The second category of media includes the general-interest print media, particularly newspapers and news magazines which allow for some internal content specialization. Typically newspapers have sections concerned with business and sports news and other regular features of interest to only a minority of the readers. The average reader is expected to read a small subset of the total available content. The third category includes the more specialized media, whose entire content is targeted at a special-interest audience. These media include special-interest magazines, newsletters, and books.

Although systematic information on the political content of individual media is rare, much of the available work concludes that the political content of the mass media tends to be quite homogeneous. One study covered the national news magazines, three prominent metropolitan dailies, and the three network news programs (Carey, 1976). Another study examined twenty newspapers from around the country as well as network and local broadcasts (Graber, 1980). Still another study reviewed the three television networks and the Associated Press wire (Hofstetter, 1976). Each study identified unique characteristics of individual media but concluded that the broad trends of election coverage are remarkably similar. There are strong pressures within the journalistic community for consensual interpretation of campaign events (Crouse, 1973). On national issues, the local television stations depend on feeds from the networks and the local newspapers rely on the major wire services for coverage. As a result, there is relatively little geographical variation in coverage of national politics.

Two other phenomena about the circulation patterns of the various media are relevant to the pluralism issue. The first phenomenon is that the specialized political media, those which cover politics in depth or from a unique point of view, are consistently low-circulation. This is another instance of the inverse law. The second phenomenon is that, although hundreds or indeed thousands of such political conduits may be in existence, the pattern of "the more, the more" means that they are consumed by relatively small overlapping audiences, the political elite of the population.

The potential thus exists for a rich and pluralistic media environment of commentary and interpretations of political life. It exists for the most part in the editorial pages of the newspapers and news magazines and in specialized, small-circulation political magazines, newsletters, and books. But while the environment is rich, the amount of specialized, truly pluralistic content to reach the average citizen is very small.

The data on the public's selective news interests are a little more complete. In one study respondents were told they could tailor-make a newspaper to match their own interests. They reviewed a list of thirty-four potential news topics and were asked in each case whether they would allocate a lot, some, a little, or no space to each interest category. There is a great deal of variation across categories, the most popular category being allocated a lot or some space by 78 percent of the sample, the least popular by only 22 percent. But a pattern of convergent common interests appears in different demographic categories. The "tailor-made" newspapers for both male and female, high school and college educated, young and old, and black and white are almost identical, with only a few predictable exceptions. The average difference in percentage interest between each of the demographic groups in the overall national average is only 5 percent. There are only five topics with a greater than 20 percent difference between men and women, only eight such topics between educational levels (Neuman, 1982).

As anyone who has ever served on a committee will attest, the human potential for diversity of opinion is awe-inspiring. How is it, then, that the data reveal so little diversity on public interests and concerns? The answer to that question goes to the core of what public opinion is. The apparent homogeneity of public concerns is explained by the "climate of opinion," based on the social psychological insight about human sensitivity to the social environment (Noelle-Neumann, 1974, 1984). Over time individuals develop a sense of both what are the public issues and what is the dominant direction of public opinion (Fields and Schuman, 1976; O'Gorman and Garry, 1976).

Thus, the content of the mass media is relatively homogeneous, as is the pattern of political concerns of the mass electorate. But the less public side of the audience's response to the political media raises the question of selective exposure recall and interpretation, which might reveal a more deeply rooted pluralism in response to media messages. There is evidence of different patterns of exposure and recall of media messages for those at different levels of political interest and sophistication. Indeed, the increased ability of the more sophisticated individuals to recall and make sense of political information as it is presented in the media lies at the core of the self-reinforcing persistence of the sophistication continuum. But the question at this point does not concern the vertical dimension of sophistication so much as the horizontal dimension of political pluralism, or the extent to which different groups in the mass public selectively attend to different types of issues.

There is a standard model of selective attention, which has become integrated into the theory of minimal effects of the mass media (Festinger, 1957; Klapper, 1960): "So what must the sensible audience member do? . . . He will build up his own complex 'safety mechanism' for screening incoming information; he will see less and less that does not agree with his dominant dispositions (selective exposure) . . . he uses propaganda to simply reinforce—not challenge—his basic attitudes and predispositions. If he did not do this, he would quickly fly into a million emotional pieces in the face of unverifiable and disharmonic information and opinion that surround him every day" (Merrill and Lowenstein, 1971, pp. 226–227). But further work has raised fundamental questions about these basic assumptions. Although there may be some de-facto differences in exposure to different media messages, people are not necessarily inclined to avoid contradictory messages. In fact, people are often motivated to keep track of what "the other side" on a particular issue is arguing (Sears and Freedman, 1967). Another study confirmed these conclusions: "While the statistical phenomenon of greater exposure to one's own candidate than to the opponent was found in many prior studies, the tendency in this direction was not particularly strong. The motivational assumptions underlying the traditional reinforcement hypothesis have been strongly called into question by our findings, consistently across a variety of variables and tests" (Chaffee and Miyo, 1983, p. 31).

One study that went beyond the issue of selective attention to measure patterns of selective recall and interpretation found that viewers of television news are 3 percent more likely to remember details from stories about candidates from their own party. The corresponding figure for newspapers is 5 percent (Patterson, 1980). These effects do not seem to be tremendously strong. Similar results were found in a nonelection setting where the recall of news about the Pope by Catholic and non-Catholic audience members was compared. The level of news recall is only 5 percent higher for Catholics (Adams et al., 1969).

Although there is relatively weak evidence of selective exposure and recall, there is a fair amount of data about selective perception and selective interpretation of political information. The clearest examples come from the research on political debates. Consistently viewers interpret their own favorite candidate as having "won" the debate.

Unfortunately, no evidence is yet available that settles the matter one way or another. One's own day-to-day political experiences show that people are generally willing to accept a theory of political pluralism that posits differentiated interests and concerns across the citizenry. They are also alert and attuned to the political slants of the various newspapers and to the subtle differences between newspaper and television coverage of political events. Again, personal experience suggests that people know about a rich diversity of available political media. The accumulated data about the flow of mass communications, however, serve as an important corrective. Although there may be a pluralism of views and a rich political environment, the flow of political communications and the major concerns of the electorate reflect more homogeneity than diversity.

The New Electronic Media

Significant changes are taking place in the structure and technology of mass communications which could have an effect on the mass public and the mass media. The engine of change is the evolution of new communications technologies. A related and equally important development is the changing regulatory structure. The new technologies include two-way cable television, direct-to-home satellite broadcasting, home computers which can access remote databases and process news and other forms of text information, and a variety of specialized broadcast services which allow broadcasters to target special audiences for special information. These new services include scrambled satellite or cable television broadcasts, special text services superimposed on the broadcast signal (teletext), and a new form of local broadcasting, low-power television, which permits many more broadcast transmitters in a given geographical area than previously possible. In addition, optical fiber and new forms of electronic switching allow the telephone system to provide a much broader array of information and communication services. Ultimately the telephone system will be able to deliver specialized video programming and video-based text (videotex) directly to the home.

This explosive growth in new electronic highways to the home and the increased ability of the citizen to process and filter information have stimulated a change in the pattern of federal and local regulation. Originally because of the constraints of the limited broadcast spectrum, the Federal Communications Commission was established to ensure that the few available broadcast channels would be consistently utilized in the public interest. Individual radio and television stations had to renew their broadcast licenses every three years, provide detailed information on the variety of public service programming they had broadcast, and follow further procedures for balanced coverage of controversial public issues. But given the expanding technological possibilities for public communications, Congress and the FCC have increasingly felt uncomfortable about the federal role in regulating the content of the media. If the new technologies provide almost unlimited pathways of communications, they argue, the scarce spectrum argument no longer holds. Perhaps open competition would do better at protecting the public interest (Pool, 1983). The net result is that the presumptions and ground rules of media regulation and media economics are in a state of flux.

The effect of these changes on the process of political communications has prompted a number of inquiries (Neustadt, 1982; Arterton et al., 1984; Rice et al., 1984; Dizard, 1985; Meadow, 1985; Abramson et al., forthcoming). But the studies are inconclusive as yet. It is still too early to get a meaningful behavioral measure of the new developments. The use of existing political media, however, suggests some skepticism about whether the new technical developments will lead to dramatic changes in citizen attitudes. Take, for example, the issue of content diversity. Despite a rich pluralism of print resources, the average citizen, as a result of deeply ingrained media habits, skims the headlines and only rarely dips into the specialized media. So the expansion of electronically delivered specialized resources, which may change the behavior of political elites and activists, is not likely to change the habitual patterns of the average citizen. Evidence comes from the first of the new media to expand into the average household, cable television. The new cable systems offer upward of 35 channels of video programming, but the typical viewer watches only a few of them, on average less than 10 channels for more than 10 minutes over a two-week period (Lemieux, 1983). Thus, although channels devoted exclusively to the coverage of news and public affairs may become available through cable, all but a small politically inclined elite will opt most of the time for sports, reruns, and movies.

The other critical development in the new media is the increased control the audience member can exert over the flow of information. Thus the technology of videotex—scanning a news database from a personal computer or terminal—allows readers to prefilter the categories of news to which they will be exposed. Although this seems to change the logic of the political communications process, it is in fact how print communications has worked from the beginning. The kind of scanning and filtering behavior that has been taken for granted in the reading of newspapers and magazines now becomes possible in the electronic media as well.

Some amount of filtering and skipping of news will continue to take place, but such filtering is balanced against the convenience and habitual reliance of the half-attentive audience member on the editorial judgment of news professionals. The average citizens want to review the headlines to make sure they are at least aware of the basic events and issues that everyone else is likely to know about.

Sorting Out Media Effects

The research on the political media has focused on the issue of media effects, especially as they are associated with the notions of propaganda and persuasion. The media are seen as potentially powerful forces, and the audience is seen as relatively defenseless. The power of the media, however, has been exaggerated. There are a number of constraints and limitations of the ability of the media to persuade and inform. Perhaps the most ironic and persistent thorn in the side of the theory of powerful media effects is the repeated demonstration of widespread political ignorance despite the plentiful opportunities for exposure to political information in the media. Critics have attempted to redress this issue by reforming the media. Great hopes are pinned on public television and new two-way technologies to mobilize and inform the public (Neustadt, 1982). But like the early studies of propaganda, such hopes presume powerful media effects.

Although there are subtle differences between the various media, such subtleties are likely to be lost in the massive flow of entertainment communications and the half-attentiveness of the individual citizen. The process of learning from the mass media is best described as the gradual accumulation of information which is repeated frequently and consistently in the different media. There is a pattern of stratification by which the more sophisticated citizens attend to the more political media and are better able to recall and interpret abstract political communications. The process involves a spiraling between increasing levels of interest and increasing knowledge and understanding. But the spiral works in the other direction as well. The bottom know-nothing stratum continue to ignore and perhaps actively fend off the flow of political communications in their environment, judging it to be both uninteresting and irrelevant.

The system of political communications could certainly be improved by new structures and technologies. Expanding the flow and the diversity of political communications are noble ideals in their own right. But such changes, if they are possible, are not likely to resolve the paradox of mass politics. Until and unless the media are able to tap the central motivational core of political attention, the fundamental orientation known as political empathy, the effects of the political media will be deeply constrained by the character of its audience.

7 The Shallow Roots of Democratic Norms

> If someone is caught red-handed beating and robbing an older person on the street, it is just a waste of taxpayers' money to bother with the usual expensive trial. Do you agree or disagree?
>
> Civil Liberties Item

A DARKER and more curious side of American mass politics involves the impact of political knowledge and ignorance on support for basic democratic values. Political life has two pathologies which are of particular interest here—authoritarianism and alienation. Although traditionally seen as distinct and independent, these phenomena are related and in fact complementary (Gamson, 1968; Sniderman, 1981). They represent the end points of a fundamental continuum of attitudes toward government. The authoritarian has too much faith in government, the alienated individual has too little. The authoritarian is overly ready to yield to authority and likely to be fearful of the open expression of diverse political views. The alienated individual is unrestrained in protest and confuses a difference of opinion on policy with a need to change the structure of the political system itself. In this sense, both authoritarianism and alienation reflect similar characteristics of intolerance, rigidity, and the inclination toward moralistic and simplistic, black-and-white thinking. Most important, both seem willing to abandon the "rules of the game" of the democratic process. The proposed remedy for the pathologies of authoritarianism and alienation is thus to increase education and political participation. The basic premise is that political knowledge breeds moderation.

Authoritarianism

The concern of social science with authoritarianism and the authoritarian personality has its roots in the dramatic upheavals of European fascism. After the Second World War the F-scale was designed to measure susceptibility to fascist tendencies (Adorno et al., 1950). Its items show a consistent coherence, and the scale exhibits a strong correlation with other critical political attitudes and measures of social background.

The purpose of the F-scale is to measure "susceptibility to fascist propaganda." Thus an implicit concern of the research is the possible reemergence of fascist movements. Although the scale links authoritarianism to underlying personality traits, it also explicitly ties the phenomenon to low levels of political knowledge: "The ultimate reason for [political] ignorance might well be the opaqueness of the social, economic and political situation to all those who are not in full command of the resources of stored knowledge and theoretical thinking. In its present phase our social system tends objectively and automatically to produce 'curtains' which make it impossible for the naive person really to see what it is all about" (Adorno et al., 1950, p. 661). Quotations from individuals of limited education were used to demonstrate the correlation of political ignorance to simplistic and extremist politics.

According to another view, it is a critical dilemma for liberal democrats, but an unavoidable fact of life, that extremist and intolerant political movements in modern society tend to be based on lower-class rather than middle-class support. The factors that apparently generate a rigid and intolerant approach to politics among the lower classes are:

Low education, low participation in political or voluntary organizations of any type, little reading, isolated occupations, economic insecurity and authoritarian family patterns . . . To sum up, the lower class individual is likely to have been exposed to punishment, lack of love, and a general atmosphere of tension and aggression since early childhood—all experiences which tend to produce deep-rooted hostilities expressed by ethnic prejudice, political authoritarianism and chiliastic transvaluational religion. His educational attainment is less than that of men with higher socio-economic status, and his association as a child with others with similar background not only fails to stimulate his intellectual interest but also creates an atmosphere which prevents his educational experience from increasing his general social sophistication and his understanding of different groups and ideas. (Lipset, 1960, pp. 100, 114)

This thesis has been criticized for equating authoritarianism with conservatism and with lower-class status (Hyman and Sheatsley, 1954; Miller and Riessman, 1961; Lipsitz, 1965; Hamilton, 1972). But no one has criticized it for equating authoritarianism with ignorance. Although the concept of authoritarianism and the corresponding F-scale have fallen out of fashion in the social sciences, the basic questions of political sophistication and political tolerance persist.

Alienation

Research on authoritarianism is a child of the 1930s and 1940s. The empirical study of political alienation, however, is a child of the turbulent 1960s. Although the concepts of alienation and self-alienation have their roots in Marx, they are now generally used as a generic label for political distrust, cynicism, and disaffection. A democratic system should not only permit but also encourage a healthy skepticism and open airing of dissent. But if disagreement leads over time to a fundamental discontent with the system for substantial numbers of the electorate, the viability of the system itself is called into question. This dynamic is a potentially dangerous one:

The rise and fall of the number of distrustful citizens over time is a sensitive barometer of social conflicts and tensions. When any sizable group becomes distrustful and begins to make demands, the government is prompted to re-allocate its resources or change its institutions to accommodate these new pressures. If the political system is flexible and adaptive enough, needed adjustments can be made without any consequent outbreak of violence, but if distrustful groups are denied access to decisionmakers or if institutions are too rigid to change, destructive conflict and a breakdown of the social order are possible. (Aberbach and Walker, 1970, p. 1200)

An irreversible spiral of increasingly desperate attempts to influence the course of political events leads to yet higher levels of frustration and intensity (Gamson, 1968). A well-known tactic of radical groups is to provoke a repressive response to mobilize their own supporters and further isolate them from the political mainstream.

Alienation is equated with political ignorance in two senses. In the mass population, there is a negative correlation between education and political cynicism (Levin, 1960; Agger et al., 1961; Templeton, 1966). The pattern is self-reinforcing. People withdrawn from politics generate a cynical rationalization based on a perceived unresponsiveness of governmental authorities. This posture reinforces further isolation from politics. And in the student population, as the argument goes, their susceptibility to extreme leftist appeals is correlated with the isolation of the student role from the mainstream of American economic life. Students are not unintelligent but rather naive and inexperienced in the practical dealings and patterns of compromise of real world politics.

The Social Learning Hypothesis

The complementary dynamics of authoritarianism and alienation are demonstrated by the common remedy each evokes, the need for more political participation and learning. This might be termed the social learning hypothesis. The premise is that the failure is not one of the system but one of the individual's understanding of how the system works. The failure of the individual to support freedom of speech for unpopular political groups is simply a failure to internalize the dominant democratic norms. The role of education is central to this thesis:

Education, though usually treated as a single unidimensional variable, is in reality an indicator of a complex of variables that not only includes schooling but the nature and style of life. Those who have graduated from college are likely to take a greater interest in political matters than people who have had only a grade school or high school education. At work and in their personal lives, they are more likely to associate with other educated people who are also interested in public questions, who discuss them frequently and may even act upon them. Similarly, people who have had the benefit of higher education are more likely than the less educated to read materials, listen to broadcasts and watch television programs about public affairs. They are more likely to join and participate in voluntary organizations that devote attention to community and international questions. For these and related reasons, they are more exposed to the dominant libertarian norms of the culture and they acquire more cosmopolitan perspectives. (McClosky and Brill, 1983, p. 420)

This is a central theme of the research tradition concerning attitudes toward civil liberties, and the finding is replicated in comparative research (Stouffer, 1955; Almond and Verba, 1963). Data on the willingness of the mass electorate to permit the expression of politically unpopular views show recent increases. This change is presumed to be a result of increased levels of higher education (Davis, 1975; Nunn et al., 1978).

A study of racism and religious prejudice expanded the concept of authoritarianism. The basic, underlying phenomenon is not so much one of explicit authoritarian beliefs as one of cognitive simplism: "Democratic principles are abstract and complex, and their apprehension requires cognitive sophistication. For this reason alone one would expect the uneducated to be less committed to them" (Selznick and Steinberg, 1969).

These arguments are a reprise of the mass society theory of the 1950s. It is thought to be best for citizens to participate in numerous voluntary associations as well as in the wider political scene in order to develop an appreciation of the rules of the game and to understand that, in losing a political battle, one need not abandon the political system altogether. A central threat of alienated and authoritarian groups is that what may appear as political apathy and lack of interest at one time may at another time of crisis erupt as a sudden mobilization to extremist politics. Thus there was great concern at the discovery that Joseph McCarthy's appeal in the 1950s was even stronger among nonvoters than among voters (Kornhauser, 1959).

The Paradox of Immoderate Politics

The social learning hypothesis appears persuasive on a number of grounds. It has wide currency among analysts in the field. It finds support in a number of empirically grounded studies. It is a coherent, common sense argument. The notion of social learning appeals as well to one's democratic instincts and optimism about the long-term future and stability of democratic regimes. There is only one problem. The data do not support the hypothesis.

The paradox of immoderate politics is that education and political sophistication do not necessarily lead to political moderation. This finding places in question the basic assumptions about what political sophistication is and why it should be nourished. At least the reverse is not true. There is no evidence that increasing sophistication leads to immoderate and simplistic ideology. The traits of authoritarianism and alienation are related to patterns of sophistication and political participation only weakly and inconsistently. So it is necessary to develop an alternative to or refinement of the original social learning theory.

There is a moderate negative correlation between the F-scale and sophistication. There is a much weaker negative relationship between sophistication and the related reverse F-scale and authoritarian conservatism scale, which presumably measures the same phenomenon (Figure 7.1).[1] The relationship between authoritarianism and what education is supposed to engender—political sophistication—is thus of modest

1. These are simple bivariate correlations. Appropriate controls for education or other intervening factors would weaken the relationships still further. The original F-scale measured authoritarianism by the number of authoritarian-conservative items agreed to. Some critics argued that such a technique is biased, because those who tend to agree to any items put to them, having the so-called acquiescence response bias, might falsely be identified as authoritarian. Other critics argued that the measure should also test for authoritarianism of the left. Efforts to resolve these disputes and to measure an authoritarianism of the left have generally not been successful (Kirscht and Dillehay, 1967).

strength in the mass population and not subject to confirmation by measures other than the original F-test itself.

There is an even more complex set of relationships between political sophistication and alienation or cynicism. The core trust-in-government item, based on the statement that, "The government in Washington can be trusted to do what is right," is only weakly related to sophistication, having a correlation of only .09 (Figure 7.2). Even the item stating that, "People like me don't have any say about what the government does," which taps both political alienation and political efficacy, finds no meaningful relationship with sophistication. The more sophisticated are known to participate more actively in politics, so the fact that they do not feel politically efficacious provides a clue to the curious phenomenon of alienation. Items measuring tolerance and beliefs about civil liberties would provide further help here but are not available in the National Election Studies. One item on support for protest does provide some evidence, since there is no meaningful correlation between sophistication and toleration of protest activities.

These findings of noncorrelation have surfaced before. There is no correlation between political tolerance and education: "While those who participate a great deal in politics are more tolerant than those who participate less, the relationship is spurious and results from other factors, related both to participation and tolerance . . . While the highly educated are more tolerant than the less educated, this relationship also results from other factors" (Sullivan et al., 1982, p. 251). Likewise, there is a lack of correlation between alienation and cognitive simplism: "It is tempting . . . to write off the disaffected as simply lacking an appreciation of complexity or a tolerance of ambiguity, to see them as prone to thinking in overly simplified, black-and-white terms, to detect in their lack of a balanced judgment of government a familiar sign of an ignorant and intolerant mind . . . The disaffected's judgment of government is overly simplified; but is it because they are given to simplistic thinking? Evidently not" (Sniderman, 1981, pp. 104–105). Comparison of measures of alienation with measures of IQ, political awareness, and exposure to political information shows no evidence of the expected pattern of cognitive simplism, and in some cases the extemely alienated and allegiant exhibit slightly higher levels of cognitive ability.

There is another related paradox of political alienation (Citrin, 1974). Since the politically cynical and alienated presumably participate less in political life, the likelihood of voting should be negatively correlated

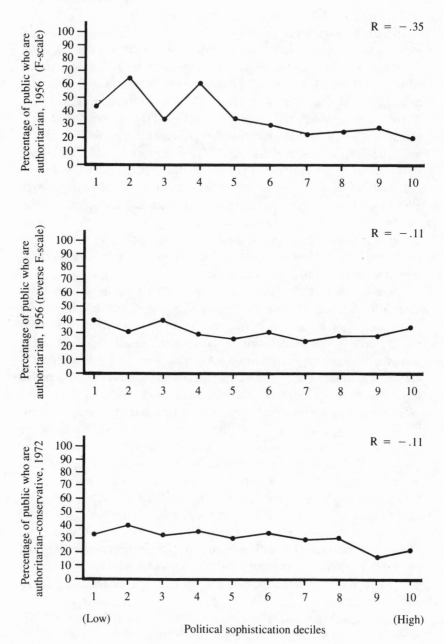

Figure 7.1. Sophistication and Authoritarianism. *Source:* NES 1956, 1972.

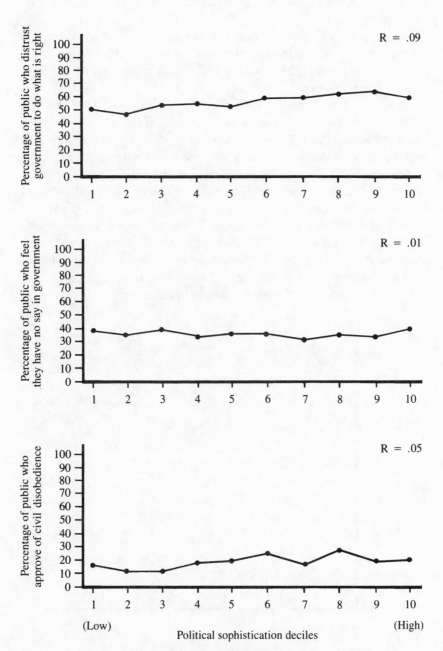

Figure 7.2. Sophistication and Alienation. *Source:* NES 1956–1980.

with cynicism. But again the expected correlation does not appear (Figure 7.3).

This is a curious pattern. One would expect political sophistication strongly and consistently to counteract simplistic authoritarianism or alienated withdrawal. How is it that cynicism is not related to lower levels of participation?

There are three possible explanations for the paradox, each of which clarifies both the persistence of authoritarianism and alienation in the mass public and the delicacy of democratic norms. The first explanation is that authoritarianism and alienation may represent verbal response styles which are not meaningfully related to political behavior. One study, for example, developed measures of extreme political attitudes by constructing a scale of political lying (McClosky, 1975). A series of questions dealt with self-reported civic behavior which was so clearly preposterous that only individuals lying about themselves could score high on this index. Simplistic authoritarians with lower levels of education were expected to score high. Surprisingly, an elite group of ministers, civic leaders, and college-educated respondents actually scored

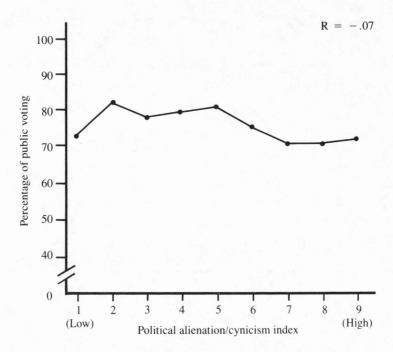

Figure 7.3. Alienation and Participation. *Source:* NES 1972.

highest. The items in fact tapped an especially strong conviction about the importance of civic participation. People responded in terms of what individuals ought to do rather than what they themselves had actually done. As a result, the educated elite showed no reluctance to take an extreme position.

This finding was confirmed in the NES data on American political alienation (Citrin, 1974). Increasing trends toward cynicism and distrust of the government were found to reflect a stylized world-view and fashionable manner of speaking. Although large numbers of the citizenry feel that the government is less responsive than it ought to be and has taken the wrong position on an increasingly large number of policy issues, they do not necessarily conclude that the political system itself has to be changed. By analogy, they might argue with great vehemence and volume to kill the umpire at a baseball game, but this pronouncement would merely be a culturally accepted manner of speech and not a statement of behavioral intent. The issue of verbal response style points up the possible distance between political opinions as measured in survey research and as manifested in the real world of day-to-day politics. Two different survey measures of tolerance, for example, show that part of the correlation between education and tolerance reflects differences in verbal style rather than in fundamental beliefs about political tolerance (Schuman and Presser, 1977).

The second explanation of the paradox of immoderate politics is that some rare phenomena by their nature simply do not lend themselves to the broadcast methods of survey research. Political extremism and protest behavior are such phenomena. When the National Election Study of 1976 asked, for example, which respondents had taken part in a "sit-in demonstration or protest concerned with some national problem," only 2 percent responded that they had. As one might expect, these protestors came from the higher rather than the lower levels of the sophistication continuum. Historical events and circumstances also change so quickly that one must be cautious about equating responses in a hermetic survey interview with the more complex patterns of happenstance, opportunity, and mood that dominate actual protest behavior (Sullivan et al., 1982).

The third explanation of the paradox of immoderate politics is that the key to political moderation lies with political elites rather than the mass polity. An important lesson in rethinking the social learning hypothesis is the realization that tolerance of democratic diversity is not a natural state but requires care and nurturance. A comparative study of authoritarianism found that in those countries which have more authoritarian elites, the overall level of mass authoritarianism is much higher (Kirscht and Dillahay, 1967). Another study reinforced this insight by showing that "the inclination to tolerate beliefs or conduct that one considers offensive or dangerous is not an inborn trait but is learned behavior. Although one might prefer that it was otherwise, history provides little evidence that men and women are led by nature to yearn for freedom much less to guarantee freedom for individuals" (McClosky and Brill, 1983, p. 415). The maintenance and persistence of democratic norms may well pivot on the behavior of the tiny elite of political activists, journalists, and public servants.

The omen of authoritarianism and alienation puts the issue of political sophistication in fresh perspective. The original theories, which simply equated sophistications with all things good and great, including carefully thought-out and stable opinions, civic virtue, and an enduring commitment to civil liberties, have been drawn into question. The connection between sophistication and opinion turns out to be complicated. The role of the tiny elite of political activists turns out to be especially important.

8 | Toward a Theory of Political Sophistication

Politics is more difficult than physics.

Albert Einstein

As is often the case in research of this sort, the accumulated findings on the nature of political sophistication in the mass citizenry have raised as many questions as they have answered. The paradox of mass politics persists. What at first glance seemed to be a self-evident positive correlation between sophistication and the expression, stability, and structuring of political opinions evaporates under closer scrutiny. Those who are more sophisticated are more likely to vote and to participate in political life beyond voting, but the relationships reflect intriguingly nonlinear patterns. The phenomenon of proxy voting seems to be more prevalent in the middle ranges of sophistication rather than, as might have been expected, among the bottom strata. Clearly the public is highly stratified in its interest in and knowledge about politics. But the character of that stratification and the relationship between sophistication and other central factors of political belief and behavior are subtle and complex.

The strategy so far has been to evaluate each set of relevant variables in search of clues to resolve the paradox. The clues have accumulated, but they have not yet fallen together into a coherent whole. A full-scale theory of political sophistication and its role in mass politics may still lie beyond our grasp.[1] But the findings do converge and provide the outline of such a theory. It is based on three central themes: the shape of the stratification curve which reveals three distinct publics, the dis-

1. The methodologists and philosophers of science have put forward explicit definitions of what is and is not a "theory" (Hemple, 1952; Nagel, 1961; Kaplan, 1964). The theory derived here does not offer rigorously derived, lawlike hypotheses and corollaries. It rather poses a set of issues and a corresponding set of operationalized core variables which allow for empirical testing. The theory draws from the original paradox a concern with the basic elements of democratic theory, in particular, the meaningful participation of the mass public in modern politics. It pays special attention to the political cognition of the individual citizen. Thus, while other voting research has emphasized demographic variables or the role of political parties, the emphasis of this research is on sophistication as the core variable.

tinction between issues and nonissues, and the distinction between attitudes and nonattitudes.

The Theory of Three Publics

The debate over whether the mass public is or is not sophisticated presents an awkward dichotomy. It is always possible to derive a seemingly straightforward test of political knowledge on which the majority of the population will fail utterly. It is equally easy to identify a critical issue or a political actor about which the electorate has accumulated a fair amount of information, thus appearing to be reasonably well informed. Such polemic loops represent a seductive distraction. The key step forward is to recognize that the shape of the sophistication distribution is more significant than its mean value.

The generalized sophistication curve is derived from the converging pattern of many previously described distributions. Although political sophistication is defined and measured as a continuous variable, the curve has two inflection points which generate the theory of three publics (Figure 8.1). There is no clear and unmistakable dividing line between these publics, but their different patterns of behavior suggest that the distinctions are politically important.

The bulk of the population, perhaps 75 percent, share a homogeneous pattern of opinion and behavior. They are marginally attentive to politics and mildly cynical about the behavior of politicians, but they accept the duty to vote, and they do so with fair regularity. This is the great middle stratum.

Another stratum of the public, about 20 percent, are markedly different. They are a self-consistent and unabashedly apolitical lot. They do not share the common norms which stress the importance of keeping informed about politics or of voting, and their behavior dramatically reflects this posture. For example, the information on voting behavior and perceived duty to vote (Figures 4.1 and 4.6) reflects this sharp falling off in the bottom two deciles. Also, those in the bottom stratum are refreshingly candid about not having any political opinions (Figure 3.2). Furthermore, content analyses of the natural language used to describe political objects reveals a number of instances of an apolitical stratum of roughly 20 percent of the population (Table 1.1).

A much smaller stratum, perhaps less than 5 percent of the population, contains the political activists. Members of this highest stratum of political sophistication exhibit uniquely high levels of political involvement

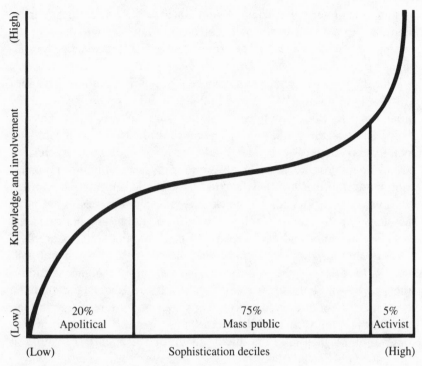

Figure 8.1. Theory of Three Publics.

(Figure 4.8). Previous research on the stratification of mass political involvement has derived similar figures (Berelson et al., 1954; Dahl, 1963).

The shape of the sophistication distribution has important political consequences. For one thing, the two ends of the curve are self-consistent. The apolitical and activist strata are both characterized by self-reinforcing values and behavior. For the large middle mass, however, the generalized norms of civic duty are at odds with their habitual political behavior. In all likelihood, falling short of the general cultural norms of political attentiveness bothers most citizens very little and contributes only in the minutest way to their accumulated guilt and neuroses. But this normative tension explains the dynamics of the opinion-giving situation which serves as the basis for survey research interviews. The proxy voting and knowledge gap phenomena, for example, characterize the coping strategies of the mass citizenry. Since so much of the statistical analysis of survey and behavioral data is based on the assumption of normal distributions and linear relationships, an empirical approach to political stratification which does not take into account the unique character of these three groups can generate misleading conclusions.

This theory is analogous to the concept of political literacy. The apoliticals can be thought of as fundamentally illiterate, so they are naturally immune to repeated attempts to politicize and mobilize them. They lie below a critical threshold which puts them outside the flow of meaningful political communications. The middle mass can then be characterized as having modest literacy. They keep track of the most important issues with modest effort, but they lack the background information and rich vocabulary necessary for the quick and convenient processing of large amounts of political information. They can communicate political ideas, but they are hunt-and-peck typists. In contrast, the activists are avid readers and lucid speakers. Since virtually all of the professional politicians, journalists, and political analysts fall into the highest stratum, they may well share an ingrained incapacity to understand that the vocabulary of politics is interpreted in somewhat different ways by the middle mass, and in stumbling across this phenomenon from time to time, they may mistake the middle mass for the apolitical stratum at the bottom of the continuum.

One reason that large proportions of the electorate are relatively inattentive has to do with the fact that processing political information has costs. This is a central finding and is fundamental to the theory of three publics. Most citizens rationally minimize the time and effort required to monitor the political environment by a variety of strategies. They monitor fundamental issues, such as war, peace, and economic health, but having determined that a crisis is not at hand, they turn their attention to more immediate and directly rewarding pursuits:

Rational citizens in an uncertain world are under great pressure to cut down the quantity of scarce resources they use to obtain political information . . . In any society marked by an extensive division of labor in the presence of uncertainty, the cost of information is bound to be different for different men. Hence the amount of data it is rational for one man to acquire can be much greater or smaller than the amount that is rational for another man to acquire. This conclusion is valid even when the returns from information are identical for all. (Downs, 1957, pp. 220, 236)

The information-processing strategies of the average citizen parallel the findings on decisionmaking in administrative organizations (Simon, 1947; Popkin et al., 1972). Unfortunately, the information costs perspective has not yet been integrated into the traditions of behavior and survey research. Thus far, the methodological disputes about issue voting have apparently overwhelmed the efforts of those who would redirect the inquiry.

Applying the notion of information cost explicitly to mass political behavior, however, puts traditional concerns in a new light. Proxy voting, for example, is generally identified as an unfortunate phenomenon. The notion of apolitical wives dependent on their husbands' advice, or of union members blindly following the voting instructions of their shop stewards, seems anathema to the basic ideals of civic duty. But from the information cost perspective, this behavior is rational and functional. When in doubt, ask someone who knows. It is unnecessary to recompile and reevaluate all the available political data when a trusted friend or colleague has already completed the task.

In a similar vein, when it appeared that General Eisenhower's avuncular personal characteristics substituted for the evaluation of his policy positions in the minds of the mass electorate, researchers were greatly concerned (Campbell et al., 1960). But in the absence of strongly differentiated policy positions, reliance on cues of personal competence and leadership ability is an entirely reasonable and rational strategy in voting. The reasonableness of proxy voting is confirmed by the fact that the middle level of political interest and knowledge, not the lowest one, is the level that exhibits the highest likelihood of proxy voting. Again, the critical swing voters and the protest voters are prominently represented in the middle and upper levels rather than at the lowest level of the sophistication continuum.

The picture of uninformed voters in the election booth staring vainly at their shoes in search of cues to help in their vote decision is in all likelihood not a hyperbole. No doubt in each election year, literally millions of crib sheets are taken into voting booths to help voters keep the names of the candidates straight. Such scenarios emphasize the information costs in mass political behavior, but they also reinforce a false dichotomy between uninformed proxy voters and well-informed, issue-oriented, rational voters. Proxy voting, and reliance on nonissue cues to the competence of political candidates are all an important part of day-to-day political behavior throughout the full range of the sophistication continuum, from the least to the most informed.

The theory of three publics presumes a bottom stratum of apoliticals whose self-consistent world view leads them to ignore political stimuli and to avoid participating in political life. The middle and upper levels of sophistication are the groups that make the biggest difference in day-to-day political conflict. But within the theory of mass society, the concepts of mobilization and extremist politics draw attention to this bottom stratum (Kornhauser, 1959).

The term *know-nothings,* drawn originally from the American movement of the 1850s, has a straightforward meaning and has been incorporated into the survey research tradition: "All persons do not offer equal targets for information campaigns. Surveys consistently find that a certain proportion of the population is not familiar with any particular event. Offhand, it might be thought that information concerning that event was not distributed broadly enough to each of them, but . . . there is something about the uninformed which makes them harder to reach no matter what the level or nature of the information . . . There exists a hard core of chronic 'know-nothings.' " (Hyman and Sheatsley, 1947, p. 413).

Marx had a similar concept of a bottom stratum "lumpenproletariat," which he felt was easily propagandized, manipulated, and mobilized to work against the interest of the working classes. He was explicit about the social character of this bottom stratum: "Vagabonds, discharged soldiers, discharged jailbirds, escaped galley slaves, swindlers, mountebanks, lazzaroni, pickpockets, tricksters, gamblers, procurers, brothel keepers, porters, literati, organ grinders, rag pickers, knife grinders, tinkers, beggars—in short, the whole indefinite, disintegrated mass, thrown hither and thither" (Marx, 1852, p. 75).

This notion of a gullible and mobilizable antidemocratic force lies at the core of mass society theory. Because the members of this apathetic stratum lack political experience, so the theory goes, at times of crisis they may turn out in large numbers to support a demagogue. Such are the critical weaknesses of extreme political stratification. Both established conservative authorities and revolutionaries like Marx eye this group suspiciously.

For the most part the findings run contrary to the mass society scenario. They are not definitive, however, because the theory posits the existence of a demagogic, charismatic, and antidemocratic leader, most prominently symbolized by Adolf Hitler. In the absence of a time of crisis and a demagogic appeal, therefore, the theory remains untested. The milder forms of demagogy represented by Senator Joseph McCarthy and Governor George Wallace give some perspective on the issue. In general, the protest voting associated with the support of McCarthy and Wallace came chiefly from the middle level of the sophistication continuum rather than the bottom stratum (Rogin, 1967; Converse et al., 1969). Under different historical conditions the results might have been different. But given the relatively mild political climate of the last three decades in the United States, the know-nothing stratum remained largely out of earshot and unavailable for political appeals of all varieties. Perhaps even more than the rest of the public, discharged jailbirds and brothel keepers are preoccupied by the day-to-day concerns of personal economic survival and have little time for political life.

The general concerns of the mass society theory nevertheless persist. The notion that active participation in the cross-cutting cleavages of political life leads to self-restraint and political maturity is wishfully naive. Student activists of the extreme left in the 1960s and their conservative counterparts of the fundamentalist religious right, as well as other single-issue constituencies, contain many of the brightest, most articulate, and most politically aware members of their cohorts. The mass society theory has been looking for trouble at the wrong end of the sophistication continuum.

The notion of a knowledge gap emphasizes the disjuncture between the relatively high levels of voting participation and the relatively low levels of political information and knowledge. There is a further gap between voting and more active forms of political behavior. Although substantial majorities of the eligible population make their way to the polls each presidential election year, less than one in twenty manage to participate beyond voting.

If voters were rationally calculating the efficient use of their political efforts, they would spend more time in smaller political groups where their efforts are more likely to make a difference than contributing an infinitesimal fraction to the aggregate vote (Olson, 1965). The notion of information costs and rationally instrumental participation is correct as far as it goes. But political participation involves more than instrumental behavior.

The overlapping motivations for voting were highlighted in the 1964 presidential election (Lang and Lang, 1968). Media reports of early election returns potentially influence the behavior of those who have not yet made it to the polls, and in 1964, when the final results from the East confirmed a landslide for Lyndon Johnson while the polls were still open in the West because of time zone differences, large numbers of Californians voted late in the day in spite of, or possibly because of, having heard the news. Potential voters became more eager to vote, rather than discouraged, as a result of having heard about the returns from the East. Thus, voting is substantially a psychological expression of political partisanship by which individuals "go on record" as continuing to support their long-standing party affiliation. Voting is an expressive act and civic obligation independent of party affiliation:

Many, perhaps most, Americans grew up with the idea that voting for president is a sacred duty. Their positive attitude toward the responsibilities of citizenship develop long before they have specific perception of who the officeholders are and the functions they perform or of the parties and what each stands for. A person's sense of obligation to cast a ballot as an expression of his civic-mindedness prevails even when the vote appears to have no purpose, as in an uncontested election or one which offers the voters a choice between Tweedledee and Tweedledum. Consequently the proportions among various population groups who vote in a presidential election reflect the prevalence of this general attitude. It is not very much affected by either the closeness of the race or the specific issues at stake.   (Lang and Lang, 1968, 140)

The ritualistic nature of voting and public political participation parallels other collective ritual acts in primitive societies and in religion (Himmelstrand, 1960; Edelman, 1964; Milbrath, 1965). But the majority of voting studies and, by definition, all of the research on issue voting emphasize the voting act as a rational calculus. The instrumental and expressive components of the voting act are not clear-cut alternatives. The two overlap in the minds of most voters. On the instrumental side, it is unlikely that a citizen's vote will tip the scale and provide victory for one candidate over another. But a surprising number of elections in the United States are relatively close races, with candidates only a few percentage points apart, and like the sweepstakes participant who faces odds of a million to one, the individual voter is psychologically inclined to expect the unexpected. The blurred lines between voting as an instrumental and an expressive act help to put in perspective the disjuncture between voting and more active forms of political participation. Voting is culturally defined as an important, symbolic, civic duty; active participation in campaigns and contact with political authorities are not.

The question of the competence of the average citizen has served as a fulcrum of tension between the widely held egalitarian-democratic ideals and the persistent results of survey research on mass political behavior. Although the aggregate level of political sophistication in the United States is not necessarily below the critical threshold for a viable political system, it is less than one might prefer. The empirical analysis of political sophistication, however, should not be defined as the study of political pathology. If individuals opt not to vote or to pay much attention to the flow of political information, that may well be a rational and quite reasonable decision to marshal scarce resources and energies for other more directly rewarding pursuts. The stratification of political attentiveness and involvement is a natural and inevitable factor of mass political life.

But because of the tension between the empirical reality and democratic norms and the tradition of survey research not to embarrass respondents, research on these issues has been awkwardly indirect and inferential. A coordinated and convergent effort at measuring political sophistication and knowledge might help to integrate democratic theory and empirical research. In time, agreed-upon measures of sophistication, like measures of party identification, could become fundamental variables in the empirical study of American politics. The measure of political sophistication used here turns out to be almost as stable over time as party identification, with self-correlations of .70 over a four-year period, compared to .80 for party identification. The roots of political sophistication are as deep in the socialization process, and its impacts on attitudes and behavior are as strong, as those of party affiliation.

Sophistication has important direct effects. It is strongly linked, for example, with both voting behavior and participation beyond voting. But a unique character of cognitive phenomena such as sophistication is their propensity toward interactive effects. That is, sophistication influences the nature of the relationships between other variables. This is critically important to the development of future research designs. Thus, if sophistication is defined as openness to political communications, it is not necessarily in itself a causal agent. For example it will not cause protest behavior. But in those circumstances where there are political stimuli to mobilize protest among a particular political group, the most sophisticated strata of that group will be the first to perceive and respond to those stimuli. In this example, sophistication is the intervening, catalytic variable which increases the likelihood that one variable, the mobilization stimuli, will influence another variable, political behavior.

At the upper end of the sophistication continuum, congressmen, journalists, or private philanthropists might, in response to a relatively small story in the newspaper, be so sensitive to the political issue involved as to devote their primary energy in the following months to an attempt to get a bill passed or to raise public consciousness about a particular episode or issue. They represent the elite. They are intellectually, professionally, and financially able to respond. At the low end of the sophistication continuum, there are individuals with limited horizons and political vocabularies who, although they are aware of the importance of strong political stimuli, such as an impending war or economic depression, do not define these world events as amenable to political influence. They simply do not respond to political stimuli in political terms. The great bulk of the citizenry fall in between these two extremes. They frequently ignore large numbers of political stimuli. They frequently interpret political stimuli in nonpolitical terms. But on occasion they respond to a political appeal by contributing time or money. More frequently, perhaps, they make a mental note that a particular event or issue ought to be taken into account the next time a major election rolls around.

Neither conservatives nor liberals are, in general, more sophisticated than the other, although both liberals and conservatives have strong intuitively based, if divergent, perceptions to the contrary. The fact of the matter is that increasing sophistication does not lead to either conservatism or liberalism. Political ideologues of both the left and the right often appear to be anything but sophisticated because of their over-reliance on simplistic catchphrases. At the same time, there are others among the citizenry who can outline the case for a conservative or liberal policy with the subtlety, thoroughness, and persuasiveness of a well-trained lawyer.

As is familiar from the legal profession, when one digs deeper into a particular case or policy issue, one can find factual examples, legal norms, and philosophical principles that might be used to support either side. Most policy debates entail trade-offs between important values, such as equity and efficiency. When liberals and conservatives differ, it is usually because their priorities among those values are different, not because the facts and principles of the matter are so obvious as to lead the sophisticated mind to an inevitable conclusion.

Issues and Nonissues

Imprecise language about what constitutes a political issue has been a principal contributor to controversy over the nature of mass politics. Examples are legion. The McCarthy era of the early 1950s in American politics was characterized by a generalized public concern, perhaps even paranoia, over the presence of Communist sympathizers or party members in positions of authority. Senator McCarthy did not invent the issue of communism, but he discovered its spectacular ability to thrust him onto the front pages of the nation's newspapers and to lead him to be described as the most influential individual in Washington next to the President, indeed to have the era named after him. The cold war dominated the international scene, the war in Korea brought it to the attention of the mass electorate in the most vivid and visceral terms, and the headlines daily echoed the charges and countercharges swirling about the senator from Wisconsin.

These were strong political stimuli indeed. But when in 1954 members of the public were asked about their fears and hopes for the future of their own lives and their country, less than 2 percent mentioned the issue of communism (Stouffer, 1955). The lesson is clear. Communism per se is not an issue. It is intimately intertwined with issues of both domestic and foreign policy. It is a political symbol of emotional weight, but it is not in itself an issue. The irony of data of this sort derives from the attempt to condense the jumble of assumptions, symbols, concerns, and strategic trade-offs that attend the historical fact of international communism into a single survey question.

Likewise, such recent historical concerns as civil rights, Vietnam, and even Watergate involved complexities and subtleties not easily captured by survey items. Lyndon Johnson, for example, was able to pull a survey from his pocket and point with pride to the clear "fact" that the majority of American citizens supported "our boys fighting in Vietnam." At the same time, other surveys revealed that an overwhelming majority of the electorate felt it was a mistake to have become involved in Vietnam in the first place.

One fundamental lesson which can be drawn from the distinction between issues and nonissues is a recognition of the procrustean character of the issue-voting model. As legend has it, Procrustes was a highwayman from ancient Attica who would stretch or abbreviate his victims when they did not conform to the length of his iron bed. One need not pause to examine the psychological roots of Procrustes' fixation on precision and order. But the vividness of the legend brings special power to the adjective procrustean.

The issue-voting model requires researchers to impute rationality to a subset of voters based on the apparent correlations between the issue preferences of the voters and the positions of the candidates. Issue perceptions and party identification are causally intertwined, and some individuals may "rationalize" a vote decision by bringing their own and their chosen candidate's perceived positions into alignment after the fact. Furthermore, although voters and candidates may thus agree on some issues, such issues may be neither salient nor relevant to the vote decision. To review a series of political issues one at a time exaggerates the importance of issue voting by continually reapportioning the same observed variance.

The issue voting model does unfortunate violence to the realities of mass political behavior. Trying to estimate the rationality and in turn the sophistication of public choice from fragmentary correlations between candidate and voter on policy issues is both unpromising and misleading. If the underlying concern of democratic theory is with the average voter's understanding of fundamental policy issues, then knowledge and understanding of issues should be measured directly.

Research on the role of issues in voting behavior is proceeding apace but is moving away from the original model of issue voting which calculates and adds together the distances between voters' opinions and the perceived positions of the candidates. The new work emphasizes political cognition, the distinction between issues and nonissues, the importance of symbolic politics, and the difficulty of rationally calculating which candidate might best serve a voter's self-interest (Fiorina, 1981; Conover and Feldman, 1984a-b; Anderson, 1985; Brady, 1985; Kinder and Sears, 1985; Miller, 1985; Sniderman et al. 1985).

Ironically, it is often in the interest of politicians to be as vague as possible when speaking out on public issues. In a two-party system both parties tend to maximize their vote appeal by adopting centrist positions. But there are systematic constraints on this practice, for if all parties adopted precisely centrist positions on all possible policy matters, the electorate would become increasingly frustrated and withdrawn. At the same time, if one party ventured toward an extremist position, it might well lose more than it gained in vote appeal. The gap between the need to appear articulate and the dangers of being too specific is often filled by artful ambiguity. Political strategists gain the most if their language can give the impression of a resonance with the opinions of voters while avoiding actually taking a position. Political rationality, in short, "leads political parties in a two-party system to becloud their policies in a fog of ambiguity" (Downs, 1957, p. 136).

A recent study disclosed that a striking feature of candidates' rhetoric is its extreme vagueness: "The typical campaign speech says virtually nothing specific about policy alternatives; discussions of the issue are hidden away in little publicized statements and position papers. Even the most extended discussions leave many questions unanswered, in short, policy stands are infrequent, inconspicuous and unspecific" (Page, 1978, p. 153). On thirty-three issue areas during the 1968 presidential campaign, Humphrey made a policy proposal in the average issue area in 6 percent of his speeches, and Nixon did so in 4 percent. And many of the "issue positions" were one-line allusions to positions taken elsewhere. Even these rare references to an issue seldom involved an unambiguous policy. In a major speech on economic policy, for example, Nixon, after criticizing the evils of inflation and lambasting the Democrats for causing it, concluded that he favored a "responsible fiscal policy." Given the backdrop of criticizing Democratic overspending, Nixon might be assumed to have meant budget cuts, but he never actually said so (Page, 1978).

In view of the fact that candidates pound the podium, list numerous issues as being important, and routinely promise to take appropriate action without explaining in detail what they have in mind, the voters' strategy of semiattentiveness makes perfect sense. Paying more attention does not mean that they will actually learn more about the candidates' positions, understand better the political controversies of the day, or use the machinery of electoral politics more effectively.

One of the central findings about the nature of political pluralism is the scarcity of issues on the public agenda at any point in time. Most individuals can handle no more than seven factors simultaneously in the process of decisionmaking (Miller, 1956). Given the diversity of individuals involved and the complexity of social and political institutions, such a limitation theoretically need not apply in the aggregate. But in order for an issue to have a meaningful impact in the electoral arena, though it need not attract the attention of a majority of voters, some meaningful plurality is required.

The 1980 election is typical. Respondents were asked, "As you know, the government faces many serious problems in this country and in other parts of the world. What do you personally feel are the most important problems the government in Washington should try to take care of?" They were encouraged to give up to three answers to that question, and their responses were indeed diverse, including over 300 distinct issues. But the number of issues receiving prominent attention was small. Inflation was the prominent concern, reflecting 19 percent of total issues mentioned, the Iranian hostage crisis and unemployment were tied for second place at 11 percent, and national defense was noted in 6 percent of the responses. Two other issues, the energy crisis and foreign affairs, garnered 3 percent of the responses, and the remaining issues did not exceed 2 percent. Most of the other issues mentioned were of potential political significance, including such obvious questions as the Middle

East, civil protection, mass transportation, immigration policy, and taxes. But they did not aggregate to significant political prominence.

The magic number seven may not be far off the mark for the aggregate public agenda. It is literally true that massive events like Watergate, Vietnam, and the Iranian hostage crisis, by grabbing the headlines and filling the front pages, push other ongoing political issues to the back pages of the paper, to the end of the television newscasts, and to the deeper recesses of public consciousness.

The distribution of public issues is similar to the distribution of political sophistication in the mass electorate (Figure 8.2). Though the shape of the curves differs a bit, the dynamic of the movement of issues up and down the curve is perhaps as significant to understanding the process of mass politics as the fundamental character of the sophistication curve. Whatever the universe of potential political issues is, the number receiving prominent attention is infinitesimal. It is not the shape of the curve but the movement of issues within it that keeps the political system as a whole alert and responsive.

Attitudes and Nonattitudes

There are three schools of thought on the use of survey research data. The first school, those scholars, pollsters, and marketing researchers who use survey research heavily, routinely gloss over the weaknesses of the methodology. The second school, those scholars and researchers who do not use survey research, are deeply skeptical of its ability to assess the beliefs and opinions of individuals in a realistic way. These scholars are much more comfortable with the richer research methodologies of the case study, participant observation, or depth interview. The third school is comprised of those researchers, including myself, who use survey research but feel uneasy about it. This group represents a small cluster of researchers who, in addition to sharing a sense of unease, feel that, with appropriate refinements and necessary qualifications in the presentation of data, survey research has an important role to play in social science research (Schuman and Presser, 1981).

The character of the survey research method deeply colors the conclusions drawn from it. This is especially true for public attitudes and political life. Researchers should build a measurement model at the same time they attempt to build a model of social processes. In that way they can incorporate their understanding of the limitations and

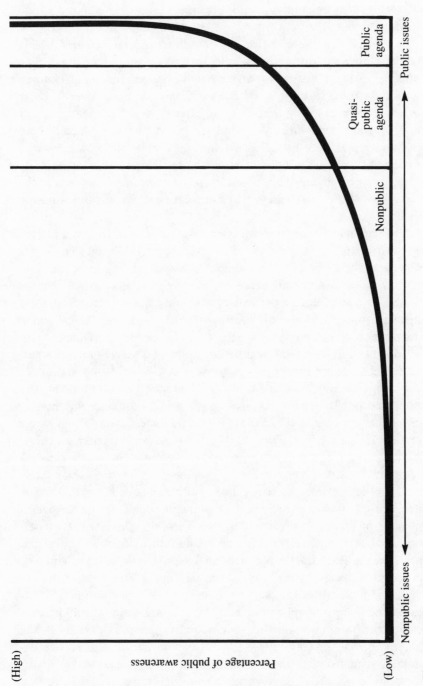

Figure 8.2. Evolution of Public Issues.

biases of measurement explicitly into their theorizing about the real world (Blalock, 1982).

It appears that the emperor has no attitudes. That wonderful fable of the emperor strutting in his underwear at the front of the parade offers a poignant lesson. It is an especially popular tale among children who understand instantly the basic psychology of pretending to know or see something in response to social expectations. In the fable, a pair of greedy and conniving tailors manipulate the emperor, his court, and the public, and then shrewdly leave the kingdom before the truth is out. In the case of public opinion research, the perpetrators are neither shrewd nor conniving. They are more like the Lockele drummers of the Congo who refused to believe that Europeans did not also communicate by drums.

The parallel with the underdressed emperor is nevertheless a limited one. Most citizens do have carefully developed opinions on some issues and partial or vague opinions on most issues. Cautious survey research, after offering respondents every opportunity to volunteer that they do not have an opinion on a particular issue, finds routinely that 80 percent of the respondents insist on offering one. Furthermore, these opinion distributions are stable in the aggregate over time and correlate in modest degree with the traditional demographic and behavioral variables. This is not a conspiracy; it is a paradox.

Perhaps these phenomena could best be termed quasi-attitudes. The measured public opinion on an issue is a mixture of carefully thought out, stable opinions, half-hearted opinions, misunderstandings, and purely random responses. In the case study of attitudes toward federal involvement in power and housing, respondents were divided into a clear dichotomy of stable versus random opinions and, by inference, an equally clear division between attitudes and nonattitudes (Converse, 1970). The item dealt with an unusually abstract and philosophical issue of government involvement in private enterprise. Thus, the estimate that 80 percent of the responses were either no-opinions or random is atypical and not necessarily characteristic of other issues. Other more salient and concrete political objects, such as the incumbent President or the enduring reputations of the major political parties, stimulate more structured and persisting opinions from the electorate, with only 20 percent expressing no opinion or offering random responses. Measured public opinion on most other issues falls somewhere between these two extremes, with from 20 to 80 percent basing their response on quasi-attitudes, a mixture of guesswork, various linguistic cues in the question wording, and the context of the item in the questionnaire. They are not strictly random. The same question wording and questionnaire context may well generate the same response if the question is later repeated. But because of the ambiguities of the language and the loose linkage between the question and the basic political beliefs held by the respondents, the question response is relatively labile.

The problem of quasi-attitudes is that they are not easily identified. Nonattitudes, quasi-attitudes, and true attitudes blur into one another. Even in response to sustained encouragement from the interviewer, most respondents cannot themselves distinguish their more deeply rooted opinions from those less clearly tied to basic political beliefs. Opinion stability over time does not help much in separating true from quasi-attitudes because there are a variety of nonpolitical as well as political sources of attitude consistency over time.[2]

Survey research ought to rely as often as possible on procedures that identify the opinion pattern for the population as a whole, as well as for smaller subpublics for whom, as best can be determined, the question at hand is politically salient and meaningfully linked to persisting political beliefs and values. Such procedures, in effect, take pluralism seriously.

Paradox Redux

This book has come full circle to the paradox of mass politics, namely, how the political system works as well as it does given the low level of political awareness and knowledge in the mass electorate. Since a paradox is by definition the simultaneous existence of two logically incompatible phenomena, the options for resolving the paradox are to discount the first phenomenon, discount the second, or demonstrate that they are not in fact incompatible. Skeptics might conclude that the average citizen is neither thoughtful nor informed, that such behaviors are incompatible with democratic theory, and that the system does not work very well. Optimists would disagree, observing that mass democracy requires a modestly attentive and knowledgeable public, the system in fact works quite well, and the data used to demonstrate low levels of

2. Perhaps the best available approach to this problem, though expensive and time consuming, is the use of multi-item indices. The apparent correlation between any two opinion indices will appear to be reassuringly strong, in the range of .20 to as high as .50. But the mathematics of most linear correlation coefficients relies heavily on the top strata of respondents whose responses are consistently distant from the mean. For the purposes of these coefficients, the 20 to 80 percent of the population who either register no opinion or lie close to the population mean are, in statistical terms, almost irrelevant.

public sophistication are erroneous, resulting from poorly designed research methods.

In fact, however, both of the propositions are correct: the mass public is for the most part uninterested and unsophisticated, and in consideration of that fact, the system does indeed work remarkably well. The political elites of this country perceive and act within the constraints of an attentive public will. Even for those many obscure and narrowly defined issues which are clearly not in the public eye, the elected and administrative elites have the shared sense that such issues could move into the public eye quite quickly, and they behave accordingly. There is a very small, attentive top stratum of the mass public which is paying close attention, writing letters, and making its presence felt in Washington along with the professional lobbying establishment The paradox is resolved because the two phenomena are not incompatible.

The key finding is that the mass public is stratified along a sophistication continuum. On most issues, the great majority of citizens are inattentive and uninformed. But, as with many social phenomena of this sort, there is a natural and effective division of labor. The division is not properly described as pluralism, because that term would imply that all citizens have developed a sophisticated opinion in specialized areas and are aligned with a demographic or organized interest group which connects them to the centers of power.

A more appropriate model is that of three publics. The bottom stratum includes the roughly 20 percent of the population who do not monitor the political realm at all and are unlikely to be mobilized to political action by even the most extreme political crisis or case of economic self-interest. At the top of the continuum is a group of active and attentive individuals, who represent approximately 5 percent of the population. For many political matters the effective size of this group could be much smaller, measuring a fraction of 1 percent of the population as a whole. The great majority of the population lie between these two extremes and monitor the political process half-attentively, but they can be alerted if fellow citizens sound the political alarm. Over the past thirty years such issues as Vietnam, Watergate, civil rights, women's rights, and a multitude of more narrowly defined issues have risen to public attention and then receded from it. The dynamism of the political agenda, the fluid movement of issues from obscurity to prominence, is a critical factor in resolving the paradox of mass politics (Neuman and Fryling, 1985).

This paradox involves the tension between the workings of the polity in aggregate, which seems to give evidence of a certain energy, intelligence, and alertness to political issues, and of the individual citizen, who does not:

> In real life, no one acts on the theory that he can have a public opinion on every public question . . . The purpose, then, is not to burden every citizen with expert opinions on all questions, but to push that burden away from him towards the responsible administrator . . . The private citizen, beset by partisan appeals for the loan of his Public Opinion, will soon see, perhaps, that these appeals are not an appeal to his intelligence . . . As his civic education takes account of the complexity of his environment, he will concern himself about the equity and the sanity of procedure, and even this he will in most cases expect his elected representative to watch for him . . . Only by insisting that problems shall not come up to him until they have passed through a procedure, can the busy citizen of a modern state hope to deal with them in a form that is intelligible. (Lippmann, 1922, pp. 250–252)

Lippmann's language emphasizes the notion of formal procedure. Actually, the complex process of setting the public agenda and the rise and decline of public issues involves a number of informal elements as well. The citizen depends on personal friends and colleagues as well as formally designated representatives for cues of what is important enough politically to require attention. The principal difference between Lippmann's perspective on the paradox and the one put forward here is the emphasis in this analysis on the shape of the stratification curve. Lippmann described a single entity, the public, and contrasted it with the corresponding role of public official. But the evidence reviewed here points to the potentially pivotal role of an informally defined activist elite within the mass public.

Ironically, because of the standard sampling procedures of survey research, there are only hints and fragments of evidence about this activist elite. Both the apolitical and the mass publics are large enough to provide ample proportions in a survey data to make their character evident. A special survey design that oversamples the activist group will be necessary to follow up the evidentiary fragments with systematic inquiry. The conflict between seeing the essence of politics in the activities of the elite stratum and seeing it in the slower tidal movements of the full electorate needs to be reformulated. The essence of politics lies in the subtle interactions between the elite stratum and the mass pubic.

Schumpeter, two decades after Lippmann, came to a similar conclusion in confronting the paradox. He contrasted a naive model of mass democracy with a revised model emphasizing the *modus procedendi* of elite-mass interaction: "Most students of politics have by now come to accept the criticisms leveled at the classical doctrine of democracy . . . centered in the proposition that 'the people' hold a definite and rational opinion about every individual question (Schumpeter, 1942, p. 269). Schumpeter describes how the workings of the system in aggregate overcome the limitations of the individual citizen.

If Lippmann and Schumpeter are still read and cited today—and they certainly seem to be—how is it that their message is so little heard? Survey research is not the culprit. It provides a very limited picture of the political process; but so do the other methodological approaches, including depth interviews with political activists. The culprit is perhaps the premium paid to specialized single-method research. One scholar becomes a specialist in the study of political parties or bureaucracies using case studies and institutional analysis. Another becomes a public opinion analyst and survey researcher. The two need not define their areas of interest as overlapping, and frequently they do not. In some measure the insights of Lippmann and Schumpeter find little resonance in modern research because such ideas run against the grain of the dominant methodologies.

The character of American political stratification also explains differences between American and other political cultures. One of the most frequent lessons of comparative politics is the fragile character of democratic institutions. The rare longevity of democratic institutions distinguishes the American case (Verba and Nie, 1972; Verba et al., 1978). The level of voluntary political stratification in the American system is as high as or higher than other developed political systems. In many marginally democratic or nondemocratic political systems, individual citizens shrug off corruption or unresponsiveness in their government, explaining either that it is not their concern or that they can do little. It is the persistent character of the American political culture to assume that, when a crisis arises, the citizenry will mobilize and respond. This is a political culture of naiveté. The widely shared naiveté shapes the character of the American political system, elites and middle strata alike.

There is another irony that emerges from the stratification of American politics. The average citizens feel that they need not study a political issue in depth in order to have a meaningful opinion on it. People find it quite natural to be asked about matters of foreign affairs and budgetary policy and to have their opinions listened to and taken seriously. Such norms are reflected in the American jury system. There is a fundamental belief that, if the populace are given the opportunity to review the facts of a case in a fair and open setting, their aggregate judgment is equal to, and in many cases preferable to, the unconstrained opinion of even the most brilliant jurists the legal system can provide.

Senator Roman Hruska was widely ridiculed when in 1970 he defended the mediocrity of Nixon's new nominee to the Supreme Court by commenting, "There are a lot of mediocre judges and people and lawyers. They are entitled to a little representation, aren't they? We can't have all Brandeises, Frankfurters, and Cardozos." The ridicule in this case was well deserved. But those many citizens who insist that they would rather be governed by the first two thousand names in the telephone book than by the faculty of Harvard University do not speak from a lack of political wisdom. In fact, they put the issue in a new light. There is a dynamic balance between the special talents of the political elite and the political system which generates the elite. It remains important to balance the specialized knowledge of the elite and the generalized common sense of the mass polity.

There is an American tradition of the man from Missouri who has to be shown. This self-made individual of rural origins and modest education is unimpressed by the sophistry and abstractions of aloof political debate. His attention focuses on the bottom line. Similarly, the unsophisticated citizen enters the voting booth, goes through the straightforward mental calculations of deciding whether the country is in an economic recession or at war, and, if it is not, votes for the incumbent. This style of political thought is not a bad yardstick in comparison with the vagaries of most campaign rhetoric. These considerations need not be the only ones to enter the voter's mind. Discussions with friends and a casual monitoring of an open political communication system will from time to time bring other concerns to the attention of the typical voter. Personal, nonpolitical concerns may also enter this voter's mind. But if an issue of fundamental political significance comes to the fore, the average voter in particular and the electorate in general are likely to recognize it as such.

Appendix A

The Concept and Measurement of Political Sophistication

THE POLITICAL sophistication of the citizenry is a central issue in theories of mass politics and democracy (Berelson et al., 1954; Campbell et al., 1960; Dahl, 1961; Key, 1961, 1966; Lane, 1962; Converse, 1964, 1970, 1975; Almond and Verba, 1965; Hamilton, 1972; Verba and Nie, 1972; Verba et al., 1976; Page, 1978; Fiorina, 1981). The issue was once listed as one of three central foci of political behavior research (Stokes, 1968). Later it was listed as one of five central concerns in the field (Sears, 1969). The sophistication issue has also been labeled as the central unifying conception to emerge from the early voting studies (Shapiro, 1969). Yet the research tradition yields no agreed-upon definition or approach to measurement. The research remains at the "preparadigmatic stage" where the domain is ill defined, theories are vague and partial, and measurement techniques are not yet convergent (Kuhn, 1962).

Perhaps the most graphic demonstration of the confusion in measurement is evident in two recent studies which independently derived similar measures of political sophistication but scored them in opposite directions, one attributing higher sophistication to those who use a greater number of dimensions of judgment, the other to those who use a single abstract liberalism-conservatism dimension in conceptualizing political issues (Marcus et al., 1974; Converse, 1964). The problem stems from the fact that "the general issue has been translated into a wide variety of specific inquiries, each with quite different implicit standards for judging the rationality or quality of an electorate's decision" (Shanks, 1970, p. 3).

There are a variety of terms by which political sophistication and its components have been identified (Table A.1). Sometimes these terms are used casually and interchangeably. At other times they are given precise, theoretically derived definitions and are tied to corresponding measurement techniques. Some terms emphasize emotional involve-

Table A.1. Terminology of Political Sophistication

Terms and concepts	Research tradition
Psychology and motivation	
Political involvement	Berelson et al., 1954
Political affect	Berelson et al., 1954
Interest in politics	Berelson et al., 1954
Political attentiveness	Key, 1961
Privitism	Kinder and Sears, 1985
Exposure to political stimuli	Milbrath, 1965
Political apathy	Rosenberg, 1954
Political salience	Czudnowski, 1968
Level of information	
Political knowledge	Glenn, 1972
Political information	Lane and Sears, 1964
Political awareness	McClosky, PAR Study
Political mass	Converse, 1962
Cognitive aspects	
Level of conceptualization	Converse, 1964
Recognition and understanding	Converse, 1964
Political cognition	Himmelstrand, 1960
Political code	Padioleau, 1974
Ideological constraint	Sullivan et al., 1978
Conceptual sophistication	McClosky, 1967
Cognitive sophistication	Pierce and Hagner, 1980
Political thinking	Barber, 1973
Political comprehension	Converse, 1962
Political alertness	Himmelstrand, 1960
Political information processing	Graber, 1984
Miscellaneous	
Political competence	Almond and Verba, 1963
Political rationality	Shapiro, 1969
Political relatedness	Eulau and Schneider, 1956
Ideological innocence	Kinder and Sears, 1985
Cultural sophistication	Trow, 1959
System proximity	Di Palma, 1970
Simplism	Selznick and Steinberg, 1969
Issue salience	Repass, 1971
Issue consistency	Nie et al., 1976
Issue voting	Kessel, 1972
Policy voting	Brody and Page, 1972
Voter sophistication	Carmines and Stimson, 1980

ment in election outcomes; others emphasize linguistic skills, current events knowledge, or the understanding of democratic principles.

Fundamental concerns of the disciplines of psychology, sociology, and political science converge in their interest in these issues (Figure A.1). In the case of psychology, the intelligence and sophistication that people bring to bear on political issues and problems is seen as a reflection of underlying personality and cognitive traits, such as intelligence, achievement motivation, and self-esteem. Psychology emphasizes rules of behavior, which generalize across different situations and domains. Thus, it focuses on issues of intelligence and open-mindedness, which remain constant across different contexts, and ignores such variables as the historical and political context (Lasswell, 1930; Reich, 1946; Adorno et al., 1950; Skinner, 1957). Sociology, in turn, sensitized to the influence of class and social structure, sees sophistication as a manifestation of education, in the sense of more highly developed verbal and intellectual

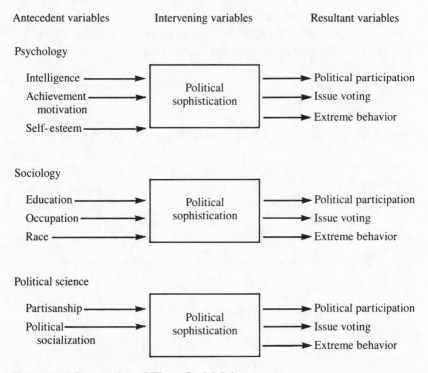

Figure A.1. Perspective of Three Social Sciences.

skills and political values. Political science, on the contrary, is characteristically concerned with the influence of the party system and focuses on partisanship or more narrowly defined political involvement measures (Campbell et al., 1954).

The term *political sophistication* is used here because it has not been closely identified with a particular operational definition. It is a general, overarching term, spanning the three concepts of salience, knowledge, and conceptualization. Furthermore, the common sense definition of sophistication conveys the importance of developing a mix of cognitive skills and knowledge through experience, emphasizing the phenomenon of general accumulation through time.

The definition of sophistication and the corresponding measurement strategy used in this study emerged from a process of moving back and forth between empirical and theoretical analyses.

The model is not dramatically different from the other models (Figure A.2). It has four distinctions. First, it includes variables from each of the three relevant social science disciplines, varying them in an attempt to identify the unique contribution of each to the overall analysis. Second, the three-component measurement model incorporates the principal definitions of sophistication into an overall index yet allows for analysis of the unique characteristics of the subcomponents. Third, since

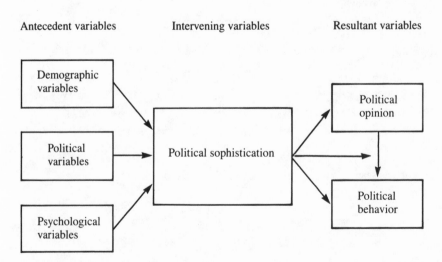

Figure A.2. Unified Model of Sophistication.

knowledge and opinion are linked in complex ways, the patterns of opinion holding, opinion consistency, and opinion structuring are separated off from the sophistication concept and measured independently. Fourth, the model focuses on interaction effects, that is, the effects of sophistication on the linkage between the variables, particularly opinion and behavior.

Political Salience

The variation in people's interest in politics has received the most attention of the three components of political sophistication, in part owing to the fact that its measurement is fairly straightforward. A political interest scale does not require a great number of items, respondents are unlikely to be insulted or frightened by such inquiries, and the public is cooperative enough to distribute itself conveniently in a normal distribution.

Items often focus on interest in elections per se, as in the question; "Some people don't pay much attention to the political campaigns. How about you, would you say that you have been very much interested, somewhat interested, or not very interested in following the political campaigns so far this year?" (NES item). Another core indicator of political salience is attentiveness to political news in the mass media. It is possible to develop an index of political interest by summing the indicators of respondents' self-reported exposure to political content in newspapers, television, radio, and magazines. Measures of actual recall of news content are inappropriate because they would tap other factors, such as cognitive skills. Another aspect of political salience is political involvement. Various indicators of this aspect are concern over electoral outcome and enjoyment in expressing political opinions. Still another element involves the affective side of involvement in politics. It is indicated by self-descriptive items such as whether a person gets upset over political events and whether politics is seen as incomprehensible.

Other concepts and corresponding indicators were rejected for inclusion in the study. For example, political efficacy is an indicator of interest in politics. Certainly the feeling that one can have no effect on political decisions justifies paying less attention to politics. But the concept of efficacy involves a number of dimensions—some psychological in nature, such as interpersonal efficacy or self-worth; others ideologically, such as belief in government's responsiveness or political alienation (Balch, 1971; Citrin, 1974). These factors are more fruitfully examined independently of sophistication. Civic duty, defined as the belief that it is important and necessary for citizens to vote and participate in politics, was also excluded as a candidate indicator of sophistication because it reflects a perceived cultural value. Political salience focuses more specifically on people's evaluation of their own level of political interest.

Political Knowledge

Political knowledge is a central dimension of political behavior: "Supposedly a citizen would need to know what the government is and does before he could make a rational judgment about political questions. This knowing, in the sense of simply having information, would seem to be about as primitive a test of citizen rationality as we could get" (Barber, 1973, p. 44).

Hidden in this brief quotation are several clues to the character of the political knowledge variable. First of all, Barber describes knowledge as a central yet primitive test of rationality. He is implying here that knowledge is a necessary but not sufficient element of political sophistication. Although indicators of knowledge are important, they tell "nothing about the capacity to use knowledge intelligently" (Almond and Verba, 1965, p. 58). One may be politically well-informed and yet, for psychological and perhaps social reasons, ignore such informational resources in making political decisions.

Another aspect of political knowledge implied by Barber is its dual character. Political knowledge is knowing both what government is and what it does. The first element refers to the basic structure of government—its basic values, such as citizen participation, majority rule, separation of powers, and civil liberties, and its basic elements, such as the two-party system, the two houses of Congress, the role of the judiciary, and the organization of the Cabinet.

An understanding of what government is represents a core of political knowledge that is accumulated from childhood and presumably grows as a result of education. Knowledge of what government does, however, reflects people's ongoing attention to politics and the mass media and hence their knowledge of current events and prominent political figures. Whether individuals untutored in textbook knowledge and lacking in formal schooling might, in following current events closely, pick up substantial information about basic governmental structure and processes remains an empirical question. But this distinction between types of political knowledge highlights the importance of not simply equating educational level with political sophistication.

The index of political knowledge used in this study has four elements: political figures, issues, structures, and groups. Political figures are the most frequently used of all indicators of political knowledge. Respondents are asked to match names to political positions or simply to list current cabinet members or party leaders. Usually a balance is set between obscure and more familiar figures and between international and national figures.

Familiarity with political issues is the core of political knowledge: "The democratic citizen is expected to be well-informed about political affairs. He is supposed to know what the issues are, what their history is, what the relevant facts are, what alternatives are proposed, what the party stands for, what the likely consequences are" (Berelson et al., 1954, p. 308). Among the issues included are labor and civil rights disputes and the controversy in the Middle East.

Familiarity with political structure, or with the basic units of government and their traditional roles, the Constitution, and the legal system, is another aspect of political knowledge. It includes understanding of such questions as the structure of the Cabinet, the congressional committee system, the meaning of separation of powers, the length of senators' terms, and the approximate allocation in the national budget to military expenses and foreign aid.

Familiarity with political groups concerns how various political units, including politicians, parties, and social groups, are aligned on prominent issues.

There are, however, problems in the measurement of political knowledge:

"The critic of such information-level findings who points out that most of the ballyhooed items come from the stray fact department, and that all sorts of vigorous and well-grounded opinions about political options can be formed without, for example, accurate recognition of the minority leader of the Senate is surely right" (Converse, 1975, p. 9).

But some facts are more "stray" than others. Some aspects of political information are more likely than others to influence overall political attitudes. Being able to identify which party is in power, for example, seems to be more revealing of a person's basic understanding of American politics than naming a particular Secretary of the Treasury.

Another problem is that political knowledge is seldom probed. One reason is that low information and low familiarity with issues are seen as a given, a phenomenon too well understood and too little changing to be included in a questionnaire. Another reason is the assumption that education is an adequate proxy indicator of knowledge. But the primary reason that knowledge is infrequently explored is the ingrained concern of investigators not to disturb their rapport with respondents. People dislike having their ignorance revealed, so the logic goes, and as a result, knowledge questions are minimized, left to the end of a questionnaire, or omitted altogether.

Political Conceptualization

The question of how individuals conceptualize social phenomena and how they organize their beliefs is a particularly difficult challenge to research: "Belief systems have never surrendered easily to empirical study or quantification. Indeed, they have often served as primary exhibits for the doctrine that what is important to study cannot be measured and what can be measured is not important to study" (Converse, 1964, p. 206). The character of a traditional closed-ended survey research interview has contributed to the difficulty of research in this area. The advantage of closed-ended items is that they allow for the systematic comparison of the responses of a large number of individuals. But this uniform structure of interviewing obscures the individual differences in how beliefs and opinions are structured. The procedure is itself a leveling process, forcing people's varied conceptions into comparable numerical properties. The interview situation is a filtering device which allows only those cognitive elements defined as relevant by the questionnaire designer to be translated into data. All other utterances, qualifications, and nonverbal clues exhibited by the respondents are ignored in the inexorable transition from questionnaire to data file (Cicourel, 1964).

The analysis of depth interviews and open-ended items, however, has proven more promising. Lane's extended depth interview, for example, explored "differentiation" and analytic thinking, the processes of separating out various political roles and institutions (Lane, 1962). The ultimate example of an undifferentiated view of politics would be the individual for whom all politicians and parties are the same, confusing the distinction even between Republicans and Communists. The same would be true of the difference between corporate leaders and government leaders and the distinction between what the government does in practice and what its charter says it should do. Such questions as the separation of powers would be meaningless if government itself is seen as an undifferentiated monolith.

Lane refers also to the phenomenon of contextualizing—spontaneously placing a particular issue in the context of an explicit, forensic ideology. His study of political ideology, involving depth interviews with 15 middle and lower-middle class men for 10 to 20 hours each and resulting in 3,750 pages of typed transcripts, turned up only one or two instances of explicit ideological contextualizing. But the political facts and utterances of these respondents were not entirely unconnected. They linked some issues with other issues, with more abstract personal values, and most often with personal experiences. Political contextualizing subsumes this full range of connections between political issues or facts and context.

Converse's work on belief systems generated a concept quite similar to Lane's notion of differentiation. Converse counted the raw number of unique, open-ended responses volunteered by respondents in evaluating the presidential candidates and the political parties—the separate factors, facts, issue positions, personality traits, or events that individuals bring to bear on the evaluation of political objects (Converse, 1962). This measure of "political mass" parallels the notion of physical mass and inertia. A large cognitive mass of facts is seen as a form of inertia which requires strong short-term forces to change voters' minds and pull them away from voting for the candidate of their party.

Converse's levels of political conceptualization correspond most closely to Lane's notions of contextualizing and organization. Converse is interested in which yardstick or organizational framework an individual brings to bear in judging political issues:

From the point of view of the actor, the idea organization that leads to constraint permits him to locate and make sense of the wider range of information from a particular domain than he would find possible without such organization. One judgmental dimension or "yardstick" that has been highly serviceable for simplifying and organizing events in most Western politics for the past century has been the liberal-conservative continuum, on which parties, political leaders, legislation, court decisions and a number of other primary objects of politics could be more—or less—adequately located.   (Converse, 1964, p. 214)

Two indicators of conceptualization derived from the work of Lane and Converse are used in the current study. The first, termed conceptual differentiation, assesses the respondents' ability and inclination to identify and discriminate among the various forces and actors involved in the political process. The measure focuses on differentiation among the candidates and the parties, such as the number of unique comments, including facts, opinions, observations, and comparative statements, which the respondents volunteered in answering why they vote for or against each candidate and each party.

The second indicator of conceptualization is conceptual integration, which parallels contextualizing and the notion of levels of conceptualization—the explicit organization of political ideas and issues, in terms of abstract or ideological constructs. Conceptual integration is complementary to conceptual integration. Individuals must differentiate elements of the political domain to some minimum degree in order to have elements to integrate. Growth in conceptualization presumably involves a spiraling back-and-forth between an increasingly differentiated understanding of the political process and the more frequent use of abstract anchoring concepts to put discrete pieces of information in some kind of manageable and accessible order. The new structuring of the political domain in turn allows individuals to assimilate and interpet further political information (Neuman, 1981).

The three components of sophistication—salience, knowledge, and conceptualization—are correlated vectors rather than independent variables. Knowledge is the central component, mediating between the salience of politics and political conceptualization.

Testing the Three-Component Model

There are nine data sets, but since in the five National Election Studies the items are worded pretty much identically, the data sets are more properly viewed as five replications with independently derived measures to explore the correlational structure of the sophistication domain. There are 349 indicators of various aspects of sophistication, but because of the overlap in the National Election Studies, the number of unique indicators is 170—still a rich resource for exploring the dimensionality of the domain. The indicators are fairly well distributed across the studies, allowing five more or less complete analyses of dimensionality. The most notable gap in measurement is political conceptualization. Unfortunately, none of the early studies included enough transcribed open-ended materials to make possible a reliable coding of conceptualization. In order to facilitate comparison, the analyses are based not on the total number of raw variables available for each study but rather on the in-

Table A.2. Principal Component Analyses (Communalities)

Variables	Elmira	PAR	Civic Culture	BAS	NES 1956–60	NES 1964	NES 1968	NES 1972–76	NES 1980
Common variance (%)	42	45	41	35	47	43	46	41	45
Salience									
Interest	.73	.66	—	.58	.83	.80	.81	.70	.80
Attentiveness	.69	.81	.79	.53	.71	.60	.74	.76	.82
Involvement	.61	.81	.68	.57	.53	.52	.79	.76	.96
Knowledge									
Political figures	.65	—	—	.66	.68	.77	.52	.96	.64
Issues	.80	.45	.72	—	—	—	—	—	—
Government structure	—	.48	.75	.66	—	—	.67	.71	.82
Political groups	.61	—	—	.58	.70	.64	.68	.63	.61
Conceptualization									
Differentiation	—	—	—	.64	.78	.75	.77	.79	.80
Integration	—	—	—	.67	.57	.63	.61	.78	.77

Table A.3. Correlation Matrix of Sophistication Indicators

Variables	1.	2.	3.	4.	5.	6.	7.	8.	9.
Salience									
Interest	—								
Attentiveness	.54	—							
Involvement	.36	.37	—						
Knowledge									
Political figures	.32	.37	.26	—					
Issues	.48	.42	.42	.52	—				
Government structure	.33	.37	.31	.48		—			
Political groups	.34	.27	.23	.44	.52	.37	—		
Conceptualization									
Differentiation	.39	.32	.24	.34		.39	.36	—	
Integration	.32	.23	.29	.30		.34	.31	.61	—

Source: Averaged from nine core studies.

dices of grouped variables. Thus, except for missing information, the factor analysis for each study involves nine variables.

The principal components of the factor analyses reveal that the indicators uniformly reflect a single underlying dimension of political sophistication (Table A.2). Each of the nine groups of indicators appear to be equally correlated with this principal component. The average common variance of 43% further illustrates the centrality of the component.

The more difficult question, however, concerns the structure of the subcomponents. Traditionally, the expectation is that correlations of indicators within each subcomponent will be higher with each other than with indicators of other subcomponents (Campbell and Fiske, 1959). The data confirm this pattern quite strongly (Table A.3). The within component correlations are, on average, one-and-a-half times higher than those across components.

In order to make the test of the component structure as stringent as possible, to allow alternative dimensions to emerge and poorly correlated indicators to be extracted off and set aside, factor analyses were conducted for each data set, rotating the number of expected factors plus one miscellaneous factor. In only one case, the 1964 National Election Study, did one of the three expected factors fail to emerge. In that case, knowledge and salience were defined as a singe factor. The miscellaneous factors turned out to be just that, a hodge-podge of different items, with no consistent pattern. The overall structure is distinctly that of three moderately independent phenomena.

The model of the three components as correlated vectors with knowledge as the central vector is supported by the data (Figure A.3). In this case the measures of integration and differentiation are reported separately. In each of the original studies the index of political knowledge is more highly correlated with the salience and conceptualization measures than those measures are with each other.

At times it is evident that the components have differential effects, as in the case of voting and more active forms of political participation. The components also appear to have somewhat distinct roots in the process of political socialization. But for the most part, they function together as elements of the same underlying phenomenon, political sophistication.

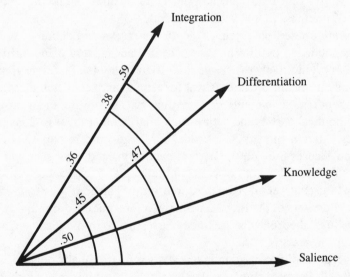

Figure A.3. Subcomponents of Sophistication. *Source:* NES 1956–1980, BAS 1972.

Appendix B

Political Conceptualization

POLITICAL CONCEPTUALIZATION, the third component of political sophistication, is the most challenging to measure and, in many ways, the most theoretically intriguing of the three components. There is a necessary trade-off between the potential richness of depth interviews, involving the study of natural language, and more systematic closed-ended survey techniques. For most applications, the rigor and generalizability of the latter are preferable. But the hour-long in-depth interviews of the Bay Area Survey offered a special opportunity to study the political vocabulary of the mass public in greater depth.

Research based on extended depth interviews and detailed study of the respondents' natural language, as in Lane's study of political ideology, is prohibitively expensive, and 10 to 20 hours of interviewing per respondent are simply impractical for larger samples. Content analysis of respondents' comments on why they might vote for or against the major political parties and their presidential candidates, as in Converse's studies, offer a more viable model for large-scale research, but this method focuses only on the current candidates and campaign and fails to tap a potential wealth of political thinking and experience on which citizens can comment if given the opportunity. The hour-long transcribed depth interviews of the Bay Area Survey offer a middle ground, a viable, general-use theoretically grounded assessment of political cognitive structure in mass publics.

Conceptual differentiation in this study is operationally defined as the number of discrete, concrete elements of political information that the individual utilizes in the course of an hour-long depth interview. It is an indication of a political orientation, the interpretation of issues and events in political terms. It is also akin to political knowledge, but actual knowledge is better measured by a focused exam. Conceptual differentiation is knowledge in use. Its focus is on patterns of cognitive discrimination, or the ability and inclination of the individual to identify and separate the various issues, political figures, units of government, interest groups, events, and social trends. Only spontaneous, volunteered references to a specific issue or political entity are coded in this measure. An undifferentiated view of politics is presumably self-perpetuating because, without a certain minimum awareness of basic political processes and institutions, political news from television and newspapers is a meaningless and confusing jumble of strange words, unfamiliar faces, and vaguely familiar reporters standing in front of buildings in Washington.

Conceptual integration in this study reflects the other common component of sophistication and ideology, the use of abstract concepts in the structuring of belief elements. It is complementary to the first dimension in the sense that an individual must differentiate elements of the political domain to some minimum degree in order to have elements to integrate. Conceptual integration is operationally defined as the spontaneous and persistent use of abstract concepts to structure beliefs and opinions in the course of the depth interviews on American politics.

The complementarity of the concepts of differentiation and integration is useful for understanding the process by which some citizens come to have a full and sophisticated understanding of the political process and others do not. Growth in political sophistication involves a spiraling back and forth between an increasingly differentiated understanding of the political process and a more frequent use of abstract anchoring concepts to put the discrete pieces of information in some kind of manageable and accessible order. This new structuring of the political domain in turn allows the individual to assimilate, retain, and interpret further political information. As an analogy, imagine what a game of chess looks like to the uninitiated—a confusng array of strangely shaped pieces which jump and zigzag around the chess board until someone miraculously wins. Gradually, however, through observation and an occasional question, the observer is able to differentiate the pieces and their characteristic movements and, ultimately, to understand how the individual movements fit together into unified strategies and styles of play. The notion of a spiraling process between differentiation and integration in a person's acquisition of knowledge in a particular sphere has antecedents in education, psychology, and political sociology (Whitehead, 1948; Piaget, 1952; Berelson et al., 1954; Bruner et al., 1956; Gardner and Schoen, 1962; Schroder et al., 1967; Zajonc, 1968). The original purpose of the depth interviews in the Bay Area Survey was to validate new scales of political alienation-allegiance and dissatisfaction with the quality of life. Data on a battery of over 500 closed-ended items had been collected in a previous interview and a self-administered questionnaire. The depth interview technique of measurement validation was explained to respondents, and then the interviewers reviewed a number of broad questions on politics, allowing the respondent to set the pace and tone of the interview.

Several characteristics of these depth interviews made them an attractive medium for exploring political conceptualization. Initial questions were diffuse and general, allowing the respondent to define the salient issues. There were extensive follow-up probes to clarify, for example, whether individuals dissatisfied with their economic situation blamed themselves, their boss, or the political or economic system in some way for their fate.

After respondents were given ample opportunity to mention issues and events, a number of the more prominent issues of the day were raised by interviewers, including economics, crime, race relations, the environment, and the quality of education. One section of the interview probed the respondent's thoughts on abstract principles of politics, including political freedom, equality, democracy, and the legitimacy of political institutions in America. Interviewers were instructed to probe and challenge each comment in an attempt to bring out whatever reasoning lay behind the opinions, exploring patterns of logic and the individual's ability to organize facts and ideas. Graduate students in the fields of political science, sociology, and law coded the transcripts for patterns of political conceptualization.

The first step in coding the transcripts for patterns of political conceptualization was to count and code each spontaneous reference to a political object or issue. The unit of analysis was the passage, a question and response and one or two follow-up probes concerning the same topic. Some passages were brief and involved yes, no, or I-don't-know responses. Other passages dealing with high salience issues ran much longer. The references had to be common, identifiable political issues, such as unemployment or high taxes, and political figures, groups, general constituencies, events, and units of government. Statements that were volunteered were distinguished from those where the respondent was simply repeating a term or issue raised by the interviewer.

The next step in coding was to establish that the volunteered reference was made in a political context. This was often a difficult process. Take, for example, a respondent raising the issue of crime. If the reference was to "increasing crime in the streets, the government ought to do something about it," or if it concerned lenient judges or an unworkable penal system, it was obviously political in nature. If instead the comment involved an incidence of crime in which the respondent or a relative was personally involved, it was not clear whether the individual actually saw the issues as a social or political problem requiring the coordinated response of the community. The key analytic concept was supraindividuality. Thus, if an event or object was seen by the respondent as being caused by or requiring the response of more than one individual, it was judged to be a political reference. This rule was not hard and fast but took into consideration the context of the particular interview. References to such clearly political entities as Congress or the Constitution and to such concepts as socialism or free speech were automatically coded as political references.

The final step in the coding process was to ensure that references to specific objects and issues were counted only once. The point of interest was the number of distinct political objects and issues mentioned by the respondent, not the frequency with which issues were raised.

Conceptual Differentiation

The key phenomenon underlying the measurement of conceptual differentiation is specificity, that is, the number of specific political issues, actors, and events that respondents bring up in the course of the interview. The fewest political references made in the course of the hour-long interview was one; the most was 94. The average was 27; the standard deviation was 17.

How can an hour-long interview on politics be conducted without a respondent's mentioning any more than one political object? The answer is straightforward enough. They talk about themselves. Their mode of thinking is overwhelmingly self-centered and concrete. Asked whether they are satisfied about the way things have been going in this country, they responded only about their job, family, friends, and other aspects of their own life. A probe about the respondents' economic situation elicits comments on the price of bread at the market last week or a decision to put off buying a new television. Questions concerning racial problems elicit a detailed description of the "black lady who was elected head of our PTA." There is no reference to social or political causes or consequences. Patterns of thought that translate all political and social questions into personal ones, however, are not the modal response. The political discourse of most people reflects some mixture of social and personal concerns. The salient political objects mentioned by the respondents can be grouped under three headings: political issues, actors, and events (Figure B.1).

The coin of the realm in the political speech of the mass citizenry is the political issue, a topical policy question or cluster of policy questions usually identified in the media and interpersonal discussion by a key term or phrase such as "busing," "taxes," "civil liberties," "crime in the streets," or "the energy crisis." Respondents do not actually have to take a position on each issue or mention a key term. They need only raise the issue in some way. The typical interview goes as follows:

Q: Could you tell me some of the things about America you're well satisfied with?

A: Well, I'm glad to see we're out of Vietnam, and it looks like latest announcements are that we might try to solve our trade deficit problems, I think also racial relation problems, I think maybe we're making progress there.

In this case, the original question is very broad, asking respondents to list issues that are salient to them.

Another type of question raises a general issue area, and respondents translate that key term into more specific issues that are meaningful to them:

Q: How about the environment? Are you satisfied with the quality of the environment around here?

A: I think we're moving in the right direction toward the environment to try to restrict automobile traffic into San Francisco, for example. It's interesting that many of the new office buildings are being built without any new parking facilities whatsoever. It's a step to encourage people to take mass transit and BART [Bay Area Rapid Transit].

If this respondent had answered simply that the environment was getting better or worse, the response would not have been credited as raising the question. The essence here is not having an opinion but being aware of currently discussed policy questions. In one case an elderly gentleman mentioned prohibition, which is not at the moment, in most circles, a hotly debated topic. This case, accordingly, was coded as a reference to a historical event. On the average, respondents volunteered references to about 10 issues in the course of the depth interview.

A distinction was made between specific and general issues. In order to qualify as a specific issue, the reference had to concern a particular bill or proposal recently considered by the voters or a legislative body, such as a school bond referendum, a proposed freeway, or a bill in

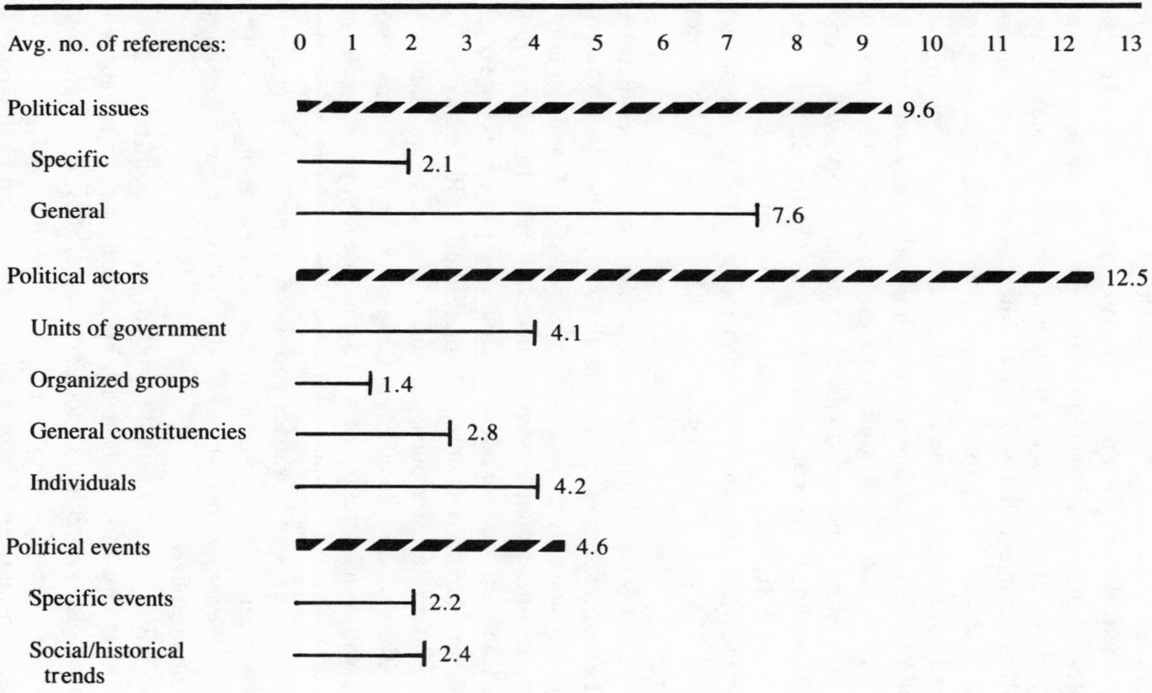

Avg. no. of references:	0	1	2	3	4	5	6	7	8	9	10	11	12	13

Political issues

Specific — 2.1

General — 7.6

Political actors — 12.5

Units of government — 4.1

Organized groups — 1.4

General constituencies — 2.8

Individuals — 4.2

Political events — 4.6

Specific events — 2.2

Social/historical trends — 2.4

Political issues — 9.6

Figure B.1. Political References in Depth Interviews. *Source:* BAS 1972.

Congress. Most references were to more general issues, at the rate of about four to one.

In the course of discussing issues and events, various political actors were mentioned, such as the President or a Congress person, an organized interest group, or a private citizen. References to units of government involved distinctions among the judicial, legislative, and executive branches of government, between the two houses of Congress, among federal, state, and local authorities, or among any of the various federal agencies and bureaus. For some individuals, the term *government* may refer to an undifferentiated bureaucratic monolith. They may have no notion of differentiated responsibility or of checks and balances. The bulk of the citizenry, however, do differentiate units and levels of government. Accordingly, the number of references to the State Department, the IRS, FBI, the Supreme Court, the mayor, the local zoning commission, and the like was used as an index of the extent of such differentiation. On the average, about four such references of distinction were made.

The notion of organized political groups refers to a political party or an interest group of some sort, such as the AMA, the Home Owners Association, the John Birch Society, or the NAACP. Almost all interviews involved some volunteered reference comparing the Democratic and Republican parties. Since references to the major parties were often linked together, they were counted as one reference. References to all other parties and interest groups were each counted as an additional reference. At times, individuals forgot the proper name of a group, got it confused with other groups, or asked the interviewer to recall the name. Thus, the American Independent party was referred to as "that other party . . . you know, Wallace and those people." As long as the referent was clear, it was included in the differentiation index. The average respondent mentioned between one and two organized political groups in the interview.

General Constituencies constitute another possible political referent. This includes groups of citizens, who, by reason of their racial, geographic, ideological, religious, or social characteristics, are singled out by respondents. The group can be a very broad one, such as poor or rich people, or a more specific one, such as people on fixed incomes, blacks, or Mexican Americans. There were about twice as many references to broad constituencies as to actual organized nongovernmental groups.

Political figures were also frequently mentioned. Archie Bunker's name was mentioned several times as typifying an approach to politics. Despite the fact that he is a fictional character, it was decided to include such references because of their prominence in popular culture. At times Archie Bunker may have been responsible for getting more individuals to think about political questions than the President and leaders of Congress combined. Most references were to prominent political figures, particularly the President or former presidents. With the exception of the governor of California, all individual political figures mentioned by more than 10 percent of the respondents had occupied the presidency. A little more than four references to various political figures were made in the average interview.

A somewhat smaller category was devoted to political events, such as Watergate or a recent presidential trip, and ongoing governmental programs, such as Medicare or the Work Incentive Program for welfare recipients. Also included were references to broader historical trends, such as increasing bureaucratization or a weakening of the role of religion in American life. There were about five of these references in the average interview.

Conceptual Integration

The measurement of conceptual integration included a different type of content analysis of the interview transcripts. In addition to scrutinizing passages and enumerating each reference to an abstract concept, coders rated the interview as a whole, functioning in this case as expert judges. They were asked to characterize the predominant pattern by which respondents organized, linked, contrasted, or put in context the various political issues, actors, and events mentioned in the interview. The typology used paralleled the levels of conceptualization measure, its generalizability beyond the election context to a broader evaluation of styles of political thought (Converse, 1964).

This proved to be a remarkably valid, robust, and viable approach to the measurement of conceptual integration. Only 2 percent of the interviews were judged unclassifiable, and an additional 8 percent were judged codable despite ambiguities. Coders assigned respondents to identical or adjacent categories 82 percent of the time. The definitions of each of the five levels were revised slightly to make them more general and appropriate to the evaluation of a full-length, ranging depth interview (Table B.1). The liberal-conservative continuum was frequently and characteristically used as a conceptual yardstick by respondents in

Table B.1. Conceptual Integration

Level of conceptualization	Original term and percentage, 1956	Revised definition	Total sample			Mean number of references			
			Percentage making at least one such reference	Average no. of references	Percentage of total sample classified in level	Central to abstract concept	Peripheral to abstract concept	Group interest	Free-floating issue
I	Ideologue, 2.5	Unambiguous use of abstract concepts to structure and link political actors, issues, events	61	1.5	13	3.9	12.5	9.7	22.9
II	Near-ideologue, 9	Peripheral or unclear use of abstract concepts	89	5.6	15	1.6	7.4	5.7	13.2
III	Group interest, 42	Structuring of political issues and objects based on group interest	98	5.5	34	1.1	4.5	6.0	11.1
IV	Nature of times, 24	Primarily free-floating reference to political issues, occasionally structured with incumbent's political performance	99	12.2	30	0.9	4.0	3.8	10.1
V	No issue content, 22.5	Residual category			8	0.7	1.0	2.3	4.9

the highest category, but its use was not a prerequisite for inclusion in that level.

Following are examples of the spontaneous and unambiguous use of political abstractions in the day-to-day political discourse of citizens whose active political participation was limited for the most part to voting and an occasional campaign contribution. These remarks were typically neither profound nor original, but they reflected the ability of the individual to put issues in a more abstract context:

Q: If you were trying to imagine an ideal system of government, how close do you think our present system of government comes to that ideal?
A: Well, I don't know of anything that is more satisfactory. I have some pretty reactionary ideas. I would go back to the idea that if anyone's going to vote on taxing property owners who would be paying they should be property owners who would be paying the taxes. That idea went out a couple of hundred years ago, but it's still a pretty good idea . . .
Q: Are there any other areas of life that we haven't talked about that you think are very important?
A: Yes, the medical. I think there should be more research done on it . . . Finding the why-nots of the human body is important to the future.
Q: Do you think that is the responsibility of government?
A: Yes, I think the government should have that responsibility—that is a big responsibility of the government. They should apportion more money into it.
Q: If they had to raise taxes to do these things, would you want it done?
A: Yeah, I would be in favor it it. That sounds like socialism, but that is the way it has to be. The type of socialism that is bad that I am talking about is the complete authoritative power of the President of the United States— not programs that have to be implemented for the welfare of the people.

In this example, the respondent's vocabulary was tied to the liberal-conservative continuum. In other examples of conceptual integration the emphasis was more historical, as in one case where the respondent contrasted America's role in Vietnam with that of England during the American Revolution. In another case the respondent anchored many remarks with references to abstract principles of freedom of speech and freedom of the press, including an extended explanation of why the right of reporters to protect their sources is essential to a healthy democracy.

The second level of conceptualization is interstitial, reflecting peripheral, vague, occasional, or restricted use of abstract concepts. This category is populated by two types of individuals—those who have a sophisticated grasp of most political abstractions and concepts but are not inclined to use them often, and those whose use of abstract concepts reflects limited understanding or some confusion. Several respondents, for example, restricted their use of the liberal-conservative dimension to spend-save issues; another respondent equated those terms exclusively with the politics of the young versus the old. Political thought characteristic of this second level is not necessarily unsophisticated, just contracted and less explicit than that of the first level. For example, individuals referred to democracy or the principle of freedom of speech in passing, without making it clear whether they had a full understanding of the historical and philosophical roots of those concepts, or they used the terms simply as symbolic phrases signifying American ideals of government.

The hour-long interviews generated substantially higher estimates of the use of abstract concepts and conceptual integration in the mass population than had earlier been found, or about five times for Level I and about 2½ times for Levels I and II. Part of this difference may be due to the more active political climate of the 1970s and the more extensive opportunity in the depth interviews for individuals to demonstrate their approach to political issues and current events. Nonetheless, those making significant use of abstract political concepts represent less than a third of the citizenry.

Although a substantial number of citizens do not make consistent use of the left-right continuum or similar abstractions to organize their assessment of American politics, they use two more concretely focused anchoring points for organizing political discourse. In one case, corresponding to Level III, citizens organize their response to politics on the basis of group interest. Passages in the depth interviews characteristic of this level defined liberalism and conservatism in group interest terms:

Q: In politics we often hear the terms *liberal* and *conservative*. What do those terms mean to you?
A: Well, it means that the Democrats are liberal and the Republicans are conservative. That's the way I look at it, and I find that it's just true.
Q: And what is there that makes the Democrats liberal and the Republicans conservative? What are their characteristics?
A: Well, the Democrats are for the people and the conservatives are for big business and the big financial interests in the country. And they are governed by those big financial interests. And you see, they believe that they should control the finances and the big business in the country. And then they should hand out the jobs to the people. That's been always the way. But the Democrats don't feel that way about it. That's why we have unions.

Equally often, group interests are more precisely focused in narrower and more straightforward self-interest terms. A retired army sergeant, for example, answered the questions on his satisfaction with American government, the quality of life in America, race relations, political leadership, and patriotism with 18 specific references to the interests of retired military personnel. This group-interest mode of cognitive organization characterized roughly a third of the sample.

Another alternative to a reliance on abstract concepts to organize political discourse is characteristic of Level IV. Some citizens organize their response to government by a seemingly straightforward mechanism of electoral reward and punishment based on the incumbent's ability to generate peace, prosperity, and a sense of administrative competence. Among these respondents, references to issues were seldom linked to abstract concepts or to each other. They were occasionally linked to social groups, but most often existed as free-floating political observations. To the extent that issues were structured, they were seen as being either successfully or unsuccessfully resolved by recent government action. Skeptical of abstract arguments of political philosophy on how the problems should be approached and who might differentially benefit, these respondents reflected the stereotype of "the man from Missouri," demanding to be shown the concrete result. One respondent came right to the point:

Q: Do you think there is anything you can do about the things you are dissatisfied with?

A: No, I don't. Just keep voting and trying to find the right candidates and just trying to do what I should do—like a decent moral life and do what I can in the community.

Q: In some way, can you have an effect?

A: A slight effect, yes. But it takes a while. If you vote somebody in, you are not sure what he can do. No man can promise anything, but I can certainly work to defeat him if I find somebody I prefer more. Or if he disappoints me, I can work very hard to defeat him next time. I always help in politics.

This group represents a little less than a third of the sample.

The fifth level includes those consistently apolitical respondents who made an occasional reference to a political issue or two but showed little evidence of any of the identified patterns of cognitive organization. Less than 10 percent of the sample are so categorized.

The levels of conceptualization can be seen as independent dimensions rather than as mutually exclusive, hierarchical categories. Much of the attractiveness of the hierarchical typology Converse developed was its parsimony and clearly ordered types of belief systems in mass publics. But because references to political abstractions, groups, and issues were measured independently, it is possible to test the cumulative nature of these phenomena and to explore the theory of three publics. The references to abstract concepts, to group interest, and to free-floating issues in each of the five levels of conceptualization reveal an interesting pattern.

A visual inspection of this pattern appears to confirm the three-publics theory in that two distinct cutting points set off Levels I and V from the middle mass. The small group classified in Level I relied heavily on abstract concepts to structure their comments (abstractions appeared three to four times as often as in the rest of the sample). Yet they made, on the average, 3.7 more references to group interest and twice the number of issue references as the rest of the sample. The small apolitical counterpart at the other end of the continuum reflected an equally unique behavioral pattern in its strong lack of interest in matters political or abstract.

Because of the prominence of abstract references at all but the lowest level of conceptual integration, a review was made of the use of abstractions and their occasional linkage to the overarching liberal-conservative continuum. The first step was to identify clusters of abstract concepts by enumerating natural terms and phrases that respondents used to denote them, forming a complete lexicon for the 137 depth interviews. Only 287 distinct political terms, phrases, or clichés were in fact counted. All of these references were spontaneous, volunteered by respondents rather than by interviewers, thereby reflecting the salience of these organizing concepts to the public rather than to the inquiring scientists. Six groups of prominent concepts were identified following McClosky's typology of political orientation (McClosky, 1975). The dominant group was the status quo versus change dimension (Table B.2). Since this part of the analysis was especially sensitive to the substantive focus of the depth interview and the groups themselves were ad hoc, these results are suggestive rather than definitive. But they hark back to the characterization of the American perspective as practical, centrist, and suspicious of utopian ideologies of radical reform (Tocqueville, 1840).

Although the American public does not routinely use the left-right spectrum to identify a richly articulated and overarching philosophy of governance, they do find occasional use for related terms to identify, and most often to condemn, noncentrist political perspectives. Americans, despite a mode of language which reflects a cynicism about the motives and abilities of politicians, bureaucrats, and government, are in general pleased with the functioning of their political system as a

Table B.2. Spontaneous Use of Abstract Concepts

Average no. of references per interview	Concepts	Definition	Typical terms
1.2	Status quo vs. change	Concepts basic to liberal-conservative continuum, focusing on patterns of political change	Revolution, militancy, reactionary, extremism
.6	Political structure and process	Abstractions focusing on due process, balance of power, and governmental organization	Two-party system, pressure group, pork-barrel politics, power structure
.5	Governmental responsiveness to public opinion	Abstractions focusing on democracy or its absence	Majority rule, dictatorship, town meeting, one-man one-vote
.4	Law and order versus individual rights	Constructs associated with liberalism-conservatism, focusing on tension between authority and individual freedom	Freedom of speech, inalienable rights, law and order, subversive activities
.2	Government intervention versus economic individualism	Concepts focusing on general principles of government involvement in economic life	Free enterprise, laissez-faire, socialist economics, capitalism
.2	Equality/ inequality	Concepts focusing on patterns of economic, political, and social inequality and ameliorative strategies	Social darwinism, affirmative action, quota system, civil rights
4.0	Miscellaneous	Concepts, terms, and phrases that either span dimensions above or denote other concepts	Justice, isolationism, pacifism, propaganda

whole. Even critical events, such as Watergate, seem not to have shaken this faith. For many citizens, especially in the middle mass, a collapsed form of the liberal-conservative continuum proves useful. Ignoring left versus right, they simply identify political actors and issues as more or as less distant from the status quo. A more philosophical conception of modern liberalism which emphasizes government intervention, redistributive strategies, and abstract conceptions of equality is notably less prominent.

Appendix C

The Data Sets

THE FINDINGS reported in this book are based on an analysis of nine American political attitude surveys. The Elmira; Participation, Awareness, and Responsibility; and Civic Culture studies represented pioneering work on voting behavior. The Bay Area Survey represents a mixture of depth interview and traditional survey techniques (Neuman, 1981). The National Election Study series (NES) for 1956–1960 provided the principal data for the early understanding of mass political sophistication (Campbell, et al., 1960; Converse, 1962, 1964). The National Election Studies for 1964, 1968, 1972–1976, and 1980 have been the principal basis for arguments on both sides of the political sophistication debate. To a great extent these nine core studies represent the raw data from which the established wisdom of American mass political behavior, such as it is, was developed. Further information on the variables used and the coding of the indices is available from the author.

The Elmira Study was a three-wave panel survey conducted in Elmira, New York, in 1948 (Berelson et al., 1954). It expanded on the earlier Erie County Study of opinion formation conducted in 1940 (Lazarsfeld et al., 1944). The study focused on national politics, chiefly attitude change in response to the ongoing presidential campaign. The principal investigators were sociologists, and they characteristically concentrated on how social class, religion, and participation in voluntary associations might influence attitudes and the vote.

The Participation, Awareness, and Responsibility Study (PAR), conducted by McClosky, dealt with the beliefs and opinions of American citizens and political elites. The 316 respondents represented a subsample of a larger study undertaken in the Minneapolis–St. Paul area. The 66 knowledge and awareness items were by far the largest and most varied pool of such items available to date. Unfortunately, they were not included in later studies, so it is impossible to compare them with national-level data. The questionnaire included some 519 survey items.

The focus was not on specific policy issues but on broader ideologically linked attitudes toward government, social class, society, and civic duty. The study included numerous social-psychological scales, tapping such phenomena as paranoia, dominance-submission, compulsiveness, and rigidity.

The Civic Culture Study, conducted in 1959 as part of a five-nation comparative study of political culture and behavior, represented one of the few full-scale national political surveys in which the thrust of measurement and item selection was developed independently of the NES series. The study emphasized issues of civic duty, political awareness, and participation but unfortunately did not deal in depth with issues of policy and ideology.

The Bay Area Survey (BAS) was conducted at the University of California, Berkeley, as part of an ongoing project on social indicators. The first wave of the study resulted in a sample of 963 respondents from the San Francisco-Oakland Bay Area and focused on political alienation, the status of women, and racial prejudice. This original sample was divided up for further intensive survey and depth interviewing. The data used here were drawn from a 143-case subsample used by the political alienation study group, selected in a way to maximize the number of highly allegiant and highly alienated respondents, so it is not strictly a random sample of the original respondent pool. Numerous checks, including reweighting the sample, established that the selection procedure did not appreciably affect the marginal or correlational patterns of the data. The first interviews were conducted in the respondents' homes in 1972. The hour-long, open-ended depth interviews and 480-item mail-back questionnaires were in the field in 1973.

The NES series were conducted biannually at the University of Michigan (Campbell, et al., 1954, 1960, 1966). These broad, almost encyclopedic surveys were concerned with the mediating role of party identification in the overall "funnel of causality" between demography and life situations and the vote. The particular item wording may have had an unduly influential effect on one collective perception of American politics. As an election year approaches, there are conflicting pressures, on the one hand, to change questions and broaden the scope of the inquiry and, on the other, to continue the same content and item wordings for the purpose of trend analysis.

The NES multiyear panels were weighted to correct for respondent attrition. Overall, the sampling did not receive a great deal of attention because the prime focus was on the analysis of structural relationships rather than the estimation of national parameters on specific variables such as voting rates. For the same reason, the local and national studies were used more or less interchangeably without regard for potential geographical differences.

The Elmira and National Election studies were conducted in the context of a national presidential election. They might be expected to have had high levels of politicization and awareness as a result of the ongoing campaigns. However, no distinct causal patterns emerged to suggest that the election context represented a special difficulty in analysis.

Although few of the analyses paid much attention to knowledge and salience variables, all of the questionnaires included numerous measures within the sophistication domain. Only political conceptualization, which requires a coding of open-ended responses, was not tapped in each of the studies. Most of the studies included a broad range of political attitude items, and all included the usual complement of demographic variables. In general, the measurement of psychological traits and variables associated with patterns of socialization was less adequate. Except for the National Election Studies, the question wordings and approaches to measurement varied from study to study, giving further evidence for the robustness of the findings. Furthermore, almost all of the studies generated the same distinct causal patterns.

References

Aberbach, Joel, and Jack Walker. 1970. "Political Trust and Racial Ideology," *American Political Science Review* 64 (Dec.): 1199–1219.

Abramson, Jeffrey, Christopher Arterton, and Gary Orren. Forthcoming. "The New Communications Technology, Public Policy, and Democratic Values." Institute of Politics, John F. Kennedy School of Government, Harvard University, Cambridge, Report to Markle Foundation.

Abramson, Paul R. 1976. "Generational Change and the Decline of Party Identification in America," *American Political Science Review* 70:469–478.

Achen, Christopher. 1975. "Mass Political Attitudes and the Survey Response," *American Political Science Review* 69:1218–1231.

Adams, J. B., J. J. Mullen, and H. M. Wilson. 1969. "Diffusion of a 'Minor' Foreign Affairs News Event," *Journalism Quarterly* 46:545-551.

Adorno, T. W., Else Frenkel-Brunswik, Daniel J. Levinson, and R. Nevitt Sanford. 1950. *The Authoritarian Personality*. New York: Harper and Row.

Agger, Robert E., Marshall N. Goldstein, and Stanley A. Pearl. 1961. "Political Cynicism: Measurement and Meaning," *Journal of Politics* 23 (Aug.): 477–506.

Almond, Gabriel, and Sidney Verba. 1965. *Civic Culture*. Boston: Little, Brown.

Andersen, Kristi. 1985. "Causal Schemas and Political Thinking." Paper for Midwest Political Science Association, Chicago, Illinois.

Arterton, Christopher, Edward H. Lazarus, John Griffen, and Monica C. Andres. 1984. "Telecommunication Technologies and Political Participation." Roosevelt Center, Washington, D.C. Report to Markle Foundation.

Bagdikian, Ben H. 1971. *The Information Machines*. New York: Harper and Row.

Balch, George I. 1971. "Multiple Indicators in Survey Research: The Concept 'Sense of Political Efficacy.' " Paper for American Political Science Association, Chicago.

Barber, James David. 1973. *Citizen Politics,* 2nd ed. Chicago: Markham Publishing.

Barnouw, Erik. 1970. *The Image Empire*. New York: Oxford University Press.

—— 1975. *The Tube of Plenty*. New York: Oxford University Press.

—— 1978. *The Sponsor*. New York: Oxford University Press.

Bechtel, Robert B., Clark Achenpohl, and Roger Akers. 1972. "Correlates Between Observed Behavior and Questionnaire Responses on Television Viewing," in Eli A. Rubinstein et al., ed., *Television and Social Behavior,* IV, 274–344. Washington, DC: U.S. Department of Health, Education, and Welfare.

Becker, L. B., and J. W. Fruit. 1980. "The Growth of TV Dependence: Tracing the Origins of the Political Malaise." Paper for International Communication Association, Acapulco, Mexico.

Becker, L. B., I. A. Sobowale, and W. E. Casey. 1979. "Newspaper and Television Dependencies: Their Effects on Evaluation of Public Officials," *Journal of Broadcasting* 23:465–475.

Becker, L. B., and D. C. Whitney. 1980. "Effects of Media Dependencies: Audience Assessment of Government," *Communication Research* 7:95–120.

Bell, Daniel. 1962. *The End of Ideology.* New York: Free Press.

—— ed. 1963. *The Radical Right.* Garden City: Doubleday.

Bem, Daryl J. 1965. "An Experimental Analysis of Self-Persuasion," *Journal of Experimental Social Psychology* 1:199–218.

Bennett, W. Lance. 1975. *The Political Mind and the Political Environment.* Lexington: Lexington Books.

Berelson, Bernard. 1949. "What 'Missing the Newspaper' Means," in Paul Lazarsfeld and Frank Stanton, ed., *Communication Research, 1948–49.* New York: Harper and Row.

Berelson, Bernard, Paul Lazarsfeld, and William McPhee. 1954. *Voting: A Study of Opinion Formation in a Presidential Campaign.* Chicago: University of Chicago Press.

Bishop, George F., R. W. Oldendick, A. J. Tuchfarber, and S. E. Bennett. 1980. "Pseudo-Opinions on Public Affairs," *Public Opinion Quarterly* 44:198–209.

Bishop, George F., Alfred J. Tuchfarber, and Robert W. Oldendick. 1978. "Change in the Structure of American Political Attitudes: The Nagging Question of Question Wording," *American Journal of Political Science* 22:250–269.

Blalock, Hubert. 1982. *Conceptualization and Measurement of the Social Sciences.* Beverly Hills: Sage.

Blumler, Jay G., and Denis McQuail. 1969. *Television in Politics.* Chicago: University of Chicago Press.

Bogart, Leo. 1967. "No Opinion, Don't Know, and Maybe No Answer," *Public Opinion Quarterly,* Fall, pp. 331–345.

—— 1972. *Silent Politics: Polls and the Awareness of Public Opinion.* New York: Wiley.

—— 1977. *How the Public Gets Its News.* New York: Newspaper Advertising Bureau.

Boorstin, Daniel J. 1961. *The Image: A Guide to Pseudo Events in America.* New York: Harper and Row.

Boyd, Richard. 1972. "Popular Control of Public Policy: A Normal Vote Analysis of the 1968 Election," *American Political Science Review* 66 June: 429–449.

Brady, Henry E. 1985. "Chances, Utilities, and Voting in Presidential Primaries." Occasional Paper No. 85–5, Center for American Political Studies, Harvard University, Cambridge, Massachusetts.

Brody, Richard A., Benjamin I. Page. 1972. "Comment: The Assessment of Policy Voting," *American Political Science Review* 66.2 (June):450–458.

Brown, Roger. 1965. *Social Psychology*. New York: Free Press.

Brown, Steven R. 1970. "Consistency and the Persistence of Ideology: Some Experimental Results," *Public Opinion Quarterly* 34 (Spring): 60–68.

Bruner, Jerome, Jacqueline J. Goodnow, and George A. Austin. 1956. *A Study of Thinking*. New York: Wiley.

Burdick, Eugene. 1959. "Political Theory and the Voting Studies," in Eugene Burdick and Arthur J. Brodbeck, ed., *American Voting Behavior,* pp. 136–149. New York: Free Press.

Burnham, Walter Dean. 1965. "The Changing Shapes of the American Political Universe," *American Political Science Review* 59 (March): 7–28.

—— 1970. *Critical Elections and the Mainsprings of American Politics*. New York: Norton.

Campbell, Angus, Philip E. Converse, Warren E. Miller, and Donald E. Stokes. 1960. *The American Voter*. New York: Wiley.

—— 1966. *Elections and the Political Order*. New York: Wiley.

Campbell, Angus, Gerald Gurin, and Warren E. Miller. 1954. *The Voter Decides*. New York: Row, Peterson.

Campbell, Donald T., and Donald W. Fiske. 1959. "Convergent and Discriminant Validation by the Multitrait-Multimethod Matrix," *Psychological Bulletin,* March, pp. 81–105.

Carey, John. 1976. "How Media Shape Campaigns," *Journal of Communication* 26.2 (Spring): 50–57.

Carmines, Edward G., and James A. Stimson. 1980. "The Two Faces of Issue Voting," *American Political Science Review* 74:78–91.

Chaffee, Steven H., and Yuko Miyo. 1983. "Selective Exposure and the Reinforcement Hypothesis: An Intergenerational Panel Study of the 1980 Presidential Campaign," *Communication Research* 10.1:3–36.

Christie, Richard, and Marie Jahoda, ed. 1954. *Studies in the Scope and Method of the Authoritarian Personality*. New York: Free Press.

Cicourel, Aaron V. 1964. *Method and Measurement in Sociology*. London: Collier-Macmillan.

Citrin, Jack. 1974. "Comment: The Political Relevance of Trust in Government," *American Political Science Review* 68 (Sept.): 973–988.

Citrin, Jack, Herbert McClosky, Merrill Shanks, and Paul M. Sniderman. 1975. "Personal and Political Sources of Alienation," *British Journal of Political Science* 5:1–31.

Clarke, Peter, and Eric Fredin. 1978. "Newspapers, Television, and Political Reasoning," *Public Opinion Quarterly* 42:143–160.

Compaine, Benjamin M., ed. 1982. *Anatomy of the Communications Industry: Who Owns the Media?* White Plains: Knowledge Industries Press.

Compton Advertising. 1975. *National Survey on the American Economic System*. New York: Advertising Council.

Comstock, George, Steven Chaffee, Natan Katzman, Maxwell McCombs, and Donald Roberts. 1978. *Television and Human Behavior*. New York: Columbia University Press.

Conover, Pamela Johnston, and Stanley Feldman. 1984a. "How People Organize the Political World: A Schematic Model," *American Journal of Political Science* 28 (Feb.): 95–126.

―――― 1984b. "Where Do They Stand? Inference Processes and Political Perception." Paper for Annual Meeting of American Political Science Association, Washington, D.C.

Converse, Philip. 1962. "Information Flow and the Stability of Partisan Attitudes," *Public Opinion Quarterly* 26.4 (Winter): 578–599.

―――― 1964. "The Nature of Belief Systems in Mass Publics," in D. Apter, ed., *Ideology and Discontent*, pp. 206–261. New York: Free Press.

―――― 1966. "The Concept of a Normal Vote," in A. Campbell et al., ed., *Elections and the Political Order*, pp. 9–39. New York: Wiley.

―――― 1970. "Attitudes and Non-Attitudes: The Continuation of a Dialogue," in Edward Tufte, ed., *The Quantitative Analysis of Social Problems*, pp. 168–189. Reading: Addison-Wesley.

―――― 1975. "Public Opinion and Voting Behavior," in F. Greenstein and N. Polsby, ed., *Handbook of Political Science*, IV, 75–169. Reading: Addison-Wesley.

―――― 1976. *The Dynamics of Party Support: Cohort-Analyzing Party Identification.* Beverly Hills: Sage.

―――― 1979. "Rejoinder to Abramson," *American Journal of Politcal Science* 23:97–100.

Converse, Philip, and Gregory B. Markus. 1979. "Plus ça change . . . The New CPS Election Study Panel," *American Political Science Review* 73: 32–49.

Converse, Philip, W. E. Miller, J. G. Rusk, and A. C. Wolfe. 1969. "Continuity and Change in American Politics: Parties and Issues in the 1968 Election," *American Political Science Review* 63:1083–1105.

Coveyou, Michael R., and James Piereson. 1977. "Ideological Perceptions and Political Judgment: Some Problems of Concept and Measurement," *Political Methodology* 4:77–102.

Crouse, Timothy. 1973. *The Boys on the Bus.* New York: Ballantine.

Dahl, Robert. 1961. *Who Governs? Democracy and Power in an American City.* New Haven: Yale University Press.

―――― 1963. *Modern Political Analysis.* Englewood Cliffs: Prentice-Hall.

Davis, James. 1975. "Communism, Conformity, Cohorts, and Categories: American Tolerance in 1954 and 1972–73," *American Journal of Sociology* 81:491–513.

Dizard, Wilson P., Jr. 1985. *The Coming Information Age: An Overview of Technology, Economics, and Politics,* 2nd ed. New York: Longman.

Doob, A., and G. E. MacDonald. 1979. "Television Viewing and Fear of Victimization: Is the Relationship Causal?" *Journal of Personality and Social Psychology* 37.2:170–179.

Downs, Anthony. 1957. *An Economic Theory of Democracy.* New York: Harper and Row.

Dubin, Robert, and R. Alan Hedley. 1969. *The Medium May Be Related to the Message.* Eugene: Center for Advanced Study of Educational Administration.

Edelman, Murray. 1964. *Symbolic Uses of Politics.* Urbana: University of Illinois Press.

Erbring, L., E. M. Goldenburg, and A. H. Miller. 1980. "Front Page News and Real World Cues: A New Look at Agenda-Setting," *American Journal of Political Science* 24:16–49.

Erikson, Robert S., Norman R. Luttbeg, and Kent L. Tedin. 1980. *American Public Opinion: Its Origins, Content, and Impact,* 2nd ed. New York: Wiley.

Erskine, H. G. 1963. "The Polls: Textbook Knowledge," *Public Opinion Quarterly* 27.1:133–141.

Eysenck, H. J. 1954. *The Psychology of Politics.* London: Routledge and Kegan Paul.

Festinger, Leon. 1957. *A Theory of Cognitive Dissonance.* Evanston: Row-Peterson.

Fields, J. M., and Howard Schuman. 1976. "Public Beliefs about the Beliefs of the Public," *Public Opinion Quarterly* 40.4:427–448.

Fiorina, Morris P. 1981. *Retrospective Voting in American National Elections.* New Haven: Yale University Press.

Flanigan, William H. 1972. *Political Behavior of the American Electorate,* 2nd ed. Boston: Allyn and Bacon.

Free, Lloyd A., and Hadley Cantril. 1968. *The Political Beliefs of Americans: A Study of Public Opinion.* New York: Simon and Schuster.

Gamson, William. 1968. *Power and Discontent.* Homewood: Dorsey Press.

Gans, Herbert. 1979. *Deciding What's News.* New York: Pantheon.

Gardner, Riley W., and Robert A. Schoen. 1962. "Differentiation and Abstraction in Concept Formation," *Psychological Monographs: General and Applied* 76:1–21.

Gaziano, Cecilie. 1983. "The Knowledge Gap: An Analytic Review of Media Effects," *Communication Research* 10.4 (Oct.): 447–486.

Gerbner, George, and Larry Gross. 1976a. "Living with Television: The Violence Profile," *Journal of Communication* 26.2:173–199.

―――― 1976b. "The Scary World of TV's Heavy Viewer," *Psychology Today* 9 (Apr.): 41–45.

Gerbner, George, Larry Gross, M. F. Eleey, M. Jackson-Beeck, S. Jeffries-Fox, and N. Signorielli. 1977. "TV Violence Profile No. 8: The Highlights," *Journal of Communication* 27.2:171–180.

Gerbner, George, Larry Gross, M. Jackson-Beeck, S. Jeffries-Fox, and N. Signorielli. 1978. "Cultural Indicators: Violence Profile No. 9," *Journal of Communication* 28.3:176–206.

Gerbner, George, Larry Gross, Nancy Signorielli, Michael Morgan, and M. Jackson-Beeck. 1979. "The Demonstration of Power: Violence Profile No. 10," *Journal of Communication* 29.3:177–196.

Gerbner, George, Larry Gross, Michael Morgan, and Nancy Signorielli. 1980. "The 'Mainstreaming' of America: Violence Profile No. 11," *Journal of Communication* 30.3:10–29.

―――― 1981. "A Curious Journey into the Scary World of Paul Hirsch," *Communication Research* 8.1 (Jan.): 39–72.

Gill, S. 1947. "How Do You Stand on Sin?" *Tide,* Mar. 14, p. 72.

Glenn, Norval D. 1972. "The Distribution of Political Knowledge in the United States," in Nimmo and Bonjean, ed., *Political Attitudes and Public Opinion,* pp. 273–283. New York: David McKay.

Gollin, Albert E., and Nicolas Bloom. 1985. "Newspapers and American News Habits," Newspaper Advertising Bureau, New York.

Graber, Doris. 1980. *Mass Media and American Politics.* Washington, DC: Congressional Quarterly Press.

——— 1984. *Processing the News: How People Tame the Information Tide.* New York: Longman.

Greenstein, Fred I. 1967. "The Impact of Personality on Politics: An Attempt to Clear Away Underbrush," *American Political Science Review* 61:629–641.

Hamilton, Alexander, James Madison, and John Jay. [1787–1788] 1961. *The Federalist Papers.* New York: New American Library.

Hamilton, Richard. 1972. *Class and Politics in the United States.* New York: John Wiley.

Hemple, Carl. 1952. "Fundamentals of Concept Formation in Empirical Science," *International Encyclopedia of United Science* 2:7.

Himmelstrand, Ulf. 1960. *Social Pressures, Attitudes, and Democratic Processes.* Stockholm: Almquist and Wiksell.

Hirsch, Paul. 1980. "The 'Scary World' of the Nonviewer and Other Anomalies: A Reanalysis of Gerbner et al.'s Findings on Cultivation Analysis, Part 1," *Communication Research* 7.4:403–456.

Hofstetter, C. Richard. 1975. "Television and Civic Education." Report to American Enterprise Institute, Washington, DC.

——— 1976. *Bias in the News.* Columbus: Ohio State University Press.

Hovland, Carl I. 1959. "Reconciling Conflicting Results Derived from Experimental and Survey Studies of Attitude Change," *American Psychologist* 14:8–17.

Hughes, M. 1980. "The Fruits of Cultivation Analysis: A Reexamination of Some Effects of Television Watching," *Public Opinion Quarterly* 44.3:287–302.

Hyman, Herbert H., and Paul B. Sheatsley. 1947. "Some Reasons Why Information Campaigns Fail," *Public Opinion Quarterly* 11.3 (Fall): 412–423.

——— 1954. "The Current Status of American Public Opinion," in D. Katz, D. Cartwright, S. Eldersveld, and A. M. Lee, ed., *Public Opinion and Propaganda,* pp. 34–48. New York: Holt, Rinehart, and Winston.

Inkeles, Alex. 1969. "Participant Citizenship in Six Developing Nations," *American Political Science Review* 63:1120–1144.

Judd, Charles M., and Michael M. Milburn. 1980. "The Structure of Attitude Systems in the General Public," *American Sociological Review* 45:627–643.

Kagay, Michael R., and Greg A. Caldeira. 1975. "I Like the Look of His Face." Paper for American Political Science Association, San Francisco.

Kaplan, Abraham. 1964. *The Conduct of Inquiry*. San Francisco: Chandler.

Katz, Elihu, and Paul Lazarsfeld. 1955. *Personal Influence*. New York: Free Press.

Kessel, John J. 1972. "Comment: The Issues in Issue Voting," *American Political Science Review* 66.2 (June): 459–465.

Key, V. O., Jr. 1949. *Southern Politics in State and Nation*. New York: Alfred A. Knopf.

———— 1961. *Public Opinion and American Democracy*. New York: Alfred A. Knopf.

Kinder, Donald R., and David O. Sears. 1985. "Public Opinion and Political Action," in Gardner Lindzey and Elliot Aronson, ed., *The Handbook of Social Psychology*, 3rd ed., II, 659–741. New York: Random House.

Kirscht, J. P., and R. C. Dillehay. 1967. *Dimensions of Authoritarianism*. Lexington: University of Kentucky Press.

Klapper, Joseph T. 1960. *The Effects of Mass Communication*. New York: Free Press.

Klingemann, Hans D. 1973. "Dimensions of Political Belief Systems." Paper for European Consortium for Political Research Workshop on Political Behavior, Mannheim, Germany.

Kohlberg, Lawrence. 1964. "Development of Moral Character and Moral Ideology," in Martin L. Hoffman and L. W. Hoffman, ed., *Child Development Research*, I, 383–431. New York: Russell Sage.

Kornhauser, William. 1959. *The Politics of Mass Society*. New York: Free Press.

Kraus, Sidney, and Dennis Davis. *The Effects of Mass Communication on Political Behavior*. University Park: Pennsylvania State University Press.

Kuhn, Thomas. [1962] 1970. *The Structure of Scientific Revolutions*. Chicago: University of Chicago Press.

Lane, Robert E. 1959. *Political Life*. New York: Free Press.

———— 1962. *Political Ideology*. New York: Free Press.

———— 1973. "Patterns of Political Belief," in Jeanne Knutson, ed., *Handbook of Political Psychology*, pp. 83–116. San Francisco: Jossey-Bass.

Lane, Robert E., and David O. Sears. 1964. *Public Opinion*. Englewood Cliffs: Prentice-Hall.

Lang, Kurt, and Gladys Lang. 1968. *Politics and Television*. Chicago: Quadrangle Books.

Lasswell, Harold. 1930. *Psychopathology and Politics*. Chicago: University of Chicago Press.

Lau, Richard R., Thad A. Brown, and David O. Sears. 1978. "Self-Interest and Civilians' Attitudes Toward the War in Vietnam," *Public Opinion Quarterly* 42:464–483.

Lazarsfeld, Paul F., Bernard Berelson, and Hazel Gaudet. 1944. *The People's Choice: How the Voter Makes Up His Mind in a Presidential Campaign*. New York: Columbia University Press.

Lemieux, Peter. 1983. "The Multi-channel Media Environment," Report of Future of the Mass Audience Project, Massachusetts Institute of Technology.

Lerner, Daniel. 1958. *The Passing of Traditional Society*. New York: Free Press.

Levin, Murray B. 1960. *The Alienated Voter*. New York: Holt, Rinehart and Winston.

Lippmann, Walter. [1922] 1965. *Public Opinion*. New York: Free Press.

Lipset, Seymour Martin. 1960. *Political Man*. New York: Doubleday.

Lipset, Seymour Martin, and Earl Raab. 1970. *The Politics of Unreason*. New York: Harper and Row.

Lipset, Seymour Martin, and Stein Rokkan. 1967. "Cleavage Structures, Party Systems, and Voter Alignments: An Introduction," in Seymour Martin Lipset and Stein Rokkan, ed., *Party Systems and Voter Alignments*, pp. 1–64. New York: Free Press.

Lipsitz, Lewis. 1965. "Working-Class Authoritarianism: A Reevaluation," *American Sociological Review* 30:103–109.

Luttbeg, Norman. 1968. "The Structure of Beliefs among Leaders and the Public," *Public Opinion Quarterly* Fall, pp. 398–409.

Manheim, Jarol B. 1976. "Can Democracy Survive Television?" *Journal of Communication* 26. (Spring): 84–90.

Marcus, George E., David Tabb, and John L. Sullivan. 1974. "The Application of Individual Differences Scaling to the Measurement of Political Ideologies," *American Journal of Political Science* 18 (May): 405–420.

Marcuse, Herbert. 1964. *One-Dimensional Man*. Boston: Beacon Press.

Margolis, M. 1977. "From Confusion to Confusion: Issues and the American Voter, 1956–72," *American Political Science Review* 71:31–43.

Marx, Karl. [1852] 1963. *The 18th Brumaire of Louis Bonaparte*. New York: International Publishers.

McClosky, Herbert. 1958. "Conservatism and Personality," *American Political Science Review* 52:27–45.

—— 1964. "Consensus and Ideology in American Politics," *American Political Science Review* 58 (June): 361–382.

—— 1975. Personal correspondence.

—— 1967. "Survey Research in Political Science," in C. Y. Glock, ed., *Survey Research in the Social Sciences*. New York: Russell Sage.

McClosky, Herbert, and Alida Brill. 1983. *Dimensions of Tolerance: What Americans Believe about Civil Liberties*. New York: Russell Sage.

McClosky, Herbert, Paul Hoffman, and Rosemary O'Hara. 1960. "Issue Conflict and Consensus among Party Leaders and Followers," *American Political Science Review* June, pp. 406–427.

McCombs, Maxwell E., and D. L. Shaw. 1972. "The Agenda-setting Function of the Media," *Public Opinion Quarterly* 36:176–187.

McDonald, Daniel G. 1983. "Investigating Assumptions of Media Dependency Research," *Communication Research* 10.4 (Oct): 509–528.

McGuire, William J. 1985. "Attitudes and Attitude Change," in Gardner Lindzey and Elliot Aronson, ed., *The Handbook of Social Psychology*, 3rd ed. II, 233–346. New York: Random House.

McQuail, Denis. 1969. *Towards a Sociology of Mass Communication*. London: Collier-Macmillan.

Meadow, Robert G. 1973. "Cross-Media Comparison of Coverage of the 1972 Presidential Campaign," *Journalism Quarterly* 50:482–488.

—— 1985. *New Communication Technologies in Politics.* Washington: The Washington Program of the Annenberg School of Communication.

Mendelsohn, Harold A., and Irving Crespi. 1970. *Polls, Television, and the New Politics.* San Francisco: Chandler.

Merrill, J. C., and R. L. Lowenstein. 1971. *Media, Messages, and Men.* New York: David McKay.

Mickiewicz, Ellen Propper. 1981. *Media and the Russian Public.* New York: Praeger.

Milbrath, Lester. 1965. *Political Participation.* Chicago: Rand McNally.

Miller, Arthur. 1985. "Information Processing and Political Candidates." Paper for Midwest Political Science Association, Chicago.

—— 1983. "Is Confidence Rebounding?" *Public Opinion Quarterly* 6.3 (June/July): 16–20.

Miller, Arthur, E. Goldenberg, and L. Erbring. 1979. "Type-set Politics: Impact of Newspapers on Public Confidence," *American Political Science Review* 73:67–84.

Miller, Arthur, and Warren E. Miller. 1976. "Ideology in the 1972 Election: Myth or Reality—A Rejoinder," *American Political Science Review* 70:832–849.

Miller, Arthur, Warren E. Miller, Alden Raine, Thad Brown. 1976. "A Majority Party in Disarray," *American Political Science Review* 70:753–778.

Miller, George A. 1956. "The Magical Number Seven, Plus or Minus Two: Some Limits on Our Capacity for Processing Information," *Psychology Review* 63:81–97.

Miller, M. Mark, and Stephen D. Reese. 1980. "Media Dependency as Interactions Effects of Exposure and Reliance on Political Activity and Efficacy," *Communications Research* 9.2 (April): 227–248.

Miller. S. M., and Frank Riessman. 1961. "Working-Class Authoritarianism," *British Journal of Sociology* 12:263–276.

Miller, Warren E., and Teresa E. Levitin. 1976. *Leadership and Change.* Cambridge: Winthrop.

Miller, Warren E., et al. 1975. *The CPS 1972 American National Election Study.* Ann Arbor: Inter-University Consortium for Political Research.

Minow, Newton N., J. B. Martin, and L. M. Mitchell. 1973. *Presidential Television.* New York: Basic Books.

Miyo, Yuko. 1983. "Knowledge-Gap Hypothesis and Media Dependency: Is Television a Knowledge Leveler?" Paper for International Communication Association, Dallas, Texas.

Nagel, Ernest. 1961. *The Structure of Science: Problems in the Logic of Scientific Explanation.* New York: Harcourt, Brace, and World.

Naples, Michael J. 1979. *Effective Frequency: The Relationship Between Frequency and Advertising Effectiveness.* New York: Association of National Advertisers.

Neuman, W. Russell. 1976. "Patterns of Recall among Television News Viewers," *Public Opinion Quarterly* 40.1:115–123.

—— 1977. "The Visual Impact of Presidential Television." Photocopy, Yale University.

—— 1981. "Differentiation and Integration: Two Dimensions of Political Thinking," *American Journal of Sociology,* 86:1236–1268.

—— 1982. "Communications and Cultural Diversity." Paper for American Sociological Association, San Francisco.

—— 1984. "The Inverse Law." Photocopy, Massachusetts Institute of Technology, Cambridge.

—— Forthcoming. "Parallel Content Analysis: Old Paradigms and New Proposals," in George Comstock, ed., *Public Communication and Behavior.* New York: Academic Press.

Neuman, W. Russell, and Ann C. Fryling. 1985. "Patterns of Political Cognition: An Exploration of the Public Mind," in Sidney Kraus and Richard Perloff, ed., *Mass Media and Political Thought.* Beverly Hills: Sage.

Neustadt, Richard. 1982. *The Birth of Electronic Publishing.* White Plains: Knowledge Industry Publications.

Newcomb, Theodore M. 1943. *Personality and Social Change.* New York: Dryden Press.

Newcomb, Theodore M., K. E. Koenig, R. Flacks, and D. P. Warwick. 1967. *Persistence and Change: Bennington College and Its Students after 25 Years.* New York: Wiley.

Nie, Norman H., and Kristi Andersen. 1974. "Mass Belief Systems Revisited: Political Change and Attitude Structure," *Journal of Politics* 8:545–591.

Nie, Norman H., and James N. Rabjohn. 1979. "Revisiting Mass Belief Systems Revisited: Or, Why Doing Research Is Like Watching a Tennis Match," *American Journal of Political Science* 23 (Feb.): 139–175.

Nie, Norman H., Sidney Verba, and John R. Petrocik. 1976. *The Changing American Voter.* Cambridge: Harvard University Press (rev. ed., 1979).

—— 1981. "Reply," *American Political Science Review* 75.1:149–152.

Niemi, Richard G., and Herbert F. Weisberg. 1984. *Controversies in American Voting Behavior.* San Francisco: W. H. Freeman.

Noelle-Neumann, Elisabeth. 1974. "The Spiral of Silence: A Theory of Public Opinion," *Journal of Communication* 24:43–51.

—— 1984. *The Spiral of Silence.* Chicago: University of Chicago Press.

Nunn, C. Z., H. J. Crockett, and J. A. Williams, Jr. 1978, *Tolerance of Nonconformity.* San Francisco: Jossey-Bass.

O'Gorman, H., and S. L. Garry. 1976. "Pluralistic Ignorance—A Replication and Extension," *Public Opinion Quarterly* 40.4:449–458.

O'Keefe, G. J. 1980. "Political Malaise and Reliance on Media," *Journalism Quarterly* 57:122–128.

O'Keefe, G. J., and H. Mendelsohn. 1978. "Nonvoting: The Media's Role," in C. Winnick, ed., *Deviance and the Mass Media.* Beverly Hills: Sage.

Olson, Marvin. 1965. *The Logic of Collective Action: Public Goods and the Theory of Groups.* Cambridge: Harvard University Press.

Owen, Bruce, Jack H. Beebee, and Willard G. Manning, Jr. 1975. *Television Economics.* Lexington: Lexington Books.

Padioleau, Jean. 1972. "Survey Research and the Study of Change." Ph.D. dissertation, University of Paris.

Page, Benjamin. 1978. *Choices and Echoes in Presidential Elections*. Chicago: University of Chicago Press.

Page, Benjamin, and R. A. Brody. 1972. "Policy Voting and the Electoral Process: The Vietnam War Issues," *American Political Science Review* 66:979–995.

Paletz, David L., and Robert M. Entman. 1981. *Media, Power, Politics*. New York: Free Press.

Patterson, Thomas. 1980. *The Mass Media Election: How Americans Choose Their President*. New York: Praeger.

Patterson, Thomas, and Robert D. McClure. 1976. *The Unseeing Eye: The Myth of Television Power in National Elections*. New York: Putnam.

Petrocik, John R. 1978. "Comment: Reconsidering the Reconsiderations of the 1964 Change in Attitude Consistency," *Political Methodology* 5:361–368.

——— 1979. "Level of Issue Voting: The Effect of Candidate-Pairs on Presidential Elections," *American Politics Quarterly* 23:303–327.

——— 1980. "Contextual Sources of Voting Behavior: The Changeable American Voter," in John C. Pierce and John L. Sullivan, ed., *The Electorate Reconsidered*, pp. 257–277. Beverly Hills: Sage.

Piaget, Jean. 1952. *The Origins of Intelligence in Children*. New York: International University Press.

Pierce, John C. 1970. "Party Identification and the Changing Role of Ideology in American Politics," *Midwest Journal of Political Science* 14:25–42.

Pierce, John C., and Paul R. Hagner. 1980. "Changes in the Public's Political Thinking: The Watershed Years, 1956–1968," in John C. Pierce and John L. Sullivan, ed., *The Electorate Reconsidered*, pp. 69–90. Beverly Hills: Sage.

Pierce, John C., and Douglas Rose. 1974. "Nonattitudes and American Public Opinion: The Examination of a Thesis," *American Political Science Review* 68 (June): 626–649.

Pierce, John C., and John L. Sullivan, ed. 1980. *The Electorate Reconsidered*. Beverly Hills: Sage.

Pomper, Gerald M. 1972. "From Confusion to Clarity: Issues and American Voters, 1956–1968," *The American Political Science Review* 66.6:415–428.

——— 1975. *Voters' Choice: Varieties of American Electoral Behavior*. New York: Dodd, Mead.

——— 1977. "Communication," *American Political Science Review* 71.4 (Dec.): 1596–1597.

Pomper, Gerald M., Ross K. Baker, Kathleen A. Frankovic, Charles E. Jacobs, Wilson Carey McWilliams, and Henry A. Plotkin. 1981. *The Election of 1980*. Chatham: Chatham House Publishers.

Pool, Ithiel de Sola. 1963. "The Mass Media and Politics in the Modernization Process," in Lucian W. Pye, *Communications and Political Development*, pp. 234–253. Princeton: Princeton University Press.

——— 1983. *Technologies of Freedom*. Cambridge: Harvard University Press.

Popkin, S., J. W. Gorman, G. Phillips, and J. A. Smith. 1976. "Comment: What Have You Done for Me Lately? Toward an Investment Theory of Voting," *American Political Science Review* 70:779–805.

Protho, James. W., and Charles M. Grigg. 1960. "Fundamental Principles of Democracy: Bases of Agreement and Disagreement," *Journal of Politics* 22:276–294.

Putnam, Robert D. 1973. *The Beliefs of Politicians: Ideology, Conflict, and Democracy in Britain and Italy.* New Haven: Yale University Press.

Ranney, Austin. 1972. "Turnout and Representation in Presidential Primary Elections," *American Political Science Review* 66 (Mar.): 21–37.

Reese, Stephen D., and M. Mark Miller. 1981. "Political Attitude Holding and Structure," *Communication Research* 8:167–188.

Reich, Wilhelm. 1946. *The Mass Psychology of Fascism.* New York: Orgone Institute Press.

Repass, David E. 1971. "Issue Salience and Party Choice," *American Political Science Review* 65 (June): 389–400.

Rice, Ronald E., et al. 1984. *The New Media.* Beverly Hills: Sage.

Robinson, John P. 1971. "The Audience for National TV New Programs," *Public Opinion Quarterly* 35.3:403–405.

Robinson, Michael J. 1975. "American Political Legitimacy in an Era of Electronic Journalism: Reflections on the Evening News," in Douglass Cater and Richard Adler, ed., *Television as a Cultural Force: New Approaches to TV Criticism,* pp. 97–139. New York: Praeger.

—— 1976. "Public Affairs Television and the Growth of Political Malaise: The Case of 'The Selling of the Pentagon,' " *American Political Science Review* 70:409–432.

Robinson, Michael J., and Margaret A. Sheehan. 1983. *Over the Wire and on TV: CBS and UPI in Campaign '80.* New York: Russell Sage Foundation.

Rodman, Hyman. 1963. "The Lower-Class Value Stretch," *Social Forces,* Dec., pp. 205–215.

Rogers, Everett M. 1973. "Mass Media and Interpersonal Communication," in I. Pool and W. Schramm, ed., *Handbook of Communication,* pp. 290–310. Chicago: Rand McNally.

Rogin, Michael Paul. 1967. *The Intellectuals and McCarthy: The Radical Specter.* Cambridge: MIT Press.

Rokeach, Milton. 1960. *The Open and Closed Mind: Investigations into the Nature of Belief Systems and Personality Systems.* New York: Basic Books.

Roper Organization. 1983. *Trends in Attitudes Toward Television and Other Media: A Twenty-Four Year Review.* New York: Television Information Office.

Rosenberg, Morris. 1954. "Some Determinants of Political Apathy," *Public Opinion Quarterly* 18.4:349–366.

—— 1968. *The Logic of Survey Analysis.* New York: Basic Books.

Rusk, Jerrold E. 1981. "The Michigan Election Studies: A Critical Evaluation." Paper for American Political Science Association, New York.

Sabato, Larry J. 1981. *The Rise of Political Consultants.* New York: Basic Books.

Sartori, Giovanni. 1969. "Politics, Ideology, and Belief Systems," *American Political Science Review* 6:398–411.

Scammon, Richard, and Ben Wattenberg. 1970. *The Real Majority.* New York: Coward, McCann, and Geoghegan.

Schattschneider, E. E. 1960. *The Semi-Sovereign People.* Hinsdale: The Dryden Press.

Schlozman, Kay Lehman, and Sidney Verba. 1979. *Injury to Insult: Unemployment, Class, and Political Response.* Cambridge: Harvard University Press.

Schroder, Harold M., Michael J. Driver, and Sigfried Streufert. 1967. *Human Information Processing.* New York: Holt, Rinehart, and Winston.

Schuman, Howard, and Stanley Presser. 1977. "Attitude Measurement and the Gun Control Paradox," *Public Opinion Quarterly* 41.4:427–438.

——— 1981. *Questions and Answers in Attitude Surveys: Experiments on Question Form, Wording, and Context.* New York: Academic Press.

Schumpeter, Joseph A. 1942. *Capitalism, Socialism, and Democracy,* 3rd ed. New York: Harper and Row.

Sears, David. 1969. "Political Behavior," in Gardner Lindzey and Elliot Aronson, ed., *The Handbook of Social Psychology,* 2nd ed., V, 315–458. Reading: Addison-Wesley.

Sears, David, and Jonathan L. Freedman. 1967. "Selective Exposure to Information: A Critical Review," *Public Opinion Quarterly* 31.2:194–213.

Sears, David O., Richard R. Lau, Tom R. Tyler, and Harris M. Allen, Jr. 1980. "Self-Interest vs. Symbolic Politics in Policy Attitudes and Presidential Voting," *American Political Science Review* 74.3 (Sept.): 670–684.

Selznick, Gertrude, and Stephen Steinberg. 1969. *The Tenacity of Prejudice.* New York: Harper and Row.

Shanks, J. Merrill. 1969. "The Quality of Electoral Change: 1952–1964," Paper for American Political Science Association, New York.

——— 1970. "The Impact of Voters' Political Information on Electoral Change: A Reexamination of the Quality of American Electoral Decision." Ph.D. dissertation. University of Michigan.

Shapiro, Michael J. 1969. "Rational Political Man: A Synthesis of Economic and Social Psychological Perspectives," *American Political Science Review* 63 (Dec.): 1106–1119.

Shaw, Donald L., and Maxwell McCoombs. 1976. *The Emergence of American Political Issues.* St. Paul: West Publishing.

Shepsle, Kenneth A. 1972. "The Strategy of Ambiguity: Uncertainty and Electoral Competition," *American Political Science Review* 66 (June): 555–568.

Shibutani, Tamotsu. 1966. *Improvised News: A Sociological Study of Rumor.* Indianapolis: Bobbs-Merrill.

Simon, Herbert A. [1945] 1976. *Administrative Behavior.* New York: Free Press.

Skinner, B. F. 1957. *Verbal Behavior.* New York: Appleton-Century-Crofts.

Sniderman, Paul. 1974. *Personality and Democratic Politics.* Berkeley: University of California Press.

——— 1981. *A Question of Loyalty.* Berkeley: University of California Press.

Sniderman, Paul M., Michael G. Hagen, Philip E. Tetlock, and Henry E. Brady. 1985. "Reasoning Chains: A Causal Model of Policy Reasoning in Mass Publics." Working Paper No. 75, Survey Research Center, University of California, Berkeley.

Sniderman, Paul, W. Russell Neuman, Jack Citrin, Herbert McClosky, and J. Merrill Shanks. 1975. "Stability of Support for the Political System: The Initial Impact of Watergate," *American Politics Quarterly* 3.4 (Oct.): 437–457.

Star, S. A., and H. M. Hughes. 1950. "Report on an Educational Campaign: The Cincinnati Plan for the United Nations," *American Journal of Sociology* 55:389–400.

Stimson, J. A. 1975. "Belief Systems: Constraint, Complexity, and the 1972 Election," *American Journal of Political Science* 19:393–418.

Stokes, Donald E. 1968. "Voting," in *International Encyclopedia of Social Science*. New York: Free Press and Macmillan.

Stolzenberg, Ross M., and Kenneth C. Land. 1983. "Causal Modeling and Survey Research," in P. Rossi, J. Wright, and A. Anderson, ed., *Handbook of Survey Research*, pp. 613–675. New York: Academic Press.

Stouffer, Samuel A. 1955. *Communism, Conformity, and Civil Liberties*. New York: Doubleday.

Sullivan, John L., James E. Piereson, and George E. Marcus. 1978. "Ideological Constraint in the Mass Public: A Methodological Critique and Some New Findings," *American Journal of Political Science* 22:233–249.

——— 1982. *Political Tolerance and American Democracy*. Chicago: University of Chicago Press.

Swanson, Charles E. 1950. "Predicting Who Will Be Informed about Government." Research Division, School of Journalism, University of Minnesota.

Templeton, Fredric. 1966. "Alienation and Political Participation," *Public Opinion Quarterly* 30.2:249–261.

Tichenor, Philip J., George A. Donohue, and Clarice A. Olien. 1970. "Mass Media Flow and Differential Growth in Knowledge," *Public Opinion Quarterly* 34:159–170.

De Tocqueville, Alexis. [1856] 1961. *Democracy in America*. New York: Schocken Books.

Trenaman, J. M. 1967. *Communication and Comprehension*. London: Longmans Green.

Trodahl, V. C. 1966. "A Field Test of a Modified 'Two-Step Flow of Communication' Model," *Public Opinion Quarterly* 30.4:609–623.

Truman, David. 1951. *The Government Process*. New York: Knopf.

Tsuneki, Teruo. 1979. *Psychological Experiment on Formats of Information Presentation*. Tokyo: Research Institute of Telecommunication and Economics.

Tufte, Edward R. 1974. *Data Analysis for Politics and Policy*. Englewood Cliffs, Prentice-Hall.

Verba, Sidney, and Norman Nie. 1972. *Participation in America*. New York: Harper and Row.

Verba, Sidney, Norman Nie, and J. Kim. 1978. *Participation and Political Equality*. New York: Cambridge University Press.

Weaver, David H., Doris A. Graber, Maxwell McCombs, and Chaim H. Eyal. 1981. *Media Agenda-Setting in a Presidential Election*. New York: Praeger.

Weston, Av. 1982. *Newswatch: How TV Decides the News.* New York: Simon and Schuster.

Whithead, Alfred North. 1948. *Science and the Modern World.* New York: New American Library.

Wiggins, L. M. 1955. "Mathematical Models for the Interpretation of Attitude and Behavior Change." Ph.D. dissertation, Columbia University.

Wiley, David G., and James A. Wiley. 1970. "The Estimation of Measurement Error in Panel Data," *American Sociological Review* 35:112–117.

Zajonc, Robert B. 1968. "Cognitive Theories in Social Psychology," in Gardner Lindzey and Elliot Aronson, ed., *The Handbook of Social Psychology,* 2nd ed., vol. I. Reading: Addison-Wesley.

Zukin, Cliff. 1981. "Mass Communication and Public Opinion," in Dan D. Nimmo and Keith R. Sanders, ed., *Handbook of Political Communication,* pp. 359–390. Beverly Hills: Sage.

Index